D0108336

Taking Back the Constitution

TAKING BACK THE CONSTITUTION

ACTIVIST JUDGES AND THE NEXT AGE OF AMERICAN LAW

• • •

MARK TUSHNET

Yale
UNIVERSITY PRESS
New Haven and London

Published with assistance from the foundation established in memory of James Wesley Cooper of the Class of 1865, Yale College.

Yale University Press books may be purchased in quantity for educational, business, or promotional use. For information, please e-mail sales.press@yale.edu (U.S. office) or sales@yaleup.co.uk (U.K. office).

Set in Gotham and Adobe Garamond types by Tseng Information Systems, Inc. Printed in the United States of America.

ISBN 978-0-300-24598-1 (hardcover : alk. paper)
Library of Congress Control Number: 2019952447
A catalogue record for this book is available from the British Library.

This paper meets the requirements of ANSI/NISO Z39.48-1992 (Permanence of Paper).

10 9 8 7 6 5 4 3 2 1

Frontispiece: Francisco Goya, *The Sleep of Reason Produces Monsters,* circa 1799 (The Metropolitan Museum of Art, gift of M. Knoedler & Co., 1918)

Contents

Introduction   vii

PART ONE

WHERE WE ARE NOW   1

1   Calling Balls and Strikes   3

2   Originalisms   19

3   Playing Politics   44

4   "We've Done Enough": The Constitutional Law of Race   66

5   The Court and Conservative Movements   79

6   Culture Wars, Yesterday and Today   99

PART TWO

WHERE A MODERN REPUBLICAN SUPREME

COURT MIGHT TAKE US   109

7   Strengthening a New Constitutional Order: Partisan Entrenchment and Fulfilling Campaign Pledges   113

8   The Business Agenda   133

9 Deconstructing the Administrative State   147

10 Possibilities Thwarted and Revived   164

11 The Weaponized First Amendment   174

PART THREE

PROGRESSIVE ALTERNATIVES—THE SHORT RUN   189

12 Winning Elections, Enacting Statutes   191

13 Putting Courts on the Progressive Agenda   207

14 Playing Constitutional Hardball   223

PART FOUR

PROGRESSIVE ALTERNATIVES—THE LONG RUN   241

15 Popular Constitutionalism Versus Judicial Supremacy   243

16 Amending the Constitution   258

   Conclusion: 2020 and After   273

   Appendix: Strategies of Supreme Court
   Decision-Making   277

   Notes   283

   Index   301

Introduction

The last time the Supreme Court had a chief justice nominated by a Democratic president was in 1953, just before Fred Vinson passed away. The last time the Supreme Court had a majority of justices nominated by Democratic presidents was May 1969, just before Abe Fortas resigned under pressure. There used to be Republican-nominated justices who were only moderately conservative—Lewis F. Powell, Harry Blackmun, Sandra Day O'Connor, David Souter, Anthony Kennedy—whose presence on the Court slowed what we now can see was a sustained move to the right. With the polarization of our political parties, that move has become a march. Republicans have shifted more quickly and substantially to the right than Democrats have to the left.

Where has the march to the right brought us? Republican control of the Supreme Court—and intermittent control of Congress and the presidency—has built a constitutional system animated by conservative principles. Political scientists have shown that the United States has gone through cycles in which a constitutional order (or regime, or system—all terms I use interchangeably) is built by adherents of a political coalition that controls the government for a decade or more. These constitutional orders, which have characteristic institutions, ideologies, and policies, decay as their political projects, leadership, and ideas come under pressure from new realities and persistent opposition. Each is then replaced by something quite different, though each also leaves a permanent residue with which successors must deal.[1]

The United States has experienced two constitutional orders since the 1930s and may now be entering a third. From the 1930s through the late 1960s there was the New Deal/Great Society constitutional order. Among its characteristic institutions were the bureaucracies of what we came to call the administrative state; its characteristic ideology was interest-group pluralism and associated practices of political bargaining and compromise; its characteristic policies were civil rights laws, Social Security, Medicaid, and the rest of the U.S. social safety net. Its constitutional doctrine culminated in the Warren Court's liberalism and an approach to constitutional interpretation that came to be described as "living constitutionalism."

This order was replaced from the 1980s to the early 2000s by a constitutional order associated with Ronald Reagan. The Reagan order's characteristic institutions were the old administrative bureaucracies, now charged with reducing their own reach through deregulation; its characteristic ideology was the view that government was the problem, not the solution; its characteristic policies were tax cuts.

The conservative constitutional order arose with the conservative critique of the Warren Court. It grew substantially with Ronald Reagan's presidency and developed significant intellectual backing through the work of a cohort of conservatives in think tanks and the legal academy, many of whom held positions in the Department of Justice and the White House counsel's office under Republican presidents. Its approach to constitutional interpretation involved adherence to original constitutional meanings, intentions, or understandings. Yet like "living constitutionalism," conservative originalisms were mostly catchphrases rather than coherent accounts of constitutional interpretation as actually practiced.

As constitutional orders do, the Reagan order began to decay, in part through political blunders by George W. Bush. And like the New Deal/Great Society constitutional order, the Reagan order was not replaced immediately. We can take the dozen years between 1968, when Lyndon Johnson's presidency was concluding, and 1980, when Ronald Reagan was elected, as the interregnum. Similarly perhaps with the years between 2009, when George W. Bush left office, and 2020.

The political scientists who have written about American political development focus on Congress and the presidency. Understanding the role of the courts in their framework requires attention to "judicial time" as well. Congressional and presidential elections occur at regular intervals. Membership on the Supreme Court changes irregularly and largely unpredictably. One effect is that a Court whose composition was determined during an earlier regime or during an interregnum can retain significant power even as a new regime comes into place. This book explores the effects of judicial time on changes in our constitutional order.[2]

The Trump presidency shows that the conservative constitutional order has reached the kind of inflection point that produces a new constitutional order. As election analyst Sam Wang put it after the 2018 elections, "We're at some kind of pivot point in U.S. history.... The United States is going someplace new. I wonder where that is."[3]

This book examines the possibilities. Either conservative constitutional law will reconstruct itself along new lines, or it will be replaced by a progressive alternative that is as yet unclear. Projecting the conservative Supreme Court decisions from the period of decay into the future shows what we might expect under a Supreme Court dominated by modern Republicans. The characteristic institutions of the Trump constitutional order would likely involve the deconstruction of the administrative state; its characteristic ideology is economic and social nationalism; and its characteristic policies are tariffs and immigration restrictions—in one scholar's terms, small government inside the United States and big government at the borders.[4]

What might the progressive alternative be, and how might it be brought about? Progressives are still grappling with the legacy of their political weakness under the Reagan constitutional order. It is unclear what will emerge, but there is a possibility that the progressive alternative will combine a reinvigorated system of public participation in democratic self-government with commitments to the thicker and more social-democratic government that characterized the New Deal/Great Society order at its height. It is, at least, the progressive alternative most clearly discernible today.

Taking Back the Constitution

PART ONE
Where We Are Now

Franklin Roosevelt's New Deal and Lyndon Johnson's Great Society defined the U.S. constitutional system from the mid-1930s through the late 1960s. That system had its own account of what the Constitution stood for and how it should be interpreted, put forward by the Warren Court and its supporters in the legal academy and the popular press. Over time, tensions surfaced within that account, particularly in connection with issues of racial equality and material inequality.

The New Deal/Great Society system exhausted itself in the 1960s under the strain of a war in Vietnam, widespread civic disorder, and a refusal to choose between spending on the war and social welfare spending, resulting in serious problems for the national economy. Constitutional systems don't collapse in a moment, though, and this one lumbered on for another decade.

Then came Ronald Reagan. He and his supporters articulated an alternative to the New Deal/Great Society regime, one in which, as he put it, government was the problem, not the solution. The Reagan Revolution became the new constitutional system. It produced—among many other things—a well-developed account of what the Constitution stood for and how it should be interpreted that was quite different from the Warren Court's account. As before, tensions within that account also surfaced, most notably because the preferred modes of interpreting the Constitution were inadequate to support the Reagan Revolution's substantive vision.

By 2008, political blunders, including misguided military adventures and bad economic policy culminating in the 2008 economic crisis, introduced a period of confusion. The Reagan Revolution found itself where the New Deal/Great Society system had been forty years before, its adherents exhausted and floundering to figure out what to do next. But it did leave a legacy of constitutional doctrine. That legacy is the starting point for thinking about what the Supreme Court might do if and when our current confusion and uncertainty is resolved either by the triumph of Trumpism or its displacement by some unknown alternative.

1

Calling Balls and Strikes

In his opening statement at his nomination hearing, John Roberts came up with a metaphor that later reports suggest he regretted: "Judges are like umpires. Umpires don't make the rules; they apply them.... [As a judge] I will remember that it's my job to call balls and strikes and not to pitch or bat."

On the surface, Roberts seemed to be claiming that judges don't have any discretion in interpreting the law. The statutes and the Constitution are the rules, and judges merely apply them. Anyone who knows baseball, however, knows that umpires have some discretion—and surely Roberts knew it too. It's just that umpires' discretion is limited. So is judges'—and that's all that Roberts needed to claim.

Consider a famous example. Don Larsen was working on a perfect game in the 1956 World Series. After twenty-six consecutive batters had failed to reach base, Larsen had two strikes on the twenty-seventh. If he pitched a strike, he would have a perfect game. Dale Mitchell, the batter, checked his swing, and the umpire, Babe Pinelli, called it a strike. Larsen had his perfect game. Most observers have since concluded that the pitch was probably a little wide of the strike zone and maybe a little high—in short, a ball.[1]

It's not clear, though, that Pinelli was making up a rule. Pretty much everyone knows that the strike zone grows and shrinks during a game, with umpires making implicit decisions that the game they are calling would be better if the strike zone were a little larger now, a little smaller later. A common example: If it's the eighth or ninth inning in a game where one side is ahead by four or five runs, and it looks like it's going to rain, anything plausibly near the plate will be a strike, just to get the game over. Umpires have discretion to define the strike zone to make the game they're calling a better game. We might call this an "implicit meta-rule" about baseball, one that pretty much every player and umpire acknowledges. And, of course, a perfect game in a World Series is about the best a game can be. One could speculate that Pinelli properly exercised discretion in calling a strike on Mitchell, applying the meta-rule but not making up a new rule for the occasion.

But the umpire's discretion is limited. George Will claimed that Larsen's pitch was "a foot and a half . . . high and outside." It wasn't. If it had been — or, more dramatically, if the pitch had sailed over the batter's and catcher's heads into the stands — Pinelli couldn't have (and wouldn't have) called it a strike. Here's a trickier question. Suppose Pinelli decided that baseball in general would be a better game if batters had four chances to swing at strikes rather than just three. He therefore decides to define the strike zone narrowly in every game — not so narrowly that if a batter does not swing at a pitch straight down the middle, Pinelli will call it a ball, but more narrowly than most umpires would. I'm inclined to think, and I'm sure John Roberts would think, that Pinelli was making a new rule, not applying some meta-rule about making the game the best it can be — at least if Pinelli wasn't open in explaining what he was doing.[2]

Sometimes, even openness wouldn't be enough. Suppose Pinelli persuaded the officials charged with scoring the game that baseball would be a better game if runners who scored by stealing home from third base added two runs to their team's score. They couldn't simply implement this vision, even if they told everyone what they were doing.

I could continue by introducing additional complications to the examples (what if other umpires gradually came to agree with Pinelli about four strikes?), but the point should be clear. Roberts used the metaphor to describe what he would do as a judge. His presentation was disingenuous because he failed to say as well what he surely knew: that he had a certain amount of discretion to introduce his personal political views into statutory and constitutional interpretation. The reason for his reticence is clear. He wanted to contrast his description of what he would do with an alternative that he attributed to liberal judges: They thought their job was to make the rules. As Roberts put it, liberal judges made decisions "according . . . to their own social preferences, . . . their policy views, . . . their personal preferences." They wanted to make the law the best it could be according to their own lights, no matter that doing so might lead them to say that a pitch over the batter's head was a strike or that runners who stole home from third added two runs to their team's score. Acknowledging that umpires have some discretion would have weakened the contrast's rhetorical effectiveness.

One problem with the implicit contrast is that it makes it nearly impossible to describe judges as disagreeing with one another in good faith, and that can be toxic for political discourse. "This pitch is clearly a strike; in calling it a ball, the dissenters [or the majority] can only be abusing their power to advance their personal agenda." More important, though, it doesn't describe how judges actually make decisions. I suspect that the umpire metaphor could be developed to accommodate the ideas I'm about to lay out, but it's easier to set out those ideas directly. I begin with a wonderful case the Supreme Court decided in 2015.

John Yates was a commercial fisherman. He caught some red grouper in the Gulf of Mexico. Federal law says that people who catch undersized red grouper—less than 20 inches long—have to throw them back into the water. A state conservation officer, conducting a routine inspection of Yates's boat, found about 70 undersized red grouper, nearly all of them between 19 and 20 inches long. The officer put the undersized fish into a crate and told Yates to leave the crate as it was. When the boat docked a few days later, however, the officer discovered that Yates had thrown the undersized fish overboard and replaced them in the crate with another bunch of fish, some of which were still undersized. Yates was convicted of "destroying property to prevent a federal seizure" and of "destroy[ing] ... [a] tangible object with the intent to impede ... the investigation of any matter ... within the jurisdiction of any department or agency of the United States."[3]

The Supreme Court considered only the conviction for destroying a tangible object. You might think the case easy: If, anticipating teaching the *Yates* case, I asked my students to bring in a tangible object, a student who brought in a red grouper would get full credit, just like a student who brought in a computer disk. The complication, if it is one, is where the "tangible object" law is found in the statute books. It's part of the Sarbanes-Oxley Act of 2002, which Congress adopted after a financial scandal. Investigating the scandal, Congress discovered that some people had destroyed computer disks and other records showing some of the financial misconduct, and also found out that existing statutes seemed to overlook that precise form of misbehavior. The "tangible objects" statute was enacted to criminalize what they had done—which of course had nothing to do with destroying undersized fish. The Supreme Court held that the statute didn't cover what Yates had done.

The lineup (another baseball metaphor, I guess) in the *Yates* case is intriguing. Justice Ruth Bader Ginsburg wrote the prevailing opinion. She was joined by Chief Justice Roberts and Justices Stephen Breyer and Sonia Sotomayor. Justice Elena Kagan wrote the dissent, joined by Justices Antonin Scalia, Anthony Kennedy, and Clarence

Thomas. (Justice Samuel Alito wrote a separate opinion that I won't discuss here; it agreed with much of what Justice Ginsburg wrote, but disagreed on some points that are minor in this context.) It's hard to see politics driving the justices' positions.

It's worth going through the *Yates* opinions at least sketchily to show how judges explain what they're doing. Ginsburg begins by describing the competing positions: The government argued that the "tangible objects" statute "extends beyond the principal evil motivating its passage," while Yates "urges a contextual reading" of the statute, "tying [the phrase] to the surrounding words, the placement of the provision within the Sarbanes-Oxley Act, and related provisions." She conceded that standard dictionary definitions would lead you to think that a red grouper was a tangible object. But, "In law as in life, . . . the same words, placed in different contexts, sometimes mean different things." There follows a page of citations to cases saying that "identical language may convey varying content when used in different statutes, sometimes even in different provisions of the same statute." In one important setting, though, it was clear that "tangible objects" really had a comprehensive meaning, but that setting involved discovery in criminal cases. "In that context, a comprehensive definition . . . is fitting." The provision invoked against Yates was different because it was a statute making something a crime rather than regulating criminal procedure.

Ginsburg then turned to "familiar interpretive guides"—the statute's title and location within the statute books, for example, and what are known as "canons of interpretation." The title referred to "destruction . . . of records." The words near "tangible objects" were "records," "documents," "falsifies," and "makes a false entry," and their proximity "cabin[ed] the contextual meaning" of "tangible objects." The best interpretation of "tangible objects" was that it referred to means of preserving information. She also invoked the "rule of lenity"—that ambiguous words in a criminal statute should be construed to limit the statute's reach. So, she concluded, the statute covered only tangible objects that recorded or preserved information—such as computer disks.

Justice Kagan found the words "tangible objects" not at all ambiguous. They were "broad, but clear." Citing dictionaries and Dr. Seuss ("One Fish, Two Fish, Red Fish, Blue Fish"), she pointed out that "[a] fish is … a discrete thing that possesses physical form." That "accords with endless uses of the term in statute and rule books." (Here she stuck in a footnote: state laws "[f]rom Alabama and Alaska through Wisconsin and Wyoming (and—trust me—in all that come between)" used "tangible objects" in the broad sense—because "really, who does not?") Context mattered, she said, but here it simply confirmed that the dictionary meaning was the right one. Other statutes using the term "embrace things of all kinds," even when they also refer to "records" and "documents." Congress was worried about people doing things that interfered with investigations, and "[a] fisherman … who dumps undersized fish to avoid a fine is no less blameworthy than one who shreds his vessel's catch log for the same reason."

Then Kagan turned to the argument from the provision's title and placement. "A title is, almost necessarily, an abridgement," and the title here failed to mention "mutilation," something the statute's words expressly covered. So too, the title's reference only to "records" didn't limit the statute's coverage of other tangible objects. The canons didn't help. They were supposed to be used "to resolve ambiguity, not to create it," and anyway, records and documents preserve information but they also *provide* it—as do undersized fish (information about their size, of course). Finally, the rule of lenity "only kicks in" when the statute's words are unclear. But "tangible objects" was quite clear, though quite broad.

Kagan ended her opinion by speculating that the justices in the majority were worried about "overcriminalization and excessive punishment." Maybe that was a valid concern, but "this Court does not get to rewrite the law. . . . We are not entitled to replace the statute Congress enacted with an alternative of our own design." In short, Kagan charged Ginsburg—and Chief Justice Roberts—with calling a strike a ball because they thought federal criminal law would be better that way.

I love to teach the *Yates* case. Kagan is a more engaging writer than Ginsburg, but it's impossible for students to grapple with the arguments that each lays out and not end up thinking the two have fought pretty much to a draw—or, to revert to Roberts's metaphor, that both did a good job of calling balls and strikes. If one side sees a ball and another a strike, something else must be going on.

It's also hard to look at the lineup of justices on each side and not think that disagreeing over whether a pitch is a ball or a strike can't always be reduced to a disagreement over conservative versus liberal political beliefs. Yet most students tend to agree with Kagan that the justices who joined Ginsburg's opinion were driven by a not completely suppressed concern about how prosecutors have used broad laws abusively—a policy preference, in short, but not one that mapped neatly onto the standard political agendas.

At *her* nomination hearing, Elena Kagan offered an alternative to the umpire metaphor. She said that what judges did was law all the way down. For her, that had nothing to do with eliminating discretion—policy preferences, a political agenda, or something else—from what judges did. What does it mean to say that what judges do is law all the way down?

Let's go back to the *Yates* case. The justices have a bunch of what I'll call legal materials in hand when they think about what "tangible objects" means. Their law clerks will have prepared a "bench memo" describing the case's facts, the lower court's decision, other relevant decisions by lower courts, and more. The justices may have talked with the clerks about the case. They also have the briefs prepared by the parties, and they may have read around in some of the cases the briefs cite. They take all these legal materials and form a first impression of the case.

One judge describes this first impression as a "hunch." A theorist calls it a "situation sense." Another theorist offers a more result-oriented description of the first impression: "How I want it to come out." I prefer a somewhat weaker version: "It would be nice if I could figure out a way to interpret the statute or the Constitution to get to the result that seems initially to make sense—but I may not be able to." In many cases, no matter what their politics are, almost all judges will have the same first impression. These are "easy" cases, and judges tend to consider them unimportant. Much more interesting is what judges do in cases they think are both difficult and important.[4]

To examine that, we have to ask where the first impressions come from. The answer is banal but important: Pretty much anywhere. Here's a list of some of those places; there are many more.

- Judges may get hunches because they've previously dealt with cases that seem roughly like this one—maybe, for *Yates,* a case involving some other kind of obstruction of justice, or one involving what they saw as overreaching by the prosecution.
- They may have a sense that some outcomes are crazy and others are within bounds because of some general and (more or less) widely shared cultural norms. This sense will sometimes lead them to dismiss out of hand outcomes that might technically fit the available legal materials.
- They may have a sense of where they'd like to come out because of a general orientation to statutory or constitutional interpretation—such as textualism, originalism, "living constitutionalism,"

or pragmatism. In nomination hearings conservatives tend to call this a judicial or constitutional philosophy, and contrast it to "ideologies" that consist of policy positions unconnected to an account of interpretation. The problem is that each side thinks its nominees have a philosophy while its opponents have ideologies.

- The facts of the case might trigger a judge's sense that some important constitutional principle is at stake. Essentially everyone agrees that the Constitution is about preserving liberty from an overreaching government, about protecting vulnerable minorities from exploitation by malicious or indifferent majorities, about ensuring that the American people are able to govern ourselves, about balancing power in the national government with preserving significant scope for decision-making in state governments. Judges frame cases in terms of these substantive values, but they don't all frame them in the same way. A case that a conservative sees as primarily about federalism might be one a liberal sees as about self-government. Liberals tend to see racial minorities and LGBTQ people as vulnerable minorities, while conservatives tend to put white "ethnics" — Italian-Americans and Polish-Americans, to use examples Justice Scalia was fond of — and evangelical Christians in that category. Frames are based on substantive visions of the Constitution, and they too generate and support a judge's initial impression about the case.

- Judges may have had personal experiences that bear on the legal materials. The lore of the Supreme Court has it that Chief Justice William Rehnquist ruled in favor of the constitutionality of the Family and Medical Leave Act in part because of his daughter's experience of the difficulties single parents face in dealing with medical emergencies. President Barack Obama's references to seeking justices with "empathy" pointed in this direction too.[5]

- They might think that their friends will think better of them if they come out one way (or worse if they come out the other way). Conservatives call this the "Greenhouse effect," referring to the social pressure they think some justices felt to conform to the liberal norms of the "inside the Beltway" hothouse—or their desire to get approval from the *New York Times*'s former Supreme Court correspondent Linda Greenhouse. Liberals might talk of the "FedSoc" effect, referring to justices' desires to get plaudits at Federalist Society conferences and from op-eds written by Federalist Society members.[6]

Once they dig into the legal materials, judges can and sometimes do revise these first impressions. But as my version suggests, they prefer to end up where they started, if they can work through the materials to that conclusion.

One additional important preliminary: Judges know what their first impressions are, but they don't always know why they have them. One source of "below the level of consciousness" impressions is especially important. Judges may have adopted their constitutional philosophies before they were judges, in part because they thought (then) that those philosophies resonated with their partisan preferences.

There's nothing arcane about the process of working with the legal materials—or rather, nothing arcane once someone has gotten a legal education. That's because the point of legal education is to teach budding lawyers how to work with legal materials—how to think like a lawyer, as the cliché has it.

Here are some illustrations, mostly from the *Yates* opinions, of how judges work with legal materials. I'll use some phrases I sometimes offer my students to describe the moves judges make.

• Make it bigger or make it smaller: A case or a phrase in a statute stands for a larger principle that extends to this problem. So: "In the Government's view, [the 'tangible objects' statute] extends beyond the principal evil motivating its passage." But also: A case or a phrase has to be understood in light of the underlying facts or the surrounding statutory or constitutional language. So: "a contextual reading," focusing on "the surrounding words" and other provisions.

The jargon here is to say that the other case or phrase is "distinguishable." In holding that the Second Amendment guaranteed a right of individuals to own weapons for self-protection, and that this right was not tied to participation in an organized militia, Justice Scalia noted that in the founding era one could find what he called an "idiomatic" use of the phrase "bear Arms" that did have a close connection to the militia. But when he looked closely at the idiomatic use, he said, he found that it almost always occurred as part of a phrase: "bear Arms against." He inferred that when "bear Arms" stood alone, as in the Second Amendment, it didn't have a connection to the militia. (Here, Scalia was using a well-recognized method for dealing with original-meaning material.)

• Go north (or south): Justices may find an analogy in some similar case or statute or constitutional provision, and extend what that case held or how that statute was interpreted to the case at hand. (Of course, the other side of the argument is that the purported analogy fails because it's—aha!—distinguishable.) For Justice Ginsburg, the analogies are in cases saying that identical words can have different meanings depending on context. For Justice Kagan, the analogies are in cases and statutes expressly giving "tangible objects" a broad meaning.

There are many more "argument forms," as one jurist described them (he counted around sixty). What matters is that law—all the way down—consists of those argument forms or, more informally, moves. The Ginsburg and Kagan opinions are so wonderful to teach because they show two talented jurists deploying a slew of moves. Looking at the moves each justice makes, one has a sense of inevitability—even though the inevitable result for Ginsburg is that Yates's conviction is reversed, and for Kagan it's that the conviction stands. There's almost nothing to say—other than "I agree with the result Ginsburg [or Kagan] reached"—once you've worked your way through the opinions. We might want to think that legal analysis should not be driven by our view of what the outcome should be, but when all is said and done, the outcome is all that matters.[7]

Although I have no inside information about where Ginsburg and Kagan started—what their "hunch" or "situation sense" was—I'll use their opinions to suggest that judges who are really good at working with the legal materials can find ways to get where their first impressions pointed. Doing so often takes a lot of work, which sometimes is not worth the bother (as in the easy cases I mentioned earlier). But when a talented judge cares about the result and is willing to do the work, she or he can get there. And sometimes the initial impression, the sense of where the judge would like to come out, is generated by a policy preference, constitutional philosophy, or political agenda. When they are, I insist, the judges are still doing law, not "merely" enacting their preferences.

The picture is a little more complicated. Judges who are really good at working with the materials can get where they want to go. Today Justice Alito on the right and Justice Kagan on the left have that sort of talent. And sometimes judges know that if they took the time and put in the effort, they could get where they want to go, but don't bother. Early in their judicial careers, Justice William O. Douglas and then-Justice William Rehnquist were adept at making the moves they needed to make. But as time went on, they grew less interested in showing their work. They wrote opinions that on their face were full of gaps, knowing that the gaps could be filled in by talented lawyers who made the effort.

Other judges are not quite as talented. Like their colleagues, they start out with a hunch or an initial impression. But as they work with the materials, they find themselves blocked: There's an argument they can't quite overcome, or a step from one point to another that they can't find legal materials to support.

At that point they face a choice. One path is to say, "I hoped to be able to rule for the plaintiff, but I couldn't figure out how to do it, so I'll rule for the defendant." Or, more formally, "The opinion for the plaintiff just wouldn't write." Assigned to write an opinion upholding a prayer at a high school graduation, Justice Kennedy came back to his colleagues with a draft opinion calling the practice unconstitutional, with a cover note saying that the opinion the other way wouldn't write. The four justices who wanted to uphold the prayer practice went ahead and did so (dissenting), which suggests that whether an opinion can be written is itself open to debate. Justices sometimes point to these "wouldn't write" opinions to show that the results they reach aren't always dictated by their political or policy preferences.[8]

One particularly important obstacle is the sense that some outcome is just too far out to be acceptable even if the legal materials can be massaged to generate the outcome. No judge today will hold that our income tax system is unconstitutional because it isn't progressive enough—though a really talented and willful judge could pull together strands in equal protection law that would have a formally acceptable argument form.

The other path is to jump over the obstacles—ignore the counterargument or come up with some patently silly distinction that allows you to put the counterargument to one side. Critics seize on these cases to show how—or to show that—political agendas or policy preferences infect judicial decisions. And they are sometimes right. The only problem is that it's true all the time. Talented judges who are willing to devote the necessary time and effort know how to make the moves that conceal the line connecting their first impressions—

"It would be nice if I could come out this way"—with the outcomes. But when the first impressions flow from political agendas or policy preferences, the line is there.

I think this is the best description of law—just a compilation of moves or "argument forms." I also think that when pressed, many sophisticated legal theorists, whether liberal or conservative, agree. But they don't like to display this understanding for public consumption. They prefer to tell the public that law "is" a set of rules and standards and principles that, when properly applied, tell judges what's a ball and what's a strike. This is one of the deep hypocrisies or mystifications of the legal academy. But the unmystified view is the only way to make sense of the observation that, for judges, it's law all the way down.

John Roberts said something else about umpires in his opening statement: "Nobody ever went to a ball game to see the umpire." That's not entirely true: Some umpires use elaborate body motions to call balls and strikes and outs, and some people enjoy watching them. More important, if people don't go to the ballpark to see the umpire, why do they go? One possibility should trouble conservatives: People go to root for the home team or the visitors—they care about the results. But conservatives and progressives alike are uncomfortable with result-oriented law.

Winning, by itself, is not the only reason people go to the ballpark. Most are rooting for one team to win, but they want it to win by playing well within the rules. They like to watch the way managers position players, see a well-executed bunt or double play or stolen base, or a fastball down the middle that even the best batter can't hit. In short, they go to see the moves the players make. The law is like that too—a set of moves that can be done well or badly.

Of course there's more to the story. Outcomes matter—in death penalty cases, people live or die depending on what the judges say the law means. People gain or lose rights, businesses thrive or go bankrupt based on judges' decisions. These outcomes depend on the moves the judges make, and the moves available to judges allow them to rule as their initial impressions dictate.

Judges might "just" call balls and strikes. When they do that—when they make the moves the law lets them make—they are doing law. And yet doing law has no relation whatever to the justices' personal preferences, to justice, or to anything else. Roberts's metaphor for law isn't bad, but it doesn't do what he and other conservatives think it does. Justice Kagan was more accurate in saying that what judges do is law all the way down—and that that fact has almost nothing to do with eliminating judges' discretion to advance their policy preferences *through* law.

Saying that conservative judges advance conservative policy goals isn't a criticism. Getting from an initial impression to a result is what all judges have to do all the time, and sometimes the initial impression is related to political beliefs. The criticism is that conservatives (and sometimes liberals, but not, at least as I interpret her position, Justice Kagan) are hypocrites in claiming to be just making sure that people play by rules whose interpretation is obvious—unlike (they imply) their liberal or conservative colleagues, who don't even try to be good umpires. Every judge tries to figure out what the rules are in pretty much the same way. Some are better than others at making the moves that constitute the law, but a judge's talent level has nothing to do with politics.

We could live with the umpire metaphor for law if everyone understood what it really meant. And as it turns out, the public isn't fooled. Recent polls suggest that well over two-thirds of the American people believe that personal preferences sometimes or always influence judges' decisions.[9] So why does the umpire metaphor resonate? Perhaps because it signals to people on your side: We're virtuous umpires while those on the other side are politicians in robes. That sets up a destructive dynamic in which you think your side is just calling balls and strikes, while the other side is pretending to call balls and strikes but actually advancing an agenda. One of the sharpest contrasts between sophisticated insider understandings and what the broader public believes occurs in connection with originalism.

2

Originalisms

Speaking at a Federalist Society dinner in November 2017, White House counsel Donald McGahn said that President Donald Trump was "very committed to . . . nominating and appointing committed originalists and textualists" to the Supreme Court. At the same dinner, Justice Neil Gorsuch, greeted with a standing ovation, told the audience, "Tonight I can report, a person can be both a committed originalist and textualist and be confirmed to the Supreme Court of the United States."[1]

Why do conservatives value textualism and originalism? They are alternatives or supplements to the umpire metaphor: both are thought to eliminate or at least sharply confine judicial discretion. "Living constitutionalism" is originalism's evil twin. According to originalists, liberal living constitutionalists think the meaning of the Constitution's words changes with the times. Living constitutionalists, in their view, interpret the Constitution so that it fits with their personal preferences and advances their political agendas. Originalist judges, by contrast, must do only what the Constitution says and follow what it originally meant.

When examined closely, however, the distinction between original meaning and contemporary preferences disappears—and in their hearts, sophisticated academic proponents of originalism know it.

According to the Bible, some Israelites used the word "Shibboleth" to identify their enemies (because they couldn't pronounce it correctly). "Originalism" is Shibboleth in reverse: It's a word conservatives use to identify their friends. Otherwise it has almost no coherent content. Textualism and originalism are good rallying cries at Federalist Society dinners, but they do little to keep judges from doing what they want.[2]

We should get one thing out of the way at the start. No one really thinks that the Constitution's words have no role to play in deciding what the Constitution means. To say otherwise is ridiculous: "I'm trying to figure out what the Constitution means, but the words don't matter." And almost everyone thinks that what the words meant when they were inserted into the Constitution—when the original Constitution was ratified in 1789, or when various amendments were adopted—has an important role in constitutional interpretation. What role, though, and how exactly do they play that role?

Textualism might seem easy to define. A textualist judge requires that any interpretation of the Constitution ultimately trace back to some words in its text. The large body of free speech doctrine rarely refers to the First Amendment's precise words, but the doctrine is textualist anyway, textualists say, because they think they can burrow through the cases and find the text at the bottom.

A textualist would also rule out "interpretations" of the Constitution that are inconsistent with its text. Those, however, are hard to come by. The examples most commonly offered involve the death penalty and gender discrimination. The textualist argument about the death penalty is that the Fifth Amendment assumes that there are capital crimes and that people can be deprived of their lives through due process of law. Saying that the Eighth Amendment's ban on cruel and unusual punishments makes capital punishment unconstitutional is inconsistent with those texts. The textualist argument about gender discrimination is that Section Two of the Fourteenth Amendment, which authorizes Congress to reduce the congressional representation of states that discriminate against male inhabitants, assumes that discriminating against females is fine.

Those aren't knockdown arguments. The Fifth Amendment assumes that there will be capital crimes, but it doesn't require that there be, and it simply imposes the condition that, if someone is deprived of life, it must be done with due process. It does not guarantee that life can constitutionally be taken. And authorizing gender discrimination in one narrow context doesn't necessarily protect it against constitutional challenge in other contexts. These are standard moves that any good lawyer can make.

So, textualism gets you something, but not nearly enough. What about originalism? It's harder to get a handle on because there are so many originalisms. I start with Ronald Reagan's attorney general, Edwin Meese, who gave prominent speeches advocating a jurisprudence of original intent. If taken to mean that we should try to figure out what the Constitution's writers had in mind, the jurisprudence of original intent was vulnerable to serious objections: How could we figure out what a person had in mind (other than through the words he used—and then why bother to talk about intent)? Even if we could, how could we add up what the hundreds of delegates who voted to ratify the Constitution at the state constitutional conventions all had in mind? Often, of course, they didn't have anything specific in mind, just a sense that the words they used got close to doing what they might have hoped was worth doing. Original-intent originalism was soon reduced to an almost invisible presence in sophisticated conservative theory. But it lives on, zombie-like, in op-eds and other popular writing.

The jurisprudence of original intent morphed a bit, then more substantially. The first transformation led people to look at what the Constitution's framers did, rather than—or maybe in addition to—what they said or thought. So, for example, if Congress hired a chaplain as soon as it could, people at the time couldn't have thought that doing so violated the First Amendment's ban on the establishment of religion. If they enacted statutes requiring capital punishment, they couldn't have thought capital punishment was unconstitutional.[3]

There's a flip side to this argument: If people around the time the Constitution was adopted didn't do something, that might show that they thought doing it would be unconstitutional. So, for example, the Supreme Court held unconstitutional a federal statute requiring local sheriffs to do background checks on applicants for gun permits, because of a principle it called the "anti-commandeering" rule: Congress can't force state and local officials to do work Congress wants done. Among the reasons the Court gave for this holding was that Congress hadn't tried to commandeer state officials until quite recently, and the absence of early commandeering statutes showed that the framing generation thought that doing so would be unconstitutional.[4]

This approach was labeled "original expected applications," and it too was vulnerable to serious objections. Everything early Congresses did, they did in a specific social and historical context that differs from the one we live in now.

From one point of view, that's fine: Originalism says that whenever the context in which the framers acted remains the same, we should do what they did. The difficulty is that contexts change. When Congress hired its first chaplain, its members knew that the nation was almost entirely Christian, with only a small number of Jews and Muslims ("Mahometans," in their terms), and not that many Catholics. In *that* world, maybe hiring a chaplain didn't violate the nonestablishment rule. But we can't know what those congressmen would have done in the more religiously pluralist world we live in today. (Note that I've just made what lawyers call the "distinguish the cases" move.) More generally, practices take place in contexts, and the Constitution's framers — and contemporary originalists — understood that context might affect constitutionality. Moving from their practices to ours, and thereby moving from their contexts to ours, washes away any inferences we can draw from what they did.

Drawing inferences from what they didn't do is even more problematic. True, they might have refrained from commandeering state officials because they thought it would be unconstitutional. But it could also be that they didn't commandeer those officials because they didn't choose to — there was no problem for which commandeering was the best policy response.

After more theoretical work, conservatives settled on the current version of originalism, labeled "original public meaning originalism." There are more or less formal ways of defining it, but the core idea is this: What would ordinary people at the time the Constitution became law have understood its words to mean? A simple example: The Constitution says that the national government shall protect states against "domestic violence." Today those words might refer to violence between men and women in their households, but in 1789, people would have understood that they referred to civil disorder.

A first complexity arises from some of the Constitution's words themselves: Congress has the power "to grant letters of marque and reprisal." What would people in 1789 have understood this to mean? Most, surely, would have no idea what those words meant.* Similarly, and more consequentially today, for the text saying that the president can be impeached and removed from office for "high Crimes and Misdemeanors." Original public meaning originalism says that at least with words that clearly had technical meanings — and maybe with most of the Constitution — we should look to what reasonably

---

* They refer to the documents Congress used when it authorized the owners of private ships ("privateers") to seize the ships and goods of enemies.

well-informed people, familiar with technical language, would have understood those words to mean.

We find out the original public meaning of words by looking at how people at the time actually used them. The Constitution gives Congress the power to regulate "Commerce among the several States." Can Congress regulate manufacturing or agriculture? When original public meaning originalists look at newspapers, speeches, and other linguistic sources to see how people used the word "commerce," it turns out that they regularly referred to "commerce, manufacturing, and agriculture," which strongly suggests that manufacturing was different from commerce—and therefore that the power to regulate commerce didn't extend to regulating manufacturing.[5]

So far so good. To be an original public meaning originalist, though, you have to find and then plow through a lot of old material. That opens the practice up to distortion, mostly unintentional, when you don't look at enough old material—or when a judge relies on material presented by advocates for only one side. Originalists of this stripe, taking advantage of the rise of big-data research, have compiled a large searchable database of newspapers and other sources from the late eighteenth century, which they use in a practice known as corpus linguistics. If you want to know how people used "commerce," just plug the word into the search engine and see what comes out.[6]

Sophisticated practitioners know that simply plugging a word into a search engine is silly, because it will yield a host of results shedding no light at all on the word's use in the Constitution. So, they say, you have to do refined searches, looking for how specific words are used in proximity to other words that help limit the results to legal contexts. And, at that point, the game is close to over, because scholars exercise lots of discretion in framing the contexts in which they search. My own assessment of the corpus linguistics scholarship is that the conservative scholars doing that research have framed their searches in ways that predispose them to find results consistent with what contemporary conservatives want the terms to mean.[7]

The corpus linguistics scholarship has also brought renewed attention to a problem identified by critics of originalism's earlier versions: What *is* the original public meaning when your searches show—as virtually all searches conducted so far do—that the word was used one way 65 percent of the time, and another way 35 percent of the time? Of course the precise numbers vary, but the point remains. This sort of division indicates that there was no single original public meaning. An originalist has to give us a reason for preferring one possibility over another, if both were available when the term was adopted.

That reason has to come from somewhere—for an originalist, something about the things the framers took for granted and didn't think needed to be written down. One candidate might be a general principle of democratic self-governance. If today a majority enacts a statute consistent only with the 35 percent understanding, the original understanding taken as a whole—the term and the commitment to democracy—supports the 35 percent result. Taking the 65 percent understanding to provide the word's meaning is a choice you make today, based on something you find outside the Constitution's text, not a choice dictated by people in the past. Again, all of the corpus linguistics studies done so far have produced this sort of division.

Here's an example. Justice Scalia said that the Second Amendment's words "keep and bear arms" created an individual right to own weapons for self-defense, not a right associated only with military service. He discussed a brief submitted to the Court surveying founding-era uses of the words "bear arms" that concluded that the words had a military-related meaning. But, he said, when you look at the examples the brief provided, you see that they had that meaning only when joined with the word "against." Since he wrote this, several corpus linguistics studies have addressed the same question. One found "about 1,500 separate occurrences of 'bear arms' in the 17th and 18th centuries, and only a handful don't refer to war, soldiering or organized, armed action." Another "found that in 67.4% of the sample size, 'bear arms' was used in its collective sense, whereas in 18.2% of the sample, the phase was used in an individual sense." A third found about twice as many military-related uses as individual-related uses.[8]

Does that mean that Justice Scalia's original public meaning analysis was wrong? Not according to two conservative scholars. "Frequency is not always just about linguistic meaning, but also about facts concerning the state of the world," they write. "The fact that most references to bearing arms in 18th century writings were in the military context could very well mean that 'bear arms' has a military-only sense besides a more general sense. Or the data may show *only* that when people used the phrase 'bear arms' they did so most frequently in a military setting." The moves here are evident. It's not the words or their original public meaning that leads these scholars to their conclusion; it's their conservatism.[9]

Careful and sophisticated academic originalists, who understand all this, have come up with a solution. In its best version, the solution distinguishes between words whose entire meaning was fixed when they were written, and words that had a core of fixed meaning but that also left room for later "construction." The words in the first group are reasonably clear and concrete—"four years" for the president's term, "letters of marque and reprisal." The words subject to construction are more general and abstract: A public declaration that a specific denomination was the nation's religion would be an "establishment of religion," but so might be other forms of public support for religions, depending on how the term was construed.

As these examples suggest, much of what people care most about today in constitutional law falls within the domain of construction. So how does construction take place? In the first instance, by regular practices of legislatures and executives. They do things they think the Constitution's words permit, and by their actions they give content to those words, at least if they do similar things over a long period of time. But as the word "construction" suggests, courts have come to play their part in building out the Constitution. Their decisions upholding and striking down legislation also give content to the Constitution's words.

Once courts enter the picture, the distinction between public meaning originalism and living constitutionalism, the conservatives' nemesis, becomes quite thin. One clue is that liberal constitutional theory distinguishes between conceptions and concepts. The former are the specific things a word clearly covers; the latter are the broader principles that explain why we hold the conception we do. That segregated schools can be equal invokes a specific conception of equality; that segregated schools cannot be equal relies on the concept of equality, which is broader. The liberal distinction between conceptions and concepts underlies living constitutionalism: As we gain a "better" understanding of the concept of equality, we abandon the conceptions we once held and adopt new ones.[10]

Notably, some prominent originalists defend *Brown v. Board of Education* as a correct construction of the equal protection clause. Here is Justice Scalia:

> In my view the Fourteenth Amendment's requirement of "equal protection of the laws," combined with the Thirteenth Amendment's abolition of the institution of black slavery, leaves no room for doubt that laws treating people differently because of their race are invalid. Moreover, even if one does not regard the Fourteenth Amendment as crystal clear on this point, a tradition of unchallenged validity did not exist with respect to the practice in *Brown*. To the contrary, in the 19th

century the principle of "separate-but-equal" had been vigorously opposed on constitutional grounds, litigated up to this Court, and upheld only over the dissent of one of our most historically respected Justices.

Liberal living constitutionalists wouldn't have any problems with that formulation.[11]

The distinction between conceptions and concepts isn't quite the same as the distinction between words whose complete meaning was fixed when they were written and words subject to later construction by legislators and judges. But the distinctions are close cousins—maybe even siblings. That's why there is something called "living originalism" and why, in a recent survey of scholarship, three of the five most prominent originalists were liberals, not conservatives.[12]

So, what does it mean to have committed originalist justices on the Supreme Court? Consider the well-known *Citizens United* decision, holding unconstitutional a restriction on corporations' ability to spend their money on campaign advertisements that they came up with on their own. The *dissenting* opinion by Justice John Paul Stevens has a section, "Original Understandings," which argues that the majority "makes only a perfunctory attempt to ground its analysis in the principles or understandings of those who drafted and ratified the [First] Amendment." Stevens found "not a scintilla of evidence to support the notion that anyone believed it would preclude regulatory distinctions based on the corporate form." The majority's response? Basically, nothing—though perhaps that shows only that Justice Kennedy was not an originalist.* The majority opinion relied on "ancient

---

* And we might cut Justices Thomas and Alito some slack for joining Kennedy's opinion because quite often a justice has to swallow something to make sure that the Court has a majority opinion.

First Amendment principles." The key word is "principles," which are derived—by construction over time—from the First Amendment. Even here, the majority merely gestured in the direction of an original public understanding. Justice Kennedy wrote, "At the founding, speech was open, comprehensive, and vital to society's definition of itself; there were no limits on the sources of speech and knowledge." On its face, this is "original expected applications" originalism, and it could be the basis for an argument about construction. Instead, it is embedded in a much narrower argument—that, assuming that this broad principle was understood to be the First Amendment's meaning in 1791, "[t]here is simply no support for the view that the First Amendment, as originally understood, would permit the suppression of political speech by media corporations."

Citizens United is typical of the conservative judicial approach to the First Amendment, at least so far. Justices almost never comment on what the First Amendment meant by "the freedom of speech, or of the press" in 1791, but they occasionally wave their hands vaguely in the direction of some high-sounding principles they attribute to the Framers.

In 2018, the Court's conservatives found a First Amendment violation in a statute requiring public employees to pay a fee for the services they received from unions.[13] The unions argued that in 1791, public employees had no First Amendment rights at all. It's worth going through how Justice Alito responded to that argument, because it shows how the Court's conservatives actually do originalism. (Justice Alito made other arguments supporting the result, but I focus here only on his discussion of originalism, which was not a major part of the opinion.)

Justice Alito began his discussion by saying, "[W]e doubt that the Union—or its members—actually want us to hold that public employees have 'no [free speech] rights.'" The reason: other unions in other cases have argued for broad First Amendment rights for public employees. How this relates to an originalist argument is, to say the least, unclear.

He continued, "Taking away free speech protection for public employees would mean overturning decades of landmark precedent." Perhaps this shows that Alito is what Justice Scalia once called himself, a faint-hearted originalist. Strictly speaking, originalism shouldn't care about the consequences of following the historical materials where they lead.

Perhaps there is some "consequences matter" constraint on originalism. The usual example is paper money: Congress has the power to "coin Money," and there's strong reason to believe that the founding generation understood this to mean, "make gold and silver serve as currency." Faint-hearted originalists believe that reverting to this understanding would be a disaster for the modern economy, and they abandon their originalism in light of such consequences. You might expect, then, a discussion of why the consequences of following original understanding in the public-employee case are more significant than consequences in other cases, most notably of course in the Court's originalist holding that the Second Amendment guarantees each of us a right to possess guns for self-defense. You don't find one.

The opinion then turns to the asserted absence of "persuasive founding-era evidence that public employees were understood to lack free speech protections." It notes that the union did identify early "restrictions on federal employees' activities," but says that "most of its historical examples involved limitations on public officials' outside business dealings, not on their speech." Again, the "most" is a giveaway.

The opinion identifies two early actions—in 1801 and 1806—that did involve restrictions on government employee speech. But "those examples at most show that the government was understood to have power to limit employee speech that threatened important governmental interests (such as maintaining military discipline and preventing corruption)—not that public employees' speech was entirely unprotected." Well, not necessarily. "At most" is rhetorical sleight-of-hand where "at least" would be more accurate. The examples could illustrate a more general principle to which the founding generation was committed. This is how the Court's current understanding of the First Amendment can best be defended on originalist grounds, as standing against government suppression of views with which it disagrees—with particular examples used to illustrate the presence of an as-yet-unstated general principle.

The opinion's most extended discussion of originalist materials follows. "We can safely say that, at the time of the adoption of the First Amendment, no one gave any thought to whether public-sector unions could charge nonmembers agency fees." This is a sort of original-expected-applications originalism, though exactly how it supports the conclusion that public employees were understood to have First Amendment rights is unclear.

Alito continues, "The idea of public-sector unionization and agency fees would astound those who framed and ratified the Bill of Rights." The attached footnote observes that "at common law, 'collective bargaining was unlawful.'" One might infer from this, were it relevant, that if collective bargaining was an unlawful activity, the First Amendment couldn't have been thought to protect measures intended to enable that activity.

More generally, though, the "astound those who framed the Bill of Rights" argument raises one of the broadest objections to originalism: Legal and social circumstances have changed so much since 1791 (or, strictly speaking with respect to the public-employee case, 1868) that we can't infer from what was generally understood then what the First Amendment should mean now. That might be a good reason for rejecting the union's broad claim, but—as critics of originalism have pointed out—it would also raise questions about the precise scope of the "things have changed so much" reason for looking to things other than the original understanding. It's easy to ask that question, for instance, about gun possession.

Finally, "prominent members of the founding generation condemned laws requiring public employees to affirm or support beliefs with which they disagreed. . . . Jefferson denounced compelled support for such beliefs as 'sinful and tyrannical,' and others expressed similar views." The citation is to Thomas Jefferson and the Virginia Bill for Establishing Religious Freedom, and the attached footnotes refer to discussions of the religious-oath clause. Alito's "such beliefs" mingles coercion with respect to religious beliefs with coercion with respect to political ones. That mingling is, on its face, problematic in light of what we know generally about religion—and politics—in the founding era. At the very least, an originalist ought to present original-materials evidence that the obvious distinction was not relevant in public understandings.

Justice Alito's opinion is quite instructive about how Supreme Court justices actually do originalism. It shows that the originalist material can be, and is, manipulated in exactly the same way that precedent is manipulated—by sometimes treating specific examples as confined to their facts rather than as illustrations of a general principle (the 1801 and 1806 material), and at other times, treating specific examples as illustrations of a general principle (the assimilation of religion and politics). Conservatives tack opportunistically between a barely perceptible original-expected-applications originalism and a completely unarticulated constitutional-construction originalism. The latter is indistinguishable from conservative living constitutionalism. Opportunism in the service of conservative outcomes is more damaging to self-styled originalists than seemingly similar moves made by non-originalists because originalists purport to hold that originalism is the *only* method of constitutional interpretation that prevents judges from injecting their personal preferences into the Constitution.[14]

Cases involving race discrimination are another example of conservative living constitutionalism. The relevant constitutional text is the Fourteenth Amendment's statement that "no State shall deny ... equal protection of the laws." It's reasonably clear that those who wrote that text believed that some forms of affirmative action—race-specific laws that they believed benefited recently emancipated African Americans—were constitutionally permissible, because they enacted such statutes.[15]

Today's conservative opposition to affirmative action might be consistent with original public meaning originalism, because "equal protection of the laws" is a phrase that gets construed differently over time. The problem then is to figure out, in any given context, what that construction is. The fact that race-specific programs were adopted shortly after the Equal Protection Clause became law counts in favor of a construction allowing affirmative action. Justice Thomas, arguing against it, has cited Frederick Douglass, who wrote in 1865 that African Americans should be skeptical of claims by white people that they were adopting race-specific programs that benefited African Americans, because such programs had a terrible track record. Whether Douglass's observation was accurate or not—I tend to think that in 1865, it was—it's hard to treat Douglass, an idiosyncratic thinker then and for many years afterward, as representing a contemporary public understanding of "equal protection of the laws."[16]

For generations after the 1870s, legislatures stopped adopting affirmative action programs, so there are no constructions to build on. Affirmative action started up again in the 1960s, regularly endorsed by legislatures and executives. So, you might think, "equal protection of the laws" had received a construction compatible with affirmative action.

Yet even as affirmative action programs were revived, the Supreme Court was deploying a doctrine placing race-specific legislation that clearly disadvantaged African Americans under what it called "strict scrutiny." To survive strict scrutiny, laws had to advance an extremely important goal (in the Court's language, they had to serve a "compelling governmental interest"), and had to do so in a precise way: they had to be "narrowly tailored" so as to cause the least possible harm, consistent with advancing the compelling interest.

When the Court faced constitutional challenges to affirmative action, it had a choice between constructions: Race-specific laws that purported to benefit African Americans might be constitutionally permissible in general, or they might be permissible only if they survived strict scrutiny. Nothing in original public meaning originalism could guide the justices in choosing between those constructions. Conservatives claiming to be original public meaning originalists acted in a way indistinguishable from how conservative living constitutionalists would have acted: they agreed that construction occurs when interpretation runs out, and that it does indeed run out when we're dealing with the words "equal protection of the laws."

I want to be clear about the argument here. It's not that you can't squeeze conservative opposition to affirmative action into the framework of original public meaning originalism, by using the idea of constitutional construction. Nor is it that the conservative opposition to affirmative action is indefensible, either on policy grounds or as a construction of the Equal Protection Clause. It's just that when you invoke modern originalism against affirmative action, you can't tell the difference between an originalist and a living constitutionalist in how they go about interpreting the Constitution.

The Court's conservatives objected in 2007, dealing with cases from Seattle and Louisville. Each city's school board had adopted voluntary programs aimed at integrating their public schools and made a child's race the decisive factor in determining which school the child was assigned to. Chief Justice Roberts's opinion contains not a word about any form of originalism. It relies entirely on a principle derived from prior cases, that the government must have extremely strong reasons for expressly using race as a basis for its decisions. Again, this might be a defensible constitutional construction. Maybe conservatives could say that originalist justices don't always have to "show their work" when they are dealing with constitutional constructions. The problem is that liberal originalists offer an alternative construction that distinguishes between using race as a reason for disadvantaging African Americans and using race as a reason for conferring benefits on them. Here too, conservatives have reasons to reject the liberal construction. Yet they could deploy those reasons without being originalists at all—or, put another way, they have "living constitutionalist" reasons for the positions they hold.[17]

There's a final matter, which seems at first to be mostly a discussion *among* originalists but which on inspection turns out to say something about originalism itself.[18] The controversy among originalists is this: Suppose you think that some earlier Supreme Court decision was wrong, largely because it wasn't based upon an originalist analysis. What do you do with that precedent? Justice Thomas offers a clear example: Disregard every non-originalist precedent, and base your decision today on the best originalist analysis you can come up with.

As the question of paper money illustrates, that could destabilize a lot. More moderate originalists say that they would ignore "egregiously" wrong precedents, and follow the precedents where the originalist evidence seems merely to suggest that the first decision was wrong. And sometimes they agree that originalists can disagree among themselves about whether the older decision was wrong on originalist grounds. All this introduces a degree of flexibility and personal judgment into originalist analysis: The words "egregiously wrong" are a pretty strong signal that personal judgments are at work.

Serious originalist Supreme Court opinions are rare, and for good reasons. Doing research into original public meaning is difficult and almost certainly beyond the capacity of the justices and their clerks. They have to rely on academic articles and briefs, but the latter almost always are slanted to one or the other side, and the former quite often are. (You might hope that briefs filed by amicus curiae—"friends of the Court"—might not be slanted, but there's now a well-established practice, known as amicus wrangling, in which the lawyers for the primary litigants rustle up supportive amicus briefs.) As Justice Scalia's stumble in the Second Amendment case shows, it's easy to make mistakes—inadvertently, but also motivated by a justice's hope to reach the result suggested by his or her first impression.[19]

Originalist opinions are often unnecessary as well. Most often— as in free speech cases—decades of precedents have accumulated. They are easily available to the justices, and as lawyers they know how to use precedents to make the moves they need to make. The underlying constitutional provisions are often ones subject to construction under contemporary originalist theory, and the precedents can count as constructions. Originalism is needed only when the Court is dealing with a term that hasn't received much construction since the founding era, and after two hundred years of adjudication and practice, there just aren't many terms like that.

Two recent cases, well known to academics but not to the general public, are good examples of originalist interpretation in the absence of judicial precedents. *NLRB v. Noel Canning Co.* involved the president's power "to fill up all Vacancies that may happen during the Recess of the Senate." The case posed two questions: Could the president invoke this clause if the Senate kept its recesses very short, specifically to prevent the president from making recess appointments, and did the clause apply only if the vacancy opened up while the Senate was in recess? Relying in part on original understandings, in part on accumulated practice by the Senate and presidents, and in part on a sense of how a good government would work, the Court held that the president could make recess appointments only if the Senate recessed for ten days or more (the number came out of thin air), and the vacancy could open up while the Senate was in session as long as it wasn't filled before the Senate recessed.[20]

Lucia v. SEC involved the definition of the words "officer of the United States." The Constitution says that such officers have to be appointed by the president or by a "principal Officer." Low-level bureaucrats can be hired through the civil service system without dragging the president into the process. How do you determine who's a "principal Officer"? Justice Kagan held for the Court that principal officers "exercise significant" national authority. Justice Thomas (of course), joined by Justice Gorsuch, agreed with the result in the case but would have relied on original understandings; he cited an article written by one of his former law clerks who did a corpus linguistics study on the question.[21]

Several things jump out from these cases. First, both involve obscure constitutional provisions that have received little judicial or public attention. (But as we will see in chapter 9, they are significant in light of a potential conservative effort to dismantle the administrative state.) Second, conservatives don't have to invoke original public meaning originalism to reach the results they favor. When they do so, it's mostly icing on a cake already baked.

The cases also show how limited the domain of modern originalism really is, how few provisions are subject to interpretation but not construction. Originalists and living constitutionalists certainly disagree about where they draw the line between interpretation and construction, but they agree that most of the constitutional provisions that generate today's major controversies—"equal protection," "due process," "freedom of speech"—are within the area of construction rather than interpretation.

I could repeat these exercises with other examples: the modern law of gender discrimination, for example. Each time, we would find that conservatives could defend their positions by invoking original public meaning originalism, but they rarely bother to do so. We would also find that the language of originalism, when it appears, is only a rhetorical signal of the opinion's affiliation with conservatism. It does no work.

Original public meaning originalism could have some payoff. Even terms subject to construction might have a core of meaning that was fixed when the terms were put into the Constitution, and independent of the times' social and cultural context. Originalism should rule out contemporary interpretations inconsistent with that core meaning.

According to originalists, such interpretations are the fatal flaw of living constitutionalism. Yet this is a completely rhetorical move. I know of no case decided in the past half-century—literally, no case— in which liberal living constitutionalists have endorsed outcomes that are inconsistent with a fixed core meaning. The cases conservatives offer as examples are sometimes those in which real controversy exists over whether the meaning was fixed independent of context, and sometimes cases in which research into original public meaning shows substantial divisions—the 65 percent–35 percent problem. In the latter cases, liberals have reasons for choosing the side they choose.

A final example is marriage equality, where a majority of the Court held that the Fourteenth Amendment's Due Process Clause, that people can't be deprived of "liberty" without due process of law, protected interests in equal dignity that were infringed by limiting marriage to heterosexual couples. Justice Thomas, not surprisingly, wrote an originalist dissent. Relying on authors such as the English legal scholar William Blackstone, the philosopher John Locke, and the American legal theorist James Wilson—writers from the eighteenth century—Thomas argued that "liberty," as used in the 1780s and 1790s, probably meant only a freedom of physical restraint, or perhaps a broader freedom from unjustified government "action, not as a right to a particular governmental entitlement." Then, referring only to state court decisions between 1791 and 1868, he continued that the term "likely" meant the same thing in 1868.[22]

What's striking about the opinion is that it relies on no major sources published after 1791. There's no detailed analysis of dictionaries, newspapers, or other materials included in corpus linguistics. That's not Thomas's fault—scholars haven't yet done the corpus linguistics studies of terms like "liberty" and "due process," perhaps because the task would be massive and the results would be rife with discretionary choices that would weaken any conclusion one might draw for contemporary interpretation.

Even putting that to one side, though, other than the footnote referring to state court decisions and one reference to an 1890 law review article, Thomas's opinion says nothing at all about the possibility that constitutional construction might give the terms broader meanings. There's a reason for that omission. After 1868, substantial arguments were made and adopted by the Supreme Court—from the late 1890s to the 1930s, and then from the 1960s on—construing the terms much more broadly. To invoke modern originalism against the gay marriage decision, you'd have to show that the terms weren't among those subject to construction over time—and Thomas didn't do that.

Though Justice Scalia joined Thomas's dissent, Alito and Chief Justice Roberts did not. This might show either that they are not "committed originalists" or, more interestingly, that they recognized that Thomas's version of originalism isn't the modern public understanding-plus-construction version.

The pattern of using a stripped-down originalism that doesn't take construction into account is reproduced when conservatives try to explain why their current views about the constitutionality of affirmative action and other topics are consistent with originalism properly understood. Often we get simple-minded textualism: "The Constitution doesn't say a word about abortion, or about the ideas of 'privacy' or 'dignity' or 'autonomy' that have been invoked to support challenges to restrictive abortion laws." We don't get an account of why the general term "due process of law" doesn't fall within the zone in which constitutional construction takes place, or why construing the phrase to extend to laws restricting abortion is inconsistent with original public meaning originalism's defense of constitutional construction beyond what was fixed when the Constitution's terms became law.

Looming over all this is the "Who cares?" question. Suppose today we think some action is really important for our national well-being. Who cares that the Framers would have considered it unconstitutional—or would not have understood the Constitution as giving the government the power to do it? Here's a silly but pointed example. The Constitution gives Congress the power to "raise and support Armies" and to "provide and maintain a Navy." In 2018, President Trump proposed a Space Force. Originalists of all stripes had no difficulty with that, as long as the Space Force was located within the Army or the Navy (like the Marines) or had the mission of supporting their Earth-bound operations (like the Air Force). One prominent originalist, though, worried about the constitutionality of a Space Force operating on its own in deep space. Suppose he's right. Who cares?[23]

The closest originalists come to explaining why we should care is that the Constitution as originally understood is really good, and we risk creating an overly powerful government, or failing to protect important rights, if we let current views of what's good and necessary override the Framers' understandings. That is particularly true if we think that when we deliberate about what's good and necessary, we may not notice our mistakes of reasoning and analysis.

Still, that's an argument about good government. If, after full reflection—including reflection on the possibility that our judgments might be distorted or mistaken—we today decide that Framers were mistaken and that creating a Space Force operating in deep space is what a good government should do, we don't have a solid reason for living under a worse government than we could simply because the Constitution as originally understood pushes us to that worse government.

We could, of course, amend the Constitution to allow Congress to create a Space Force. If we think the Framers just made a mistake, though, why should we have to take the trouble, at least if there's a plausible argument connecting the Space Force to some power Congress unquestionably has—that is, as long as the most modest requirements of textualism are satisfied? I don't know of any effective counterarguments mounted by originalists.

Yet originalism does do something. In the early years of the Reagan era, it explained why courts should not strike legislation down—it offered a theory of constitutional interpretation justifying "judicial restraint." At the time, conservatives worried that courts, still in the hands of Great Society judges, would stop them from moving their program forward.

The language of judicial restraint still pops up, particularly in the mouths of conservative politicians and op-ed writers. Today, though, originalism is a theory of judicial activism, explaining why it's OK for courts to hold statutes unconstitutional—including the poster child for originalism, restrictions on gun ownership. The reason is that courts have come under conservative control—or conservatives believe that they are likely to control the courts soon and for the indefinite future. When that happens, originalism can be used to stop liberals from achieving *their* legislative goals while not interfering with conservatives' favored laws.

Law professor Eric Segall published a book, *Originalism as Faith*, making arguments much like the ones I've sketched. Responding to Segall, a prominent sort-of-originalist blogged, "There is widespread agreement among originalists that the original meaning sets tighter limits on the scope of federal power relative to the states than is currently the case under post-New Deal Supreme precedent, that the Constitution provides substantially greater protection for property rights than currently exists, and that the Second Amendment includes a relatively robust individual right to bear arms." True enough, except that the post should have read, "agreement among conservative originalists." The agreement flows from their conservatism, not their originalism.[24]

The umpire metaphor and originalism are conservatives' Shibboleths: They signal who are the insiders they approve of, and who are outsiders they shun.* Because these ideas don't actually tell us anything about how conservative or liberal judges behave, I will pretty much ignore them in the remaining chapters. Instead I will focus on what these justices *do*—how their original impressions harden into holdings, and the political significance of those holdings. I do so not

---

* Why then are there liberal originalists? Liberal originalism may be a capitulation to what German legal theorist Georg Jellinek called the "normative power of the factual." If conservative justices want to hear originalist arguments, liberals ought to be able to produce them.

because the justices always act as Republicans or Democrats when they make their decisions—although they sometimes do—but because their initial impressions, hunches, and intuitions arise from a complex social and ideological world in which politics and constitutional ideology or philosophy have some effect on those first impressions, especially when politically significant issues come before the Court.

3

Playing Politics

Election and reelection are a politician's prime directives. If you don't get elected you can't enact any of the policies you think are important—at least, you have no more power to do so than any other citizen. Politicians do many things in pursuit of that goal. They help their constituents cope with bureaucracies; they issue policy statements and send out press releases; they support policies their constituents favor; they support policies important contributors favor (which aren't always favored by constituents).

Constitutional orders, populated by politicians, have a similar prime directive: Do what you can to ensure that the order holds on to power as long as possible, even if you sense that the order is on its last legs. The tools a constitutional order has are its policies. The prime directive is then simple: Adopt policies that help your friends and hurt your opponents. Or, as political scientists elegantly put it: "New policies create a new politics."[1] Policies that help your supporters make it easier to stay in office; policies that hurt your opponents make it easier to keep them from taking over. The Affordable Care Act for Democrats, the Trump tax cuts for Republicans: these are constituency-building policies.*

---

* Embedded in the Trump tax cuts were provisions limiting the deductibility of state income and property taxes, which hurt residents of high-tax, generally "blue" states.

The Supreme Court is part of a constitutional order too. Having the president nominate and the Senate confirm Supreme Court justices is a way of coordinating the elected branches with the judicial one.* But the Court's toolkit is different from Congress's. The justices can strike down laws that help the order's opponents, uphold laws that help its supporters, and—most aggressively—hold that the Constitution requires Congress and state legislatures to enact laws helping the order's supporters. By 2018, the Court had used the first two tools to sustain the Reagan Republican constitutional order; the third was still in reserve.

Importantly, the Court's majority might not have consciously intended to sustain that order, though individual justices might have had that goal in mind. Sometimes, sustaining that order was a happy by-product of constitutional philosophies that were themselves well integrated into the very same order.

Because policies make politics, what the Supreme Court says about the constitutionality of almost anything could be treated in a chapter on playing politics. Holding that the Second Amendment protects individuals' right to own guns, for example, cements the National Rifle Association's allegiance—and contributions—to the Republican Party.[2] This chapter, though, focuses on the Court's rulings on what legal academics call the law of politics: laws governing campaign finance, elections, and the like. I also discuss decisions dealing with—and limiting—the way liberal politics is funded.

---

* The full story gets complicated because the pace of change in the Court's composition differs from the pace of change in Congress and the presidency, but the general story—that the Supreme Court is (eventually) part of the prevailing constitutional order—remains accurate.

Campaign Finance

Any story about the Roberts Court and the law of politics has to begin with *Citizens United*. That's unfortunate, for several reasons. In itself, *Citizens United* was a minor tweak to existing campaign finance law. Worse, the intuition about the First Amendment and campaign finance that drove the decision is difficult to challenge within the broader structure of First Amendment law. *Citizens United* brought that intuition into the open, and thus emboldened people—most dramatically, enormously rich people—to set up organizations, known as Super-PACs, that dramatically increased their ability to spend money to support their favored candidates. Most politicians think that all this favored Republicans; academics who have studied the topic are less certain.[3]

Understanding *Citizens United* requires a short course in campaign finance law. Begin with the line, "Money isn't speech." Of course it isn't, but in many settings, money is an essential predicate for speech. If I can't figure out the best way to explain why Bernie Sanders or Rand Paul would be a great president, surely I should be allowed to hire someone—call him a speechwriter—to put my thoughts in order. And if I'm not a compelling speaker, surely I should be allowed to hire someone to deliver the speech—or compose the advertisement—that lays out my case for Sanders or Paul. So even if money isn't speech, it is in practical terms essential to communicating ideas to the public. Limiting what I can do with my money limits my ability to get my ideas across—which should trigger First Amendment concerns.

The modern age of campaign finance law began in 1976, when the Supreme Court struck a compromise. It divided the subject into two parts, one dealing with *contributions* we can make to candidates and political parties, the other dealing with *spending* by candidates and their supporters.

The Court held that legislatures could set limits on individual contributions to candidates to protect against corruption and the appearance of corruption. Many supporters of strict campaign finance regulation understood corruption in broad terms. They thought it was corrupt, or had the appearance of corruption, if politicians got so much money from an individual, or from rich people generally, that constituents would wonder whether the politicians were serving the constituents or the contributors.

This concern about corruption, broadly defined, intersected with a feeling that there ought to be some rough equality among candidates—a "level playing field." Making sense of this idea is quite difficult: Why should a Republican candidate in an overwhelmingly Democratic district have roughly the same amount of money as the Democrat to spend on the campaign? The Supreme Court dismissed the concern for equality as "foreign to the First Amendment," and so we were left with only corruption as a permissible reason for regulating money in campaigns.

The Court toyed briefly with the broad understanding of corruption but eventually settled on a narrower one. Contributions could be limited in order to prevent *"quid quo pro"* corruption—essentially bribery, the exchange of a campaign contribution for a promise to do the contributor's bidding after the election. Once it's put that way, it's easy to see how this is narrow. Think of someone who gives money to a candidate's campaign expecting that the candidate will support the contributor's pet project after the election. If the candidate isn't already holding the seat, the contributor is betting that the candidate will win and then honor the promise. We know, though, that politicians—like the rest of us—can be ingrates, or more politely, might tell the contributor that the time just wasn't right to introduce the project.

The contributor might do better by giving money to a candidate who was already likely to win—in which case the recipient has no reason to give a promise in return. And that, pretty much, is what contributors do. They look for candidates, mostly incumbents, who are likely to favor their projects for ideological or other reasons, and also likely to be elected. They hope for gratitude in return, not the fulfilment of a corrupt promise.

The Supreme Court hasn't yet extended this argument to contributions to candidates themselves (the topic returns in chapter 11). It has said, though, that the logic applies with full force to contributions to political parties, which collect money from contributors and funnel it out to candidates based on the parties' evaluation of the candidates' prospects. The possibility of *quid pro quo* corruption from such contributions is vanishingly small.

Quid pro quo corruption and, perhaps more important, the appearance of that type of corruption do exist. Still, no serious student of campaign finance considers it a major problem. And according to the Supreme Court, if the reality isn't a problem, the mistaken belief among the public that it *is* a problem can't be the kind of appearance of corruption that the Court thinks might matter. All this is a major reason why campaign expenditures are so high: Candidates spend as much as they can raise, and the only reason the Court recognizes for limiting contributions rarely comes into play.

What about campaign spending? The basic rule is simple: The First Amendment bars legislatures from limiting what people spend on political campaigns. A candidate can spend as much as she is able to raise. And people who support a candidate can spend as much as they want, as long as their spending is "independent" of the candidate's. The "independence" requirement looks in two directions. Truly independent spending can't generate a corrupt *quid pro quo* because the candidate receives no "this" in exchange for a "that." And spending that isn't truly independent—spending that, in the field's jargon, is coordinated with the candidate—is effectively a contribution that evades the constitutionally permissible limits.

The next point is that it's difficult to explain how limits on truly independent spending are consistent with conventional understandings of the First Amendment. If I want to impoverish myself by spending everything I own to support the candidacy of Bernie Sanders or Rand Paul, how could it possibly be constitutional for the government to forbid it?

Finally, neither corporations nor labor unions can give money from their organization's treasuries directly to candidates. The Court hasn't (yet) held these limits unconstitutional—and there's little need to. Starting in the 1940s, unions and then corporations set up "political action committees" (PACs). PACs solicit money from union members, corporate executives, and others, and use it in campaigns. Sometimes they give the money directly to candidates. Those contributions are capped, but the caps are higher than those placed on individual contributions. Sometimes PACs spend the money themselves, the familiar independent spending. And the same rule applies: No limits on independent spending. If a PAC uses its money *only* for independent spending, it's known as a Super-PAC.

So, according to the Supreme Court: Campaign contributions can be limited, but only if the limits are designed to prevent *quid pro quo* corruption. Campaign spending, whether by candidates or by their supporters, can't be limited, except for spending by supporters that is coordinated with the candidate's campaign.

Citizens United was about independent spending by Hillary Clinton haters. It held that corporations couldn't be prohibited from spending money from their treasuries to support or oppose political candidates. Lurking in the background was the rule—obviously correct—that corporations can use their money on "issue advertising." A coal company can publish an ad criticizing some environmental regulation as "job destroying," just as a company making wind turbines can publish an ad encouraging Congress to spend more money on renewable energy sources. Sometimes the line between issue advertising and supporting or opposing a candidate is quite thin: The "pro-coal" ad appears near the end of a campaign in which one candidate has taken a strong "pro-coal" stance and the other has taken an anti-coal stance.

Citizens United said that corporations didn't have to worry whether the advertisements their money paid for were about issues or candidates. Big public corporations in fact don't make many contributions to candidates, largely for fear of consumer backlash. In itself, *Citizens United* didn't greatly affect campaign contributions or spending.[4]

Its rationale, though, was that limiting independent expenditures by anyone—corporation or individual—ran up against serious First Amendment problems. A lower court quickly took the ball and ran with it, holding that all limits on truly independent expenditures are unconstitutional. That in turn encouraged advisers of politically engaged rich people to tell them, "All bets are off—spend what you want to support or oppose candidates you care about." And it bolstered the creation of Super-PACs. All this might have happened even without *Citizens United*. But the decision seems to have emboldened contributors and to have accelerated changes already occurring.

Most critics of the current constitutional law of campaign finance focus not on the relatively minor ruling in *Citizens United* that corporations can spend corporate money on campaigns, but on the proposition that most nominally independent spending is in fact coordinated under the table with candidates' campaigns. It probably is, which takes us back to the beginning: Does coordinated spending pose a serious risk of *quid pro quo* corruption? Most critics think it doesn't. But they think the Court's definition of corruption is too narrow.

The concluding point about campaign finance law is paradoxical.

Most scholars who have studied the matter think the current constitutional law of campaign finance regulation is close to a partisan wash: when we look at things broadly rather than district by district, Democrats and Republicans are operating on pretty much an even playing field with respect to both expenditures and contributions, though there might be a slight Republican tilt to some of the more arcane details of existing doctrine.

The view of politicians is quite different. The names of those who challenged campaign finance rules in the Supreme Court make the point: James Buckley, a Conservative senator from New York, and Mitch McConnell, who needs no introduction here, were the key challengers. Republicans more or less uniformly oppose restrictive campaign finance regulations and Democrats more or less uniformly support them.

Perhaps politicians know better than academics how money works in campaigns. Even if not, though, Supreme Court justices might consciously or unconsciously view decisions striking down campaign finance restrictions as helping to preserve the Republican-dominated constitutional order.

Voter Identification Laws

Donald Trump claims millions of votes were cast illegally in 2016 by people who voted twice or more, or who weren't entitled to vote at all but snuck into the polling booths anyway. For Republicans, the solution to this problem is laws demanding voter identification at the polling place—requiring people who show up to vote to present proof that they are entitled to do so.

Democrats describe such laws as "voter suppression" laws. They believe that in-person voter fraud, the only thing voter ID laws prevent, is a trivial problem affecting a tiny percentage of votes. To them, voter ID laws make voting hard or impossible for people who don't have ready access to government-issued IDs. And that, they say, is their purpose. Such people fall into population groups—the poor, students, and, to some degree, the elderly—that tend to vote for Democrats.

Some voter ID laws say that only an original birth certificate will count. Coming up with a birth certificate is difficult for people who have moved a lot or don't know how to navigate the bureaucracies that issue birth certificates. Other voter ID laws say that identification issued to students by a state university doesn't count. Gun registrations and concealed-carry permits—signs of likely Republican allegiance—are often acceptable.

Party behavior seems to confirm the Democrats' view. Republican-controlled legislatures adopt voter ID laws that limit the kinds of identification that count, often by party line votes; other legislatures don't. As soon as the Republican-controlled legislature in Texas was relieved of the obligation to get approval from the Department of Justice for changes in voting rules, it jumped on the chance to enact a voter ID law.

The Supreme Court endorsed restrictive voter ID laws in 2008, with the prevailing opinion written by Justice John Paul Stevens, who may have been unduly influenced by his experience with elections in a Chicago dominated by a Democratic political machine. Indiana's law was not as restrictive as many. Voters had to present a government-issued ID, which could be a passport, a driver's license, or a special voter ID card the state had created.[5]

Justice Stevens acknowledged that Indiana had not shown that in-person voter fraud was a serious problem, but he noted "flagrant examples" of such fraud elsewhere and at other times. He referred to voter fraud in East Chicago, Indiana. Even though this example did not involve in-person fraud, it was good enough for Stevens.

What about the interests of people who wanted to vote but

couldn't get acceptable ID cards? Stevens said that the challengers had not presented evidence that it was too difficult to obtain acceptable voter ID. Most people already had drivers' licenses, for example. Stevens agreed that getting an ID might be hard for "a limited number of persons," such as "elderly persons born out-of-state," but he pointed out that Indiana allowed them to cast a provisional ballot and gave them ten days to come up with an acceptable ID. Maybe that would be too hard for a handful of people, but that possibility wasn't enough to invalidate the entire voter ID law.

The Indiana decision validated one state's voter ID laws but left room for challenging others. Lower courts have put some of the most restrictive voter ID laws on hold, not because of their partisan tilt but because they were adopted in order to suppress votes by African Americans—"with almost surgical precision," as one court put it. Careful Republican legislatures can still follow Indiana's lead and adopt voter ID laws that favor Republicans. The Court's voter ID decision protects one important attempt by Republicans to preserve their political position. (Subtler forms of vote restriction remain available as well but have not yet attracted the Supreme Court's attention.)

Yet as with campaign finance reform, the partisan effects of voter ID laws are unclear. A large recent study concludes that these laws have little effect on voter turnout (or on identifying voter fraud)—although in a world where important elections are decided by narrow margins, very small effects may matter a lot. And although the effects may be small, their direction is indeed what the politicians expect: a small tilt toward Republicans.[6]

Partisan Gerrymandering

In the 1960s, the Supreme Court held that every legislative and congressional district within a state had to have almost exactly the same number of people as every other legislative or congressional district. This eliminated "malapportionment" and benefited the then rapidly growing suburbs at the expense of rural areas, with relatively little effect on large cities.

This decision opened the way for a revival of gerrymandering. Today's gerrymanders involve districts that all have the same number of people but whose boundaries are drawn to accomplish some particular goal—sometimes racial (limiting or increasing the ability of racial minorities to elect representatives), sometimes political. Racial gerrymandering overlaps with political gerrymandering because racial minorities tend to vote for Democrats. A race-based gerrymander is usually a Republican-favoring gerrymander as well.

The Voting Rights Act of 1965 outlawed racial gerrymandering but left pure political gerrymandering untouched. Both parties use gerrymanders when they can, but in the twenty-first century Republicans proved better at it than Democrats. Democratic political strategists focused on winning elections for Congress; Republicans gave more attention to state elections. Even as Democrats were gradually losing their grip on Congress, they were being pushed aside in droves by Republicans in state legislatures. And state legislatures draw the district lines. Chance mattered too: Public disaffection with the Obama administration led to extremely large Republican victories in 2010, not only in Congress but in state legislatures. States have to draw district lines at least every ten years, when the national census tells them how many people are living in each area in the state. With the 2010 victories in hand, Republicans were well positioned to entrench themselves through partisan gerrymandering.[7]

They quickly adopted sophisticated technologies that allowed them to draw districting maps precisely to maximize the chance that Republicans would control legislatures and have a majority of congressional seats. In 2012, for example, Democratic candidates for Congress in Pennsylvania won 51 percent of the votes cast for those seats, but they elected only 5 out of 18 representatives (about 28 percent). The figures for North Carolina in 2014 were similar: Democrats won 46 percent of the votes but won only 23 percent of the seats. Republicans accomplished these results by "stacking" and "cracking": putting a large number of presumed Democrats in a few districts and distributing the rest among districts where they would be swamped by presumed Republican voters.

Democrats tried to overcome their disadvantages in legislatures by moving to the courts, but they were consistently stymied by the Supreme Court. In 1986 and 2004, it held that partisan gerrymandering could theoretically violate the Constitution, but it refused to find that unconstitutional gerrymandering had in fact occurred—and pointed out how hard it would be to come up with a sensible standard for determining when such a gerrymander had happened. The Court's more conservative justices regularly said that the entire enterprise of trying to get the courts to find a partisan gerrymander unconstitutional was misconceived.

By 2018, it was clear that none of the Court's conservatives were likely to hold partisan gerrymandering unconstitutional. The Democrats' only hope had been Anthony Kennedy, and when he retired that year, constitutional law seemed settled; with his departure, the chances of the challengers' winning disappeared. In 2019 the Court's conservative majority held that federal courts couldn't do anything about partisan gerrymandering because the Constitution gave them no standards by which they could determine whether a partisan gerrymander went too far. Partisan gerrymandering, a powerful tool Republicans used more effectively than Democrats, was here to stay.[8]

The 1965 Voting Rights Act

Enacted at the height of the civil rights movement and then regularly reenacted, the Voting Rights Act of 1965 outlawed racial gerrymandering and other changes in local election laws that made it harder for African Americans and members of other racial minorities to elect the representatives they preferred, even in areas where they might have had a shot at doing so. A simple example: A city is 60 percent white, 40 percent African American, voters are racially polarized, and the city council has ten members. Elect the city council at-large, and ten whites are elected; elect the city council by districts, and there's a decent chance that three or four members will be African Americans.

Not all election rules are that simple, though, and showing that a rule makes it hard for racial minorities to elect their preferred candidates is often difficult. That is especially so when the city or state comes up with "good government" reasons for the rule: "We're closing down a lot of polling places in minority areas because we now have technologically sophisticated polling booths that can handle many more voters, and as it happens the facilities in white areas have the kinds of electrical and internet connections needed to operate these new booths."

The Voting Rights Act and its successors dealt with this sort of problem by identifying a number of states—initially seven states in the South plus Arizona and Alaska—that had shown a historical pattern of excluding racial minorities from voting (African Americans in the South, Hispanics in Arizona, and Aleuts in Alaska).[9] Under Section Five of the Voting Rights Act, legislatures and election officials in those states couldn't change their election rules without getting approval from the Department of Justice. The department would "preclear" a change only if it concluded that the change had neither the purpose nor the effect of discriminating by race.

By far the most changes requiring preclearance were minor adjustments—moving a polling place because it had been in a school that was closed for renovation, for example—and the department approved these changes routinely. Obtaining preclearance, though, was still a burden. More important, election officials in the covered jurisdictions often resented the fact that they had been singled out for this treatment. They had to get Washington's permission to make changes their colleagues in other states could make whenever they wanted. They wanted to be in the same position: make the changes and then see if they were challenged.

Even more important, conservative constitutional scholars argued that the preclearance requirement was inconsistent with basic principles of federalism—principles that lay at the foundation of the constitutional order.

Most important of all: most of the covered jurisdictions were in the South, which by the turn of the twenty-first century had become Republican-dominated. Sometimes Republicans wanted to change the election rules to strengthen their party position. Sometimes, they thought, the Department of Justice blocked partisan changes by claiming that the election officials hadn't proved that the changes wouldn't discriminate on the basis of race. That was particularly true under Democratic administrations, Republicans thought, but they also thought the Justice Department's permanent bureaucracy was either overly fond of finding race discrimination or even biased toward Democrats. The solution was to get rid of Section Five.

Congress had regularly renewed the Voting Rights Act, typically by large margins, so—following well-established patterns—Republicans went to court. The Roberts court obliged. First it adopted an extremely creative reading of Section Five to hold that a utility district in Texas didn't have to go through the preclearance process. Chief Justice Roberts's opinion explained that the interpretation was justified because there were serious doubts about Section Five's constitutionality. The Court's liberals, relieved that the Court didn't actually hold Section Five unconstitutional, joined his opinion.[10]

Four years later, their willingness to go along turned around and bit them. In *Shelby County v. Holder,* the chief justice wrote an opinion squarely holding Section Five unconstitutional, and criticized the liberal dissenters for failing to explain why they had agreed four years earlier that there was a serious constitutional principle at stake.

What was that principle? The chief justice called it a "fundamental principle of equal sovereignty among the States." Critics said, with some justification, that the chief justice had basically made this up. The Constitution does contain a couple of provisions referring to uniformity among the states. One deals with bankruptcy law; the other, far more important, guarantees the states equal representation in the Senate regardless of their population. A textualist might say that when the Constitution identified two specific forms of equality among the states, it precluded other more general forms—or, as we saw in chapter 2, that the two specific examples were instances of a more general principle that pervaded the Constitution as a whole.

Nor were there strong precedents to rely on. The only solid one—other than Roberts's own four-year-old opinion dealing with Section Five itself, and a few passing references to the principle in cases that did not actually invoke it—was a decision from 1911. The 1906 statute admitting Oklahoma to the union said that the state's capital had to remain in Guthrie forever. After it was admitted, the state relocated its capital to Oklahoma City. The Supreme Court held the 1906 provision unconstitutional because it was inconsistent with a long-standing principle that, once admitted, all states were on an equal footing. If Texas or Indiana could relocate their capital, the equal-footing doctrine meant that Oklahoma must have the power to do the same. This is a thin platform on which to rest a decision as significant as *Shelby County.*[11]

Once again, the Court's decision furthered the Republican program of partisan entrenchment. As already noted, the Republican legislature and the governor of Texas, taking immediate advantage of their new freedom, adopted a strict voter ID law. What Texas did was replicated throughout the South, sometimes in the large, as when states restricted early voting, a practice thought to favor Democrats, and sometimes in the small, as when states and counties selectively closed polling places.

Defunding the Left

By the time Michael Avenatti became famous across the country as Stormy Daniels's lawyer, he was already well known in California as an effective trial lawyer for consumers suing large corporations. He won a $450 million verdict against Kimberly-Clark Corporation because it misled hospitals about how effective its gowns were in protecting against infection. A funeral park paid more than $80 million to settle a case he brought alleging that the owners had ordered workers to dig up graves and coffins to make room for the park's expansion. Avenatti's income came from a share of the money he won for his clients — typically for trial lawyers, between one-quarter and 40 percent of the recovery.

Many plaintiff-side lawyers like Avenatti support the Democratic Party. Representing ordinary people against large corporations, they feel an affinity for Democrats' historical position as the party of the working person — and their support has been reciprocated by Democratic-sponsored laws that expand corporations' liability for harm and make it easier for plaintiffs to sue.

Trial lawyers' political affiliations inspired a long-standing Republican strategy to "defund the left." The idea was simple. The trial lawyers won large verdicts and used some of those winnings to support Democrats. Republicans could clip their wings by making it more difficult to win large awards, thereby reducing their incomes.

The mechanisms discussed to this point in the chapter help Republicans by letting them use their legislative power to entrench themselves. Defunding the left turns that mechanism around. Instead of helping Republicans, it uses statutory and constitutional interpretation to deprive Democrats of financial resources. As Justice Kagan put it in an important decision in 2018, the Court's conservatives "turn[ed] the First Amendment into a sword," as they did with other constitutional and statutory provisions.

Because trial lawyers' income was a percentage of what they won for plaintiffs, the trick was to push recoveries down. The attack on trial lawyers' income had two prongs, one constitutional and the other statutory.

Plaintiffs can suffer actual injuries—such as infections if hospital gowns don't protect them adequately. They can recover "actual" or "compensatory" damages to cover the real costs of those injuries—such as the cost of medical treatment, lost wages while they recovered, or compensation for pain and emotional trauma. Sometimes, when juries find that the defendants' wrongdoing was particularly egregious, they can also recover "punitive" damages. The $450 million award Avenatti won against Kimberly-Clark included a large punitive component.

Ordinarily, state courts set the standards for determining when juries can award punitive damages and how much they can award. Corporations began waging a war against punitive damages around 1980—perhaps not coincidentally, just as the New Deal/Great Society constitutional order was about to stagger off into history. They mounted a constitutional challenge based on the Due Process Clause, arguing that the standards states had come up with were too vague.

The attack on punitive damages reached the Supreme Court in 1989, but the first challenge failed, as did follow-ups in 1991 and 1993. The Court took the corporations' arguments seriously but rejected them on relatively narrow grounds. In 1996, the Court held a punitive damage award unconstitutional for the first time. Then in 2003 it came up with a rule—pretty much from nowhere—that punitive damages usually couldn't exceed more than ten times the actual damages.[12]

The punitive-damages cases show why it's valuable to distinguish between the views of individual justices and the Supreme Court as an institution participating in a constitutional order. Limiting punitive damages did defund the left, but Justices Scalia and Thomas insisted that the principles of federalism and constitutional interpretation to which they were committed provided no foundation for limiting punitive damages. So, although most of the justices who supported limiting punitive damages were appointed by Republican presidents, they gained majorities for their position only by occasionally getting support from more liberal colleagues. Even so, the outcome was consistent with the program of defunding the left.

Of course ten times a large number is an even larger number. If plaintiff-side trial lawyers could come up with a large enough group of injured consumers and similar plaintiffs, they could still make a more-than-decent income. Class-action lawsuits were the vehicle of choice.

A class action pulls together everybody who has been hurt by a defendant's action—for example, everyone who owned a cemetery plot in Avenatti's funeral-park case. They are allowed when, as the relevant rule puts it, they present "common questions" of law and fact. In 2011, the Supreme Court adopted a more restrictive definition of "common question" than many lower courts had. To put it informally, to qualify as a class, members had to suffer the same kind of injury from the same kind of wrongdoing.

For many of the cases brought by plaintiff-side trial lawyers, the "common cause" requirement wasn't difficult to satisfy: The funeral park had a policy of digging up graves, and that caused the same injury to every owner of a cemetery plot. More complicated theories of "common cause" ran into difficulty. The plaintiffs in the 2011 case were female employees of Wal-Mart, who contended that the company's policy of letting local managers decide what to pay employees led to salary discrimination against them. Several justices were puzzled about what the common question was. Wal-Mart's policy of letting local managers decide salaries might be called discriminatory because it gave sexist managers permission to follow their prejudiced instincts, but several justices thought labeling that policy discriminatory was a stretch.[13]

Even more problematic for plaintiff-side trial lawyers was the requirement that the injuries be roughly of the same sort. Suppose a car maker installs defective airbags. Sometimes the bags don't deploy at all, sometimes they deploy incompletely; sometimes people die when the bags don't deploy, sometimes they suffer broken bones, and sometimes they simply suffer emotional trauma. Are these the same kinds of injuries? The point is not that the requirement of rough similarity can't be satisfied, but that it gave defendants a bargaining chip they could and did use to push down the possible recovery after trial—and therefore during settlement negotiations.

Class actions usually take place in court. Lawyers for corporations figured out another way to keep damage awards down. They included provisions in sales and employment contracts requiring that any disputes be submitted to arbitration—and then added that the arbitration had to be on a consumer-by-consumer or employee-by-employee basis, without the possibility of a class action within the arbitration process. After plaintiff-side trial lawyers persuaded some important state courts to hold that the no-class-action provisions were unenforceable as a matter of state contract law, corporations' lawyers went to the Supreme Court and persuaded it that the Federal Arbitration Act required state courts to follow the no-class-action provisions.[14]

The decisions about punitive damages, class actions, and arbitration didn't drive plaintiff-side trial lawyers out of business. There was enough serious corporate wrongdoing to support profitable cases even within the narrower parameters the Court laid out. But the Court did make these lawyers' lives more difficult. Its decisions also reduced their income, and reduced the number of lawyers able to make a living in that capacity. All that in turn reduced the contributions these lawyers could make to the Democratic Party.

The program of defunding the left through constitutional interpretation had another prong. Like plaintiff-side trial lawyers, labor unions were historically strong supporters of the Democratic Party. The first political action committee, for example, was a PAC formed by the Congress of Industrial Organizations (CIO). Union PACs gave Democrats money and union volunteers went door to door canvassing voters. Private-sector unions weakened dramatically through the late twentieth century, but unions representing public workers—teachers, city employees, police, and the like—remained strong and mostly Democratic leaning.

But public-sector labor unions faced a constitutional problem. Decades-old decisions hold that the government can't force people to say things they disagree with. And once we understand that money is closely associated with speech, we can see why the Court extended those decisions to hold that the government can't force people to pay money to be used for advocating political positions they disagree with.

Some complicated lines have to be drawn here, but the basic idea is simple: If the government tells a public school teacher who opposes the Democratic Party, "You have to pay dues to a union, which is going to give thirty percent of it to the Democratic candidate for governor," the teacher has a substantial First Amendment objection: "You can't make me spend my money to support a candidate I oppose."

The Court agreed, and in a series of decisions it said that public-sector unions had to divide their dues into two parts. One part raised money to do work-related things, like pay for representation when schools tried to discipline union members and—crucially—to pay the costs of engaging in bargaining with the public employer. The other part raised money for political spending, whether supporting candidates or issue-advertising. According to the Court, the First Amendment allowed public-sector unions to require members to pay dues for the first set of activities, but prohibited them from requiring that members pay dues for the second.

That compromise held, though shakily, for about forty years. Conservatives attacked it almost from the beginning. As they saw things, everything a public-sector union did, involved politics. Consider wages, the core of collective bargaining. When a teachers' union demands a wage increase, the school board has to find the money somewhere—by raising taxes, cutting programs, or some other means. Those choices flow inevitably from bargaining over wages, and they are quintessentially political.

A few decisions in the 2000s weakened the initial compromise, and then in 2018, the Court rejected it entirely. Justice Alito's opinion for the Court overruled the decision adopting the compromise. Indeed, everything public-sector unions did involved politics, so objectors couldn't be forced to pay dues at all. The compromise, Justice Alito wrote for the Court's conservative majority, was badly reasoned from the start, and its force had been undermined by later decisions attempting to come up with a better justification. The most recent decisions expressed skepticism about whether the compromise was consistent with the First Amendment—and that skepticism, according to Alito, was well-founded.[15]

Alito's opinion concluded with a delicate observation: "[T]he loss of payments from nonmembers may cause unions to experience unpleasant transition costs in the short term, and may require unions to make adjustments in order to attract and retain members." Public-sector unions seem to have developed alternatives to the compromise they had lived with. Yet, the Court's decision amounted to an almost literal defunding of the left—perhaps not the finishing touch on a long-term program, but certainly a major accomplishment.[16]

The Home Team

The decisions examined in this chapter have the effect of help-ing Republicans and hurting Democrats. As I argued in chapter 1, we needn't assume that the justices who did all this intended those effects—although we don't have to assume that they were entirely oblivious either. Many, perhaps all, of the decisions are defensible as law if you are inclined to defend them—although of course the opposite decisions would have been at least as defensible. Even *Shelby County*, perhaps the weakest of the lot, could be said to rest on a non-textual background assumption about federalism.

In this book, however, my aim is to look at the Court's decisions with reference not to their grounding in law but to their role in build-ing, maintaining, and defending a constitutional order—here, the Reagan constitutional order when that order was facing real stresses. The Court's conservatives (arguably like the liberals when they held the majority) called balls and strikes in a way that favored the home team.

4

"We've Done Enough":
The Constitutional Law of Race

Writing in the *Shelby County* case, Chief Justice Roberts explained why eliminating the preclearance requirement made sense: "things have changed dramatically" since the Voting Rights Act was adopted in 1965. "Problems remain, [but] ... there is no denying that ... our Nation has made great strides" in reducing racial discrimination in voting. Recently, the Court has brought the same perception to other cases dealing with race discrimination.

It still objects to blatant racism. In 2017 the Court overturned Duane Buck's death sentence. Buck's attorney inexplicably called psychologist Walter Quijano to testify against imposing the death penalty—inexplicably because Quijano regularly testified for the prosecution and equally regularly told jurors that African-American defendants were more likely to be violent in the future. Quijano did just that in Buck's case. In 1999 the Supreme Court held that using his testimony to support a death sentence was unconstitutional. John Cornyn, then the Texas attorney general, took what Chief Justice Roberts called the "remarkable step" of agreeing that death sentences in five cases where Quijano testified should be vacated. His successor Greg Abbott, now the governor of Texas, refused to do the same in Buck's case because Buck's own lawyer had called Quijano to the stand. Bulldozing through some serious procedural objections raised by Justice Thomas in dissent, Roberts relied on the 1999 holding, writing that juries couldn't "make a decision on life or death on the basis of race" and that Quijano's racist testimony, even though only one part of the state's case, was a "toxin [that] can be deadly in small doses."[1]

A few weeks later, Justice Kennedy joined the Court's liberals to relax a traditional rule barring inquiry after a conviction into the possibility that an individual juror misbehaved. In *Pena Rodriguez v. Colorado,* the misbehavior was racism—two jurors said that a third had said things like, "I think he did it because he's a Mexican and Mexican men take whatever they like." What Kennedy called the "imperative to purge racial prejudice from the administration of justice" overrode the tradition.

In a similar case, the Court described overt racism in the criminal process as "unusual." When the facts were as clear as they were in these cases, it could intervene without casting doubt on the racial fairness of the whole legal system. But faced with claims of systemic wrong, the Court balked.

School Integration

For about three decades after *Brown v. Board of Education* held segregation unconstitutional, the Court's docket of segregation cases dealt with claims that school boards were moving too slowly to eliminate it. The Court mostly agreed. The tone began to shift in the 1970s and 1980s, with a Court led by Chief Justices Warren Burger and then William Rehnquist limiting the steps it would require schools to take to desegregate. By the late 1980s and 1990s the tenor of the Court's holdings was clear: Almost everywhere, school boards had done enough to eliminate segregation.

In 2007, shortly after Chief Justice Roberts came to the Court, the tone shifted again. Now the Court held that school boards had done *too much* to eliminate racial segregation. In the late 1990s and early 2000s, school boards in Seattle and Louisville had used programs aimed at integrating their schools. They believed it was good social and educational policy for each school in the district to mirror the racial composition of the district as a whole rather than, for example, that of the neighborhood where the school was located. So they developed policies to assign students to schools to achieve this integration. Each board's program began with a complicated set of rules that didn't refer to race, but both systems used race as a tie-breaker: If the other rules hadn't achieved the desired racial makeup of a specific school, a student's race—white, African American, or (in Seattle) Asian—would determine which school he or she attended.

These programs were voluntary from the school boards' point of view, but of course they were not voluntary from the point of view of students and their parents. Groups of white parents in both cities challenged the programs, claiming they were unconstitutional because the tie-breaking rules expressly relied on race. Chief Justice Roberts agreed. Getting over racism was an important social and educational goal, but, he wrote, "The way to stop discrimination on the basis of race is to stop discriminating on the basis of race."[2]

Justice Kennedy concurred in the result but did not endorse everything the chief justice said. He did agree, though, that both cities' policies were unconstitutional—in part because they were badly administered. In Louisville, for example, it wasn't clear exactly how or when race was used as a tie-breaker. More important for Kennedy, though, was that the cities had other means available to achieve the desired integration. He suggested, for example, that they could pick locations for newly built schools with an eye to their likely racial composition—the decision would be "race conscious," as some scholars put it, but not race-specific. The suggestion was quite unrealistic, though: Student enrollments in many cities, though not Seattle and Louisville, were shrinking, and those cities were closing schools rather than building new ones.

Justices Stevens and Breyer wrote passionate dissents. Unusually, Breyer read his dissent from the bench and later called it the most important opinion he had written as a justice. Stevens pointedly wrote that "no Member of the Court that I joined in 1975 would have agreed with today's decision." That roster included William Rehnquist. Stevens's observation showed how dramatically the constitutional regime that had settled in by 2007 differed from the one it displaced.

The prior order's constitutional doctrine acknowledged that race mattered in society. It allowed government to take race into account. A decision written by Justice William Brennan in 1968 said that the goal of desegregation was "a system without a 'white' school and a 'Negro' school, but just schools." The ambiguity of the word "just"— "merely" or "consistent with justice"—was almost certainly intended. In 1968, the word may well have suggested that the vision animating the constitutional order was of a non-racial society—schools should be "merely" schools. But as affirmative action came on the scene, many people came to hold another vision, that of a multi-racial society, and the meaning of "just" shifted to "consistent with justice."[3]

Like the prior order's doctrine, the current one's acknowledges that race matters in society; that acknowledgment clearly underpinned Kennedy's observations about school locations and is the best explanation for Roberts's rhetoric. But unlike the older doctrine, the current one denies that race could matter in law. It envisions the United States as a non-racial society. Should that vision in turn be displaced, either a multi-racial or a white nationalist alternative will likely come to the fore.

Affirmative Action

Questions about quotas for important positions have bedeviled policy makers since at least the 1920s, when the possibility that the United States would become a multi-ethnic nation brought on a nativist backlash against immigration. Harvard University imposed, then removed, quotas for Jewish students; Justice Felix Frankfurter worried that campaigns by African Americans, with banners like "Lucky Won't Hire Negro Clerks in Proportion to Negro Trade—Don't Patronize," would lead to employment quotas.[4]

These questions took on wider importance in 1969, after President Richard Nixon directed government officials and contractors to take "affirmative actions" to ensure that they were not discriminating against African Americans in filling job openings. Initially, affirmative action meant only that employers would take a hard look at their hiring practices. It gradually morphed into something else—employers set targets to give them a rough guide to whether their processes were discriminatory. Then the targets became goals, and the goals hardened so that failure to meet them became a strong indication that discrimination was going on.

By the 1970s, affirmative action in employment and higher education had become politically controversial—another indication that the New Deal/Great Society constitutional order was under pressure. The Supreme Court decided a handful of cases involving affirmative action in employment. The factual settings varied, and the rulings were complex, but the outcome was a seeming compromise: Employers could use affirmative action to fill positions if they did so in a subtle, perhaps even covert manner.

The Court confronted affirmative action most explicitly in a series of cases involving higher education. The defendants were the flagship campuses of state universities in Washington, California, Michigan, and Texas. The *Bakke* case, from California in 1978, set out the terms of a compromise that stuck through the early 2000s. Universities could not take race into account to achieve some specific racial composition in their classes; enforcing an explicit quota would be unconstitutional. But they could take it into account to achieve what they, as experts in educational policy, judged to be a diversity that would benefit all students.

The compromise had a peculiar effect. Academic administrators who had started affirmative action programs because they had a vision of what their classes should look like (literally) became convinced that diversity was an important educational value, and they administered their affirmative action programs with a great deal of attention to race. Opponents of affirmative action saw the invocation of diversity as a fig-leaf for racial balance—and they weren't entirely mistaken.

The Court restated the compromise in 2003 in decisions involving affirmative action programs at the University of Michigan, one at the undergraduate college, the other at the law school. To simplify the story: Admissions officers at the undergraduate college, charged with processing thousands of applications, assigned numerical values to a variety of applicant characteristics, added them up, and offered admission to those whose scores exceeded some predetermined cut-off. One of the characteristics given a number was race. Admissions officers at the law school, in contrast, assessed applicants' files as a whole, making an intuitive evaluation about whether the applicant was likely to succeed and what qualities the applicant would bring to the classroom. They "took race into account," as they put it, but not in any hard and fast way.

The Court held that the university violated the Constitution in its undergraduate admissions program. Giving race a fixed value was too much like a racial quota. It also held that the law school's program was permissible: Taking race into account in a flexible way was an appropriate way to achieve the goal of diversity and the educational benefits associated with it.[5]

But the record of the law school case contained an embarrassing fact. The law school admitted students on a "rolling" basis — offers of admission were sent out as the admissions officers evaluated the files in front of them. The embarrassment was that the officers monitored the racial composition of the class as these offers were made and accepted. Though the university couldn't admit it openly, this meant that if the officers saw that they hadn't extended "enough" offers to members of minority groups or that not enough of such applicants had accepted these offers, they would increase the weight given to race in the remaining files. This practice made sense only if the law school had a sense of what it meant to have "enough" racial minorities, and that idea was uncomfortably close to seeking a predetermined racial balance in each class. Yet the Court had said that the Constitution barred universities from taking racial balance as a goal.

Taking race into account in a whole-file review imposed some costs on universities, which could preserve their affirmative action programs only by hiring more people to process applications. But, again, the 2003 compromise seemed to stick for a while.

At the University of Texas, the early response to the Court's affirmative action decisions was to abandon any express reliance on race in admissions to its Austin campus. With Republican governor George W. Bush's support, the legislature enacted a "10 percent plan": anyone who finished in the top ten percent of his or her high school class was automatically admitted to the Austin campus. Everyone knew that this would produce classes with a fair amount of racial diversity, because Texas's high schools were racially identifiable. Many schools had heavily African-American student bodies, others had heavily Hispanic ones. The top ten percent from those schools would come to Austin and integrate the campus. This was a "race conscious but not race specific" approach akin to the one Justice Kennedy later approved in the Seattle and Louisville cases.

After the Supreme Court approved Michigan's "whole file" review approach, the University of Texas supplemented the ten percent plan with a "whole file" approach to be used for the seats that remained unfilled after the ten percenters were admitted. Opponents of affirmative action objected. The "whole file" approach was in effect being used to achieve a desired racial balance at the Austin campus. Ultimately, in 2016, the Supreme Court upheld the Texas system on a four-to-three vote. Justice Kagan couldn't participate, because as solicitor general she had supported Texas earlier in the litigation, and Justice Scalia had passed away. Justice Kennedy, who had dissented in the Michigan cases of 2003, cast the deciding vote and wrote the Court's opinion.[6]

In the Michigan cases, Justice O'Connor had written that "race-conscious admissions policies must be limited in time." She observed that the Court had first approved diversity-based affirmative action in 1978, twenty-five years earlier. "We expect that 25 years from now, the use of racial preferences will no longer be necessary." Notably, Justice Ginsburg endorsed the idea that affirmative action programs must have a time limit. If the Court is dominated by conservatives in 2028, it will surely follow through on O'Connor's observation and say that time's up. Before then, such a Court may well find specific flaws in any affirmative action programs that come before it, with the central flaw being that, as administered, the programs actually seek racial balance rather than diversity. Or it might simply cut to the chase and overrule the compromise, holding all forms of race-conscious affirmative action—which is to say, all affirmative action programs— unconstitutional.

Most state colleges and universities have more seats than they have qualified applicants. Basically, everyone who satisfies quite lax standards of language and mathematical literacy can get in to one of those colleges, making affirmative action irrelevant. Affirmative action in education is confined to elite and "flagship" schools. These schools' administrators are committed to achieving diversity, and the formal demise of affirmative action—defined as the express use of race in admission decisions—is unlikely to end it in practice. The Court's decisions in the Michigan and Texas cases give admissions officers at elite schools enough flexibility to achieve racial balance in the guise of pursuing diversity. They will regularly face legal challenges, and if they are too overt about what they're doing they may lose some cases. But race-conscious affirmative action is likely to persist no matter what the law formally requires.

The disconnect between the principles animating the late-Reagan constitutional order and the practices and commitments of administrators at elite universities—and, more broadly, of elites generally—suggests the difficulty of constructing a new post-Reagan constitutional order. The vision of the United States as a non-racial society, which will remain important on the Supreme Court for at least as long as Chief Justice Roberts is there, will conflict with elites' vision of the nation as multi-racial. Resolving this conflict is one of the major tasks for those involved in building a new constitutional order.

Black Lives Matter and Constitutional Law

"Hands Up, Don't Shoot" and similar phrases are symbols of the Black Lives Matter movement. Brought into existence by notorious examples of police shootings of unarmed black men and boys, the movement focuses on changing the way police behave, not on bringing lawsuits to the Supreme Court. And for good reason: Supreme Court doctrine about police shootings is tilted heavily in favor of the police. Unlike the law examined earlier in this chapter, the law here is not about race as such. Yet the effect of police use of force on African-American communities means that the law is about race.

Texas state trooper Chadrin Mullenix's shooting of Israel Leija illustrates both the problem on the streets and the Supreme Court's construction of the law. Leija was in the drive-through lane of a restaurant when a local police officer came up to him with an arrest warrant. Leija hit the gas pedal and led police on a high-speed chase on an interstate highway. Other officers, trained in the technique of using strips of tire spikes, laid them along Leija's route. Trooper Mullenix also responded: he stationed himself on an overpass to try to shoot at Leija's car as it went by below, even though he had no training in how to do that safely. He asked his supervisor what the supervisor thought of the tactic and, before receiving an answer, got out of his car and got ready to shoot at Leija's car as it approached the first tire spikes. While Mullenix was waiting for the car to reach his position, his supervisor radioed, "Stand by" and "See if the spikes work first." Mullenix ignored the advice (or order) and fired six shots at Leija's car. The car hit the spikes, its tires exploded, and the car rolled over twice. When the police extracted Leija from the car, they found that he had been killed, not by the crash, but by four shots to his body—and none of Mullenix's shots had hit the car's engine block or radiator. When Mullenix met with his supervisor after the incident, his first words were, "How's that for proactive?" Beatrice Luna, the administrator of Leija's estate, sued Mullenix for damages.[7]

The applicable law about excessive force has two parts. The first goes to the constitutional merits. The Constitution prohibits "unreasonable" searches and seizures. Shooting a person to stop her from escaping is a seizure, and it has to be reasonable. The test is whether the officer has probable cause to believe that the target "poses a threat of serious physical harm." The Court didn't decide whether Mullenix had probable cause to shoot, however, because of the other half of the relevant law.

Even if Mullenix didn't have probable cause, the law gives him "qualified immunity" against being sued for damages. Police officers can't be held liable for the damage their actions cause, even if those actions violate the Constitution, unless what they did violates "clearly established . . . rights of which a reasonable person would have known." Not only does the Constitution have to be violated; it has to be violated in a way that a reasonable person would know was *clearly* prohibited. The kicker is that the judge decides whether the officer has qualified immunity, and if the officer does, the case never goes to a jury.

In Luna's case, the Court had to ask whether a reasonable person would have known that it was "clearly established" that using deadly force against Leija was excessive. Or—roughly, which is dangerous in this legal area—was it unreasonable to believe that *that degree* of force was justified? The Court takes the officer's point of view because, it says, officers "are often forced to make split-second judgments—in circumstances that are tense, uncertain, and rapidly evolving." Looking at all the circumstances, the Court held, a reasonable person wouldn't think it was clearly established that using deadly force was unreasonable: Leija's actions were threatening, and, according to the Court, Mullenix reasonably worried that the tire spike strips weren't the best way to stop him—they don't always work, and when they do, they sometimes put others in danger, typically by leading the car to crash or roll over, as Leija's did. So Mullenix won without having to face a civil jury.

The substantive law about deadly force is pretty generous to police officers, but the law of qualified immunity compounds the generosity. It takes the officer's point of view and emphasizes how unclear—and fraught with danger—are the circumstances officers face.

Some cases do go to juries, though, and Justice Sotomayor—alone, notably, among the Court's liberals—thought that Beatrice Luna's should have. For Sotomayor, the key question was whether Mullenix's decision to shoot, before waiting to see if the tire spikes worked, was reasonable or unreasonable. She thought a jury could sensibly find his decision unreasonable.

Sotomayor has been on something of a crusade against the Court's affection for qualified immunity. The Court sometimes grants review in a case, hears oral argument, and then decides. These are the cases that get media attention, and in the cases the Court has heard involving qualified immunity and deadly force, the outcomes tilt heavily in favor of the police. More significantly, though, Justice Sotomayor pointed to another part of the Court's docket—the so-called summary docket, where the Court decides cases without hearing oral argument. Many of the Court's qualified immunity cases have been on the summary docket, and Justice Sotomayor noted that it "routinely displays an unflinching willingness 'to summarily reverse courts for wrongly denying'" qualified immunity but "rarely intervene[s] where courts wrongly" grant it. The implicit charge: The majority is calling balls and strikes while favoring the home team.[8]

Neither the Supreme Court nor even lower courts as a whole can do much to curb unjustified police use of deadly force. In theory, allies of the Black Lives Matter movement can seek injunctions against ongoing police misconduct, as the Obama administration did in Ferguson, Missouri. Truly abusive officers can be prosecuted for civil rights violations, but getting convictions is difficult because the standards require prosecutors to show that abusive officers intended to deprive their victims of their civil rights, not that they simply intended to beat them up or kill them.

The remedy has to come from within police departments themselves, prodded by voters. Recent elections of reform-minded prosecutors in Philadelphia and Boston show the way. The courts could have some effects on the margins, though, by letting juries decide more often whether an officer used excessive force. Not every jury would rule against the officer, and a few widely publicized verdicts would send a message of caution to officers generally.

Under the law as it stands, the Supreme Court's message is that judges, who don't have to deal with police on the streets every day, know better than ordinary people what constitutes excessive force. Under the New Deal/Great Society constitutional order, there were hints that judges might cede some authority to the best police chiefs, taking professional best practices as a guide to determining when an officer crossed the line. Under the current order, that decision is left almost entirely to the officer on the scene, as illustrated by the Court's refusal to let a jury decide whether Trooper Mullenix's disregard of the order not to shoot was reasonable, and whether his boasting afterward revealed anything about his state of mind when making that choice. A different constitutional order might pay more attention not only to police officers and police chiefs but to the ordinary people who sit on juries.

5

The Court and Conservative Movements

When the media reported what Ralph Reed of the Freedom and
Faith Coalition, the evangelical leader Franklin Graham, and Dana
Loesch of the National Rifle Association thought about Brett Kavanaugh's nomination to the Supreme Court, nobody batted an eyelash.
Going to such leaders is part of the reporters' to-do list in covering
Court picks, because these leaders tell us how those nominations
will be received by the Republican Party. Interest groups and social
movements are important components of political parties—not formally, usually, but because their leaders can fire up enthusiasm or sit
on their hands, get voters to care about who wins and loses (or tell
them why they should be indifferent), raise money for candidates,
and much more.[1]

Party platforms combine broad statements about the party's
vision for the nation—in 2016, "Make America Great Again" and
"Better Together"—with lists of policy proposals that have no clear
relationship to those visions. We could make America great again by
cutting down on gun violence through strict gun control laws (as in
Australia), or bring America together through community-sponsored
programs to train everyone in weapons use (as in Switzerland and
Israel).

Of course we don't see that happening because interest groups
and social movements—and, importantly, their leaders—incline to
one or the other party for extended periods. Affiliations can shift:

black voters once saw the Republican Party as the party of civil rights and the Democrats as the party of white supremacy, and now the images have flipped. Such changes are both symptoms and causes of transitions from one dominant regime to another.

Sometimes interest groups and social movements place their policy issues in a constitutional frame, using constitutional arguments to support their claims about what they want. Sometimes in doing so they help shape a regime's constitutional vision. And sometimes the two kinds of constitutional arguments—policy-based and visionary—are intertwined. The Reagan constitutional order's treatment of claims by gun-rights advocates and by the Christian Right illustrate the possibilities.

Gun Rights and the National Rifle Association

In 1991, well after he had retired as chief justice, Warren Burger—a standard-issue Republican of the 1950s and 1960s—called the claim that the Second Amendment protected an individual's right to own a handgun "one of the greatest pieces of fraud, I repeat the word fraud, on the American public by special interest groups that I have ever seen in my lifetime." In 2008 the Supreme Court accepted that "fraud," in an originalist opinion by Justice Antonin Scalia.

The factual details of *District of Columbia v. Heller* (and a follow-up case from Chicago) are mostly unimportant here. Both cases involved complete bans on personal ownership of handguns—the nation's most stringent regulations at the time. Far more important are the constitutional arguments gun-rights advocates made, and how they were transformed when the Supreme Court ruled in their favor.[2]

The National Rifle Association's "fraud," in gun-control advocates' eyes, was to divide the Second Amendment into two parts and throw one away. The Second Amendment says, "A well regulated Militia, being necessary to the security of a free State, the right of the people to keep and bear Arms, shall not be infringed." In Second Amendment jargon, the reference to the militia comes in a preamble, while the right appears in the "operative" clause.

Proponents of gun control say that the preamble limits the operative clause to weapons possession in connection with a formal militia, organized to defend the state. A generation of scholarship supporting gun rights countered with a powerful explanation: For the founding generation, the word "militia" didn't refer to any organized body, but instead to the people of a locality armed to defend themselves not against marauding thieves but rather against an overreaching government. This was sometimes derided as the "anarchist" or "insurrectionary" argument for gun rights. When conservative political candidates refer to "Second Amendment remedies," that's what they have in mind.

Second Amendment remedies are *not* what the Supreme Court had in mind when it struck down bans on handgun possession. Its theory was that we each have a right to keep and bear commonly available weapons to protect ourselves from thugs. Even though the originalist evidence for the insurrectionary right was far stronger than for the self-defense right, the Court couldn't really say that the Second Amendment protects the insurrectionary right. In modern circumstances, that right would require that we be permitted to own bazookas and rocket-propelled grenades to fight a government that uses armored personnel carriers.*

The relation between the *Heller* decision and the conservative constitutional vision is a bit peculiar. *Heller* gets lauded for its originalism even though the originalist argument it develops is much weaker than

---

* I personally don't think this implication of the insurrectionary right discredits it.

it could have been, precisely because Justice Scalia based the right to bear arms on self-defense.

More important, perhaps, *Heller* leads to a doctrinal discussion of whether semi-automatic weapons are in sufficiently wide use for self-protection that they fall within the domain of the Second Amendment, whether the amendment guarantees a right to carry weapons openly, what restrictions it places on a state's ability to require permits before you can get a gun, whether restrictions on gun ownership should be given "strict" or "intermediate" scrutiny, and other questions. These are interesting subjects, but they don't have much to do with the "small government" or "oppressive large government" ideas that are part of the broader conservative constitutional vision. *Heller* has produced a legalistic discourse about gun regulation, not the political one that animates the most committed gun-rights proponents.

The Supreme Court has avoided dealing with gun rights since its initial interventions. Lower courts have divided over the route to upholding major gun regulations: Some judges think that *Heller's* originalism requires them to find early examples of regulations comparable to those being challenged, while others think they can apply a more ordinary doctrinal analysis. No matter the route, though, the lower courts have generally upheld the most common gun regulations, including bans on openly carrying guns and bans on ownership of semi-automatic weapons, while striking down a handful of regulations that seem especially egregious in the circumstances (such as a lifelong ban on weapons possession by a man who committed a single act of domestic violence many years ago).

The effect of these decisions has been to lower the temperature of court-focused discussions of gun regulations. But interestingly, gun-rights rhetoric outside the courts proceeds almost as if *Heller* had never been decided. That may be the result of *Heller's* failure to articulate the right to possess guns in terms of the insurrectionary reasoning that animates the most ardent gun-rights advocates. Constitutional vision and constitutional doctrine on the "same" side of the issue have been pulled apart.

None of this means, of course, that *Heller* didn't matter for gun-rights proponents. The decision featured the familiar conservative-liberal division on the Court, confirming the gun-rights proponents' belief that their interests lay with the Republican Party. For those seeking to extend a conservative constitutional regime while transforming its larger vision, that's all to the good.

The Christian Right

The story about the Constitution and the Christian Right is similar to that about gun rights, but more complicated. The similarity lies in the way the Court's decisions helped cement the Christian Right's commitment to the Republican Party even though the Court's doctrines weren't expressly *about* religion in the way the Christian Right would have liked. They are about free speech and religious equality rather than about religion itself. And one important set of cases was about a federal statute, the Religious Freedom Restoration Act, not the Constitution. Here too, doctrine and rhetoric pulled apart, this time with the Court's decisions feeding into a constitutional vision in which religion played a larger role than it did in the decisions themselves.

Free Exercise Decisions

The Free Exercise Clause—"Congress shall make no law ... prohibiting the free exercise of religion"—is the natural home for claims that the government has restricted religious liberty. It obviously prevents the government from telling people that they can't worship their deity. What about doing what that deity commands? Here are

some examples the courts have had to confront: ritual animal sac-
rifice; smoking marijuana; refusing to work on Saturdays; stopping
children's education at sixteen; sending children out to solicit contributions; and refusing blood transfusions and immunizations.

For about thirty years, the Court gave all these actions some protection when they were based upon religious commands. In a 1991
opinion by Justice Scalia, though, the Court retreated. The case, *Employment Division v. Smith,* involved peyote use by adherents to the
Native American Church. Everyone agreed that the Native American
Church was a real church, not something made up just so people
could use peyote. Scalia's test was simple: If the state was invoking
a neutral law—one that didn't refer to religion—that was generally
applicable, meaning that it didn't have any built-in exceptions, the
Free Exercise Clause was not violated by invoking the law against
a religiously motivated practice. Otherwise, Scalia wrote, everyone
could "become a law unto himself": The Constitution would grant
exemptions to anyone who held religious views, no matter how idiosyncratic, that bumped up against ordinary laws.

Highly controversial when handed down, the *Smith* decision
forced defenders of religious liberty to look elsewhere for protection.
They found it in an important federal statute and in the Free Speech
Clause.

The Religious Freedom Restoration Act

The *Smith* opinion observed that "a society that believes in . . .
protect[ing] ... religious belief can be expected to be solicitous of that
value in its legislation." Proving that religious liberty was not solely
a concern of the Christian Right, Democratic congressman Charles
Schumer introduced the Religious Freedom Restoration Act (RFRA)
in 1993. After some modest opposition from prison administrators,

who had to deal with claims from Muslims and Jews for special meals and other religious accommodations, Congress adopted the act by overwhelming margins in both houses.

This law applies to the general and neutral statutes that the *Smith* decision leaves outside the Free Exercise Clause. If such a statute imposes a substantial burden on someone's ability to comply with his or her religious beliefs, RFRA demands that the government accommodate those beliefs. If the statute serves a "compelling" interest, the government has to use the "least restrictive means" to advance that interest.

Alabama's prisons, for example, required that inmates be cleanshaven. That conflicted with a Muslim inmate's religiously grounded belief that he had to have a short, neatly trimmed beard. The prison administrators said that they had a compelling interest in being able to identify prisoners quickly, by sight. The Court agreed that this was a compelling interest, but noted an obvious alternative: Photograph the inmate with his beard and without it.

Although RFRA required that both national and state laws accommodate religious beliefs unless they had extremely strong reasons for insisting on strict compliance by everyone, the Court held that Congress didn't have the power to force states to comply. RFRA continued to apply to national laws, though, and several states adopted their own RFRA-like statutes.[3] In the 1990s and early 2000s, RFRA continued to have broad support among defenders of religious liberty, both conservative and liberal.

Then the political context changed, and the consensus around RFRA dissolved. Most of the problems mentioned above—drug use in religious ceremonies, Sabbath observance—pitted claims of religious liberty against general public safety and social welfare statutes. Churches cared a lot about getting exemptions from these statutes, and no other interest group cared much. That's why it was easy to enact RFRA.

The cases of the 2000s brought a new array of interest groups into conflict, because these cases dealt with the interaction between religion and antidiscrimination law. Simplifying a bit, they placed the Christian Right on one side, and women and the LGBTQ community on the other.

The new politics of religious accommodations came to a head in 2014 in the *Hobby Lobby* case. Although the Supreme Court had limited RFRA's reach, it still applied to all federal laws. The Affordable Care Act of 2010 required that employers include a package of essential benefits in the health care plans they offered employees. Among those benefits was contraception (but not abortion). Some religious believers hold that some forms of contraception work by causing the death of a fertilized egg, which in their view amounts to causing an abortion. They lobbied for an accommodation that would relieve them of the obligation to include such contraceptives in the basic benefits package.

After an extensive back-and-forth, the Obama administration agreed, but only in part: If they objected to certain contraceptives, churches and nonprofit religious institutions such as colleges and hospitals didn't have to provide those benefits themselves. Instead, their health care insurers would absorb the costs.

Some on the Christian Right thought this accommodation was too narrow. What about a company owned by a small group of people—typically, a family—who had exactly the same objection to providing insurance for the contraceptives? RFRA asked whether the Affordable Care Act placed a substantial burden on religious conscience. Why should it matter that the people who had the objections were organized as a nonprofit corporation or a profit-making one?

A sharply divided Supreme Court agreed with the objectors. It assumed that the government had a "compelling" interest in making affordable contraception available to employees who wanted it. But, the conservative majority held, requiring the employer to pay for it wasn't the least restrictive means. What was? Justice Alito said that the government could buy the contraceptives itself and give them to the employees—a government takeover of this segment of the market for medicine. More seriously but less authoritatively, he suggested that the government could offer the for-profit objector the same accommodation it gave to nonprofits. Under that accommodation, he wrote, employees themselves wouldn't pay a penny for the contraceptives, which meant that the government's interest in assuring access was fully met.[4]

But that wasn't the end of the story. The Court's opinion didn't actually hold that the accommodation given nonprofits was the least restrictive means. Another set of objections immediately arose: For the accommodation to work, the employers' insurance companies had to know that they were going to eat the cost of the contraceptives. The mechanism was a letter from the employer to the insurance company. But some employers objected that even writing such a letter would implicate them in providing abortions—make them "complicit," as it was put in the litigation.[5] Those cases were pending decision by the Court when Justice Scalia died, and the Court crafted a compromise—or rather, it strongly suggested that the government and these objectors should negotiate a compromise.[6]

In *Hobby Lobby*, the Court sided with the Christian Right— a typical role of a Court in bolstering the political coalition supporting the constitutional regime in place, even as the regime was nearing its end. That it was a statutory case rather than a constitutional one shows both that important statutes can offer significant support for a constitutional regime, and that such regimes may be more vulnerable when their supports are merely statutory.

The Christian Right continued to push for state-level RFRAs, but it had lost its allies. In 2016 Mississippi did adopt a state RFRA explicitly aimed at ensuring that people with religious objections would not have to provide services to LGBTQ people. In other Republican-dominated states, though, RFRAs ran into trouble. Conservative governor Jan Brewer of Arizona vetoed one that passed in the legislature; so did conservative governor Nathan Deal of Georgia. As governor of Indiana, Mike Pence signed an RFRA after assuring residents that it didn't mean what it said. In Missouri, where Republicans controlled both legislative houses, a proposed RFRA was bottled up in committee.

The Free Speech Clause

Even before the *Smith* decision, some Christian Right litigators had shifted their focus in cases where their clients wanted to engage in public religious exercises—mostly prayers and similar activities. When they said that they had a right under the Free Exercise Clause to say prayers around a school's flagpole, some schools responded by saying that they couldn't allow that because it would violate the principle of non-establishment of religion. The non-establishment objection might not have prevailed, but the litigators thought they had an easier path to victory: Reframe the claim under the Free Speech Clause and argue that all they were asking for was to be treated the same as any other group that wanted to gather near the flagpole to make political statements or distribute flyers about community events.

The cases were indeed winners on free speech grounds. Congress chimed in with the Equal Access Act, which gave religious groups a right to the same access to public school facilities after school hours that anyone else had.

Some advocates for religious liberty understood that these victories came with a price tag. The winning theory was that religion was a viewpoint just like any other: A prayer was no different from an op-ed column. Those most committed to their religious beliefs often thought that religion was not merely "a" viewpoint but a quite special one. They thought the law should acknowledge this specialness. To win court battles, though, their lawyers had to deny it.

The Free Speech Clause resurfaced in *Masterpiece Cakeshop v. Colorado Civil Rights Commission*. As states expanded their general nondiscrimination statutes to protect members of the LGBTQ community, clashes with religious traditionalists were almost inevitable. Some traditionalists objected to making their commercial services available to LGBTQ people. The *Smith* decision meant that the traditionalists couldn't rely on the Free Exercise Clause.

The Free Speech Clause, though, was still available—for some. You couldn't seriously claim a free speech right to refuse to sell an ice cream cone to a kid who walked into your store with her two mommies. But what about taking wedding photographs for a same-sex couple? Photography was surely covered by the Free Speech Clause. What about baking a cake for such a ceremony? Decorating a cake is an artistic activity—and maybe developing your own special recipe for undecorated cakes is a kind of creative activity to which the Free Speech Clause applies.

The Christian Right got quite exercised about these wedding cake and photography cases, partly because they were the last redoubt for a defense of traditionalist views about marriage, and partly because they saw the claims by the LGBTQ community as serious overreaches. Why would you want your wedding pictures taken by somebody who thought your lifestyle was deeply immoral? The people denied service could almost always find another photographer or baker who would happily sell them what they wanted.

The LGBTQ community replied mundanely that sometimes it

wasn't so easy to find another supplier—in small communities with only one photographer, or where the handful of photographers were all traditionalists. It also noted, more expansively, that it insults one's dignity to go into a store, describe what you want, and be told, in effect, "We don't serve your kind here."

Masterpiece Cakeshop was a wedding cake case, but the anticipated Free Speech Clause ruling wasn't forthcoming. Justice Kennedy wrote that in general, business owners couldn't raise "religious and philosophical objections" to same-sex marriage to justify their refusal to provide services "under a neutral and generally applicable public accommodations law." Ministers could do so, but that "exception" had to be "confined," because otherwise "a long list of persons who provide goods and services for marriages and weddings might refuse to do so for gay persons, thus resulting in a community-wide stigma inconsistent with the history and dynamics of civil rights laws that ensure equal access to goods, services, and public accommodations." Kennedy then described the baker's free speech argument with some sympathy. The opinion continued, though, with a caution: "any decision in favor of the baker would have to be sufficiently constrained, lest all purveyors of goods and services who object to gay marriages for moral and religious reasons in effect be allowed to put up signs saying 'no goods or services will be sold if they will be used for gay marriages,' something that would impose a serious stigma on gay persons."

Then Kennedy took a sharp turn. The baker, he wrote, was "entitled to [a] neutral and respectful consideration of his claims," but had not gotten one. Combing through the record, Kennedy found a few examples of what he described as anti-religious sentiments expressed by members of the state's antidiscrimination commission. That showed, he concluded, that the commission hadn't given the baker's request for an exemption from the antidiscrimination laws the required "respectful consideration."

Masterpiece Cakeshop is analytically unsatisfying. Though it doesn't use the magic word "compelling," Kennedy's opinion suggests that ensuring compliance with antidiscrimination laws is an important interest, which suggests that the baker wouldn't win his free speech claim. And because Colorado doesn't have a state RFRA, that should have been the end of the matter. Instead, however, Kennedy invented a peculiar religion-clause doctrine. Under *Smith,* Colorado doesn't have to have *any* exemptions from its antidiscrimination laws. So why does the commission have to give respectful consideration to the baker's request? Consider these two possible statements by the commission: "Because we think religion is a pernicious influence on society, we're glad that under state law we can't give you an exemption" and "Because we think that religion is a powerful force for good in society, we're really sorry that under state law we can't give you an exemption." Why the first makes the commission's denial of an exemption unconstitutional and the second doesn't is a mystery.*

As doctrine, *Masterpiece Cakeshop* makes no sense. As political compromise, leaving it to a future Court to reconsider *Smith* or rule definitively on the free speech claim, it worked exceedingly well. It provides a guide to agencies that think that refusing to provide wedding cakes amounts to discrimination: they simply have to be careful in what they say when they deny an exemption. Things would be different, of course, if the Court had overruled *Employment Division v. Smith,* or if it had directly confronted the free speech issue.

---

* For precision I note that the case would be different, and the Court's analysis better, had the commissioners expressed hostility to the value of free speech rather than to the value of religion.

Public Aid to Churches

The Warren and Burger Courts left a legacy of suspicion about public financial support for churches — not Thomas Jefferson's impregnable "wall of separation," to use a favorite phrase of those opposing such support, but a reasonably strong barrier. The Court prevented states from subsidizing the salaries of math and science teachers in church-affiliated schools, and from reimbursing such schools for the cost of administering state-required tests. But it allowed cities to lend schoolbooks and to send public employees to administer required tests. The results were difficult to reconcile: A common observation among specialists was that states could provide religiously affiliated schools with atlases and globes but couldn't pay for student field trips to a natural history museum.

These decisions came in an era when public aid to church-related schools meant, basically, public aid to Catholic schools — and against a historical background of anti-Catholicism in U.S. politics. The politics changed, however, with the rise of "Christian academies" in the South, sponsored by white Protestants fleeing desegregating public schools, and as Protestant evangelicals began to ally with Catholics on the issue of abortion.

In the 1980s, constitutional doctrine began to shift from suspicion of public financial aid to religiously affiliated schools, to a more generous assessment of such aid. The Court upheld tax deductions for expenses associated with attending private schools, the vast majority of which were religiously affiliated. It prevented taxpayers from challenging a system giving tax credits for the tuition paid to such schools. And it upheld a voucher program that let parents use public vouchers to pay for tuition at such schools.

Two features of all these cases stand out. In each, the government gave money to parents, who then chose — or had already chosen — to use it at a religiously affiliated school. One case came close to a direct financial outlay to these schools, allowing the state to lend computers and books to these schools, with the amount available determined by the number of children in the school. Second, the programs were neutral on their face: They assisted nonpublic schools generally, although a huge proportion of the benefits flowed to church-affiliated schools. The only brick left in the wall of separation was the one blocking cash payments to churches.[7]

Even that brick began to crumble when the Court focused not on the disproportionate effect of the programs on religiously affiliated schools, but on the programs' neutrality, the fact that they were available to nonpublic schools generally. That neutrality gave the Court a new and powerful doctrinal tool: a rule that government programs couldn't discriminate between religion and nonreligion.

A nondiscrimination rule like that had been lurking in Religion Clause doctrine for a while, though mostly it was embedded in discussions about how bad it was to discriminate in favor of one religion against another. It surfaced in a peculiar and seemingly narrow case, but the justices recognized its potential.

Missouri had an environmentally conscious program for recycling scrapped automobile tires by encouraging people to convert them into rubber playground surfaces. Schools that wanted to improve their playgrounds could apply for a grant to pay for resurfacing with these recycled tires. Relying on a provision in the state constitution that seemed to bar giving public money to churches, Missouri wouldn't give the grants to schools affiliated with churches.

The Supreme Court found this nearly a pristine violation— "odious," Chief Justice Roberts called it—of the principle that governments can't discriminate between religion and nonreligion. The school had "a right to participate in a government benefit program without having to disavow its religious character." As Justice Sotomayor observed in her dissent, the case held, "for the first time, that the Constitution requires the government to provide public funds directly to a church."[8]

This decision is a big deal. Religious institutions have rarely tried to get public aid just because they are religious institutions. Instead, they have supported general programs—voucher programs, tuition tax credits, and the like—that are available to everyone but that sometimes provide most of their benefits to churches or their affiliated institutions (generally schools and hospitals). The Missouri case seems to open the way for states to adopt much more substantial programs whose effect is to send public money to church-related institutions, and the justices knew this. Roberts's opinion contains a footnote using a standard legal move, limiting the case to its facts: "This case involves express discrimination based on religious identity with respect to playground resurfacing. We do not address religious uses of funding or other forms of discrimination." Justices Thomas and Gorsuch expressly refused to join that footnote—making another standard move, arguing that you can't limit a general principle to the facts of the case applying that principle.

Public Acknowledgment of Religion

In 2005 the Supreme Court decided two cases involving displays of the Ten Commandments, one in a county courthouse, the other on the Texas state capitol grounds. Eight justices thought the cases were the same. Four said both displays were constitutional because they memorialized the role the Ten Commandments played in the development of U.S. values, and four said both were unconstitutional. Note the similarity to the transformation of prayer into speech: Religious commandments become historical artifacts.[9]

Justice Breyer thought the two cases were different. The Texas display had been there for forty years without exciting controversy, but the courthouse display, just six years old, was controversial from the moment county officials put it up. Some academic commentators found Breyer's distinction silly: If the county's display violated the non-establishment clause today, how could the fact that Texas's was older insulate it from exactly the same constitutional defect? But Breyer was on to something. The politics surrounding religion in the public square changed from the 1950s and 1960s, to the 1990s and today. The early period was a time of diffuse public religiosity, captured in President Dwight D. Eisenhower's observation that "our form of government has no sense unless it is founded in a deeply felt religious faith, and I don't care what it is." The Texas display emerged from that political context. The later period saw the rise of the Christian Right, which pushed for public acknowledgment of Christianity's central role in U.S. life—pejoratively, a "sectarian" position. That was the context of the courthouse display.

The Supreme Court moved in fits and starts toward the Christian Right position. It didn't allow a rabbi to deliver a generically religious invocation at a high school graduation, or a student election to choose someone to recite a prayer at the start of a high school football game. Invoking long practice, it did allow Nebraska's legislature to have a long-term Christian chaplain open its session with a prayer that sometimes had specifically religious content.[10]

Justice Breyer's thought that new practices were more questionable than old ones escaped Justice Kennedy. In a case involving prayers opening city council meetings, a practice that began after a new council member was elected in 1999, Kennedy disconnected the legislative prayer decision from its historical roots, writing that the Constitution permits all legislatures to use prayers to set a "deliberative" and "solemn" tone for their meetings. Notably, for several years each prayer had been given by a Christian minister, and some content was explicitly Christian, including urging listeners to accept Christianity as the true religion.[11]

The reason was that city bureaucrats had called every religious institution in town, offering to let their pastors give the opening prayer, but the only such institutions were Christian churches. There was a Jewish synagogue a few blocks over the city line. According to the Court, that was fine—as long as the city officials didn't deliberately exclude representatives of other faiths from offering prayers and, perhaps, as long as there weren't too many proselytizing prayers.

In 2019 the Court appeared to have reached a compromise mostly favorable to public displays of religious symbols. After World War I the city of Bladensburg outside Washington, D.C., put up a war memorial to city residents who had died during the war. The memorial was a large Christian cross. Rejecting a constitutional challenge to the continued maintenance of the cross, Justice Alito wrote that over time this particular cross had come to take on two meanings. One was of course specifically Christian, the other a generic meaning associated with peace. (Justice Ginsburg's dissent argued that attributing this second meaning to the cross was implausible.) Seven justices agreed that the city could continue to maintain the cross, though there was a division—which might prove important in later cases—over whether "history and tradition" validated this specific monument, along the lines of Justice Breyer's approach, or whether "history and tradition" validated all monuments of a similar genre no matter how recently they were erected.[12]

The movement from generic religiosity—what one scholar called "ceremonial deism"—to specifically Christian imagery and messages was clear. Not clear enough, of course, fully to satisfy the Christian Right, but enough to show that the Supreme Court was on its side. And that was sufficient to keep the Christian Right within the Republican coalition.

In political terms, the Roberts Court gave quite a bit to important interest groups within the conservative Republican coalition. Gun-rights proponents got the first acknowledgment of a constitutional right for which they had been arguing for decades. The Christian Right's campaign against Jefferson's "wall of separation" basically succeeded. Never an accurate description of constitutional doctrine, the metaphor became completely inapt as the Court left the wall in ruins.

Yet Jefferson's metaphor remains a central feature of public discourse about religion and government. The first page of a Google search for "wall of separation" and "public opinion" turns up an op-ed piece from 2018, "The White House Is Tearing Down the Wall Between Church and State" (note the present tense).[13]

The disconnect between the Supreme Court and one significant segment of public opinion is reproduced within the federal judiciary. As of 2018, the lower federal courts had not enthusiastically pursued the doctrinal implications of the decisions reviewed in this chapter. Almost every significant regulation of gun possession remains enforceable. Lower courts continue to find expressions of public support for religion unconstitutional.

The reason for these outcomes is, again, political. The lower courts are, as yet, not as dominated as the Supreme Court is by Republican appointees. Judges on those courts can find loopholes in the Court's holdings or exploit ambiguities and footnoted qualifications to limit the reach of the Court's decisions.

A conservative account might be more Machiavellian. Strategically, it's often good to give allies some but not all of what they want, so they'll stay with you for the long run. Eventually they might get fed up, but that can take a long time. Doling out a pro-gun-rights decision every few years might make political sense: Give gun-rights proponents everything they want all at once, and the issue might lose its urgency; proponents might decide to vote based on something other than a candidate's support for gun rights.* Many would continue to vote for Republicans, but some would defect. An open-ended doctrine is thus more politically attractive than a definitive one. Half-victories mean that partisans have to fight in legislatures first, then in courts. The legislative battles keep interest groups tied to the political parties they support.

---

* And those same decisions might push into politics people who had been relying on the courts.

6

Culture Wars, Yesterday and Today

Justice Scalia chastised his colleagues when they struck down a Colorado referendum barring any government in the state from protecting "homosexual, lesbian, or bisexual" people against discrimination: "The Court has mistaken a Kulturkampf for a fit of spite." The reference to the nineteenth-century German attack on the Catholic Church was cute but inapt. "Culture war" would have been better.[1]

Sociologist James Davison Hunter brought the term "culture war" to public attention in his best-selling book *Culture Wars: The Struggle to Define America,* published in 1991. Like nearly every other institution in that era, the Supreme Court was drawn into these wars, particularly over the issues of free speech and political correctness, abortion, and LGBTQ rights. But even if the same groups now find themselves fighting over the same issues, yesterday's culture wars are not today's.

Yesterday's Culture Wars

Political Correctness and Campus Free Speech

Long a staple of conservative thinking, criticism of political correctness in higher education took the form of challenges to campus speech codes. The Supreme Court didn't address such codes directly, but a decision about laws banning hate speech clearly implied that almost all campus speech codes were unconstitutional.

In *R.A.V. v. City of St. Paul,* Justice Scalia wrote an opinion for the Court holding a city's hate speech ordinance unconstitutional because, he said, it discriminated on the basis of viewpoint—that is, it banned hate speech directed at some targets but not others. The opinion was analytically contorted; Scalia struggled, without great success, to explain why sexual harassment law was constitutional, for example. The analytical difficulties probably don't matter because the core idea was probably correct.

What's striking about the aftermath is this: Every court that has considered constitutional challenges to campus speech codes after *R.A.V.* found them unconstitutional. And yet they persist. No one thinks that campus speech codes can actually be enforced through formal disciplinary processes, but the codes remain part of campus culture. Some have morphed into "codes of good conduct" or "guidelines" for good behavior. The ideas underlying them continue to influence campus administrators and, it appears, many students.[2]

While conservatives won the legal battles over political correctness, they fundamentally failed in their overall campaign. Perhaps the lesson is that those of us who pay attention to constitutional law shouldn't overestimate its importance. Culture develops with little regard for legal opinion. Law may be only a small weapon in the culture war.

Gay Rights

In 1977, the pop singer Anita Bryant led a successful campaign to repeal a Miami ordinance prohibiting discrimination on the basis of sexual orientation. In 1998, Miami reenacted the ordinance.

The culture war over gay rights—later relabeled LGBTQ rights—took place all around the country. Each side could claim victories, but in the end the Supreme Court came down decisively on the liberal side, in opinions written by Justice Anthony Kennedy.

Just before Kennedy arrived at the Court, in *Bowers v. Hardwick,* the justices upheld the constitutionality of state laws that prohibit sexual relations between men. Justice Byron White's opinion for the Court was moderately homophobic, and Chief Justice Burger's concurring opinion more so. Justice Lewis Powell waffled during the Court's deliberations but eventually joined the majority. After his retirement, he expressed misgivings about having done so.

That was the high-water mark for traditionalist positions on constitutional law dealing with same-sex relations. Justice Kennedy wrote the opinion that overruled *Bowers* in 2003, saying it "was not correct when it was decided." He also wrote the Court's opinion striking down the federal Defense of Marriage Act, which denied federal benefits to members of same-sex couples.

Obergefell v. Hodges was the last real battle. Its holding that states must make marriage available to same-sex couples was the most decisive defeat imaginable for marriage traditionalists. Again, the bottom line is striking: Justice Kennedy's opinions have been about as stable as anything in constitutional law can be. It's unlikely that any jurisdiction in the country will re-criminalize same-sex relations. The Court might allow some forms of explicit discrimination against LGBTQ people. Most notably, it might require states to include in their child welfare systems organizations that refuse, mostly for religious reasons, to arrange adoptions by same-sex couples.

The Court could also eat away at *Obergefell*'s edges. It might allow a state to provide some benefits to opposite-sex married couples but not to same-sex ones, for example. And on what's probably the most sensitive issue remaining for conservatives, it might allow a state to deny same-sex couples the opportunity to adopt children. Most of these possibilities are unlikely. Even if President Trump gets additional appointments to the Court, there's essentially zero chance that the Court will overturn *Obergefell* in the quite unlikely event that someone asks it to and the even more unlikely event that the justices agree to hear the case. Unless, of course, the culture surrounding the LGBTQ community changes dramatically.

In *Lawrence* and *Obergefell,* the Court saw where the nation's culture was going and got just a bit ahead of it. Same-sex marriage probably would have come even to Mississippi sometime, but it got there in 2015 because of *Obergefell.* That's not nothing, but it's also not an example of the Court as "social justice warrior."

Abortion

Liberals basically succeeded along the campus and gay-rights fronts of the culture wars, but not on abortion. The foundation of abortion rights, *Roe v. Wade,* remained under siege and was eroded by the court until Justice Kennedy found, shortly before his retirement, that Texas had gone too far in limiting the practical availability of abortion.

We need not rehearse the history of abortion rights since *Roe v. Wade.* The *Casey* decision in 1992 simultaneously reaffirmed *Roe's* "core holding," that states could not flatly prohibit abortions, and recast the constitutional test. States could regulate the availability of abortion as long as the regulations didn't impose an "undue burden" on a woman's right to choose to have or not have an abortion.

The undue-burden test inevitably became the vehicle for judges to express their underlying views about the right to choose and the right to life. Pro-life legislators pushed the limits of the test by proposing and sometimes adopting quite stringent restrictions on when, where, and how abortions could be reformed: when, with waiting periods between requesting and obtaining an abortion; where, with regulations about the physical arrangements required in clinics where abortions were performed; and how, with bans of specific abortion methods. The effect of these regulations was to substantially limit the availability of abortions in many states. Blue states remained pro-choice, but some women in red states have to travel a long way to find a clinic where they can get an abortion, and have to give up a few days of work to get there, go through the waiting period, and return home.

Until 2016, Justice Kennedy found that nearly every regulation the Court dealt with—in only a handful of cases—didn't impose an undue burden. In *Whole Women's Health v. Hellerstedt,* however, he concluded that Texas had gone too far. Kennedy assigned the opinion to Justice Breyer, who wrote a typically fact-filled opinion explaining to his satisfaction why Texas's regulations didn't accomplish much medically while making it a lot harder for women to obtain abortions.

Even after *Whole Women's Health,* the undue-burden test weakened the right to choose, especially as applied by lower courts in red states. The pro-life side treated the undue-burden test as the material it had to work with and never abandoned hope of overruling *Roe v. Wade.*

By 2018, campus battles in the culture wars had reached an uneasy truce favorable to liberals, and liberals had routed their opponents on the LGBTQ issue. But on abortion, liberals were rather clearly in retreat. The Republican-dominated legislatures in Ohio and Georgia enacted statutes that posed nearly direct challenges to *Roe v. Wade* itself. They were teeing the issue up for the Court to decide—but whether and when the Court would respond remains unclear.

Today's Culture Wars

Culture wars don't really end. Sometimes they trail off, as the old warriors die off or move on and aren't replaced by younger ones. Sometimes major battles are replaced by skirmishes, typically provoked by the side that's lost one of the battles. And sometimes, entirely new issues arise, with new armies created from elements of the old ones. In 2019 the culture wars—with the important exception of abortion—were reduced to skirmishes conducted mostly on terrain favorable to progressives.

"Free Speech" on Campus

Conservative provocateurs occasionally seek publicity by ginning up campus controversies: Conservative students invite them to speak, knowing that the provocateurs' views are so repugnant to many students that the campus will be consumed with discussions not of the views but of whether the speakers should be allowed to come, be confronted when they arrive, or be heckled or shouted down as they try to speak. Campuses house many not-quite-mature young people and hot-heads on both sides, and the discussions can get heated.

By 2018, campus administrators had figured out what to do, with some assistance from the courts. Mostly they ramp up their security arrangements, send enough campus police to the speaking venue to keep tensions down, and allow the speaker to have his or her say. Because the point of the invitation was less to engage the speakers' ideas than to show how intolerant campuses are, most speakers back out once it's clear the campus will not prohibit them from appearing.

Most of these skirmishes have ended inconclusively. Conservatives get to show that the student culture is made up of "snowflakes" and "social justice warriors," and liberals get to point out that they are willing to let the speakers have their say, and that sometimes it's conservatives who are snowflakes that melt away when their political theater doesn't go off as planned.

Finally, traditions of academic freedom—supported by free speech principles—have allowed liberal-dominated faculties to resist efforts to impose curricular requirements from the outside. On campuses, the culture wars produced an armed truce, with liberals on the ramparts holding weapons substantially stronger than their challengers'. The defenses are occasionally probed, but the attacks almost always fail.[3]

Bathroom Battles

Those who lived through the years when gay and lesbian sexual relations were illegal can remember when the police raided public bathrooms to find out whether people were having illegal sex there. They might raise their eyebrows when told that today one of the two major controversies over gender and sex again involves public bathrooms, particularly school bathrooms—but this time as places where people just use them as intended.

Here's the issue: Which bathroom must or may transgender people use? Must they use the bathroom corresponding to the sex designation assigned to them at birth? May they use whichever bathroom they choose? A federal statute makes it illegal for public schools to discriminate in providing services on the basis of sex. The legal issue is whether schools that follow the first policy are violating the antidiscrimination law. There's no Supreme Court ruling squarely on point, and the lower courts are divided.

Again, though, the point for our purposes is that these controversies are skirmishes about the effects of a major social change that's almost completely settled in. The change can be tracked in terminology: from "homosexuals" to "gays" to "gays and lesbians" to "LGBTQ"—with the recently added "T" generating the culture wars controversy after "LG" and even "B" controversies have disappeared.

Wedding Cakes and "Facilitating" Abortion

After the Court held that states had to make marriage available to same-sex couples, defenders of "traditional" marriage retreated to a fallback position: Governments had to accommodate people who had religious objections to participating in or facilitating same-sex marriages, by allowing them to opt out of doing what they did with respect to traditional marriages.

The first big controversy involved a county clerk who refused to sign marriage licenses. After a kerfuffle about what state law allowed, the controversy ended with the licenses signed by her deputy—a decent solution for both sides.

The next controversies involved refusals by wedding bakers and photographers to sell their services in connection with same-sex marriage celebrations. These are skirmishes after the main battle has been decided. Same-sex couples may be insulted when a photographer or baker turns them down, and sometimes finding a substitute may be a nuisance. But it's better than not being able to marry at all.

Litigation over the relation between Obamacare and the Religious Freedom Restoration Act basically went away when the Trump administration expanded the scope of accommodation quite substantially—even going beyond religious objections to include conscientious nonreligious objections. The effect was to further tighten the availability of abortions to a significant number of women, even though abortions remained available as a matter of law.

Current Skirmishes and Battles to Come

Without meaning to understate the intensity of concern on both sides of these skirmishes, we ought to note how much smaller they are than earlier generations' culture wars. Many of those worried about "forcing" religious bakers to provide cakes to gay weddings, for example, are no longer worried about the fact that same-sex couples actually can get married, much less that sexual relations between people of the same sex are no longer a crime. Many of the people who worry about forcing religious objectors to facilitate contraception might not be happy that contraception is widely available, but they aren't ready to refight that battle.

Hobby Lobby may differ from *Masterpiece Cakeshop,* and not merely in the number of people actually directly affected by the decision. *Masterpiece Cakeshop* really is a skirmish in which progressives were fighting a retreating group of cultural conservatives. *Hobby Lobby* is a more substantial battle—not the ultimate one but a major engagement—in the unresolved culture war over abortion.

Justice Scalia observed that "[w]hen the Court takes sides in the culture wars it tends to be with the knights rather than the villeins . . . reflecting the views of the lawyer class from which the Court's Members are drawn." He didn't suggest how the Court could avoid taking sides—how it could somehow stand above the fray. In real wars, studied neutrality typically favors one side: Great Britain against revolutionary France during George Washington's administration, Great Britain against Nazi Germany during FDR's. Neutrality in the culture wars is an illusion.

• • •

Even before Brett Kavanaugh's arrival consolidated conservative control, the Supreme Court had already moved substantially to the right on many issues. Justice Kennedy's presence on the Court meant that progressives could occasionally win an important case. No longer—or at least, not highly likely.

We face two divergent paths of constitutional development. A post-Trump conservative constitutional order might have a program of economic nationalism and social exclusion. The alternative path would find a new Democratic coalition controlling Congress and the presidency, pursuing a program akin to European social democracy—

and confronting a Supreme Court that, at least at the outset, is firmly in conservative hands.

Along the first path constitutional development would move smoothly to the right. Along the second, we might well experience a constitutional crisis.

PART TWO

Where a Modern Republican Supreme Court Might Take Us

Part One showed how much the Supreme Court has already done to advance a conservative constitutional agenda. What it does over the next decade may depend on the nation's political choices. The Reagan constitutional order appears to have exhausted itself with nothing to replace it. We can discern the vague outlines of a new Trump-influenced constitutional order, and even vaguer outlines of a new progressive order. What the Court does will depend in part on which order ultimately prevails.

For Trump's supporters, his consolidation of conservative control over the Supreme Court is to be celebrated as a great accomplishment. This part of the book examines what that means if a new conservative constitutional order emerges. What constitutional law will a conservative Supreme Court develop in a Trump-influenced constitutional order?

I'm writing here about a post-Trump conservative Court, not the one we have now. So it doesn't count against my argument to identify cases the present Court has decided that don't fit my predictions. And, even after 2021 we might see occasional deviations from the pattern in cases where the partisan stakes, though present, are relatively low. In low-stakes cases partisans might find it easier to go with their commitments to existing doctrine or to interpretive approaches than to figure out how to reconcile all that with their partisan inclinations.[1]

A short, cynical version is this:

- Statutes, policies, and practices—law in any of its forms—that strengthen the Republican Party and weaken the Democratic Party are constitutionally permissible.
- Laws that strengthen the Democratic Party are unconstitutional.
- If leading Republicans are indifferent about a law, and leading Democrats favor it, and if the law doesn't strengthen the Democratic Party, the law might or might not be constitutionally permissible.
- If leading Republicans are indifferent and leading Democrats oppose a law, it might be unconstitutional.

All the rest is commentary.[2]

• • •

In the past, when the Supreme Court was aligned with a dominant political coalition, it could sometimes strike out on its own, taking advantage of the space made available by divisions within the governing coalition. The ideological coherence within the Republican Party today makes that path unlikely. The party used to contain people who were fiscal conservatives but social liberals—"country club" and Northeastern Republicans—but no longer. Anthony Kennedy may have been the last Republican nominee on the Court to align himself with that group, and even he was more conservative on many issues (though not on gay rights) than many "liberal" Republicans.

Today we have an almost complete convergence between the Supreme Court majority and a Republican Party united around a strongly conservative ideology. If a new Trumpist constitutional order takes hold after 2020, that convergence will lower the Court's profile relative to Congress, because Congress will seldom do things to which the Court's majority objects. That doesn't mean, however, that the Court will become a low-profile institution.

Once a conservative Supreme Court in a Trump-influenced order disposes of some discrete issues—overrules *Roe v. Wade,* further limits legislative power to regulate guns—will there be any more general themes? At the most general level, the answer has to be yes. The Court will work with Congress and the president to entrench the new constitutional order by doing work that Congress doesn't have time to do on its own.

We should keep one feature of the U.S. constitutional system in mind throughout. Federalism and the separation of powers mean that progressives will have the ability to implement some of their own new agenda in the states, in federal bureaucracies, and perhaps occasionally even in Congress: for example, increasing the minimum wage in some states and adopting state-based systems that expand the availability of health care.

Congress and the president in a consolidated new conservative order have the formal power to stifle such initiatives—or, more precisely, the Court in such an order can construe the Constitution to give them the power to do so. Sometimes Congress or the president won't have the time or political will to exercise that power. The conservative Supreme Court can take up the slack, using the Constitution to slap down whatever achievements progressives might achieve.

The role the Court plays against progressives would be even more dramatic were the nation to take the alternative path—not a new Trump-influenced constitutional order but a new progressive one. Parts 3 and 4 examine that possibility.

7

Strengthening a New Constitutional Order: Partisan Entrenchment and Fulfilling Campaign Pledges

As we saw in chapter 3, Congress and the president can do a great deal in a consolidated constitutional order. Energy replaces gridlock, and statutes fulfill campaign promises. But as we also saw, the Supreme Court has its own role to play in strengthening the major elements contributing to the order's stability. Even an entrenched order may face challenges the Court can deal with. And the politicians who built the order may have been helped by interest groups that need to be kept in line through regular policy victories. The Court can deliver some of those victories.

Partisan Entrenchment Again

In one of the last decisions in which Anthony Kennedy participated, the Court held, by the usual five-to-four majority, that a federal statute dealing with voter registration didn't prevent Ohio—with a strongly conservative election official in charge—from removing people who hadn't voted from its registration lists. The Obama administration had filed papers objecting to Ohio's process; the Trump administration reversed course and supported Ohio.[1]

In 2017, Secretary of Commerce Wilbur Ross directed the Census

Bureau to include in the 2020 census a question asking whether the person filling out the form was a citizen. Specialists believed that including that question would reduce the accuracy of the census count because some non-citizens—especially those not lawfully present in the United States—wouldn't fill out the form. This inaccuracy would weaken the voting power of people in districts where many non-citizens failed to fill out the form. In June 2019 the Supreme Court blocked the Census Bureau's plan to include the question, largely because Ross and his lawyers had been extraordinarily clumsy in how they tried to hustle the question on to the census form. (And even so, four justices would have allowed them to do so.)[2]

Those cases illustrate a more general legal concern. Some policy choices, progressives believe, are likely to reduce voting, especially by progressive-leaning groups: restrictive voter identification laws and other ways of administering elections that progressives characterize as "voter suppression." The term refers to rules that discourage and sometimes bar people from voting—and the people targeted are more likely to be Democrats than Republicans even though the rules don't explicitly refer to political parties.

In a consolidated conservative regime, challenges to voter suppression would be bound to fail. The courts would let red states tighten up the vote process, deferring to their legislatures' view that vote fraud was a serious problem whether the legislatures could bring forward any evidence of this or not. Maybe a red-state legislature might go "too far too fast," but even in striking down some voter-suppression techniques as too severe, a conservative Court would point the way to accomplishing the same result within what it viewed as constitutional limits.

A case decided in 2016 is instructive. The Court has long held that states have to use the one-person, one-vote rule to draw district lines: You take the state's population and divide it by the number of districts to get the number of people to be included in each district. Easy enough — except for the question of whom you count at the first stage. One possibility, of course, is to count everyone in the state — old, young, citizens, non-citizens. Another possibility is to count only the number of people who are eligible to vote — because, after all, what you're trying to do is give every *voter* an equal say in determining elections. The "eligible-voter population" number would reduce the effective representation of districts with many non-citizens and young people — which Republicans correctly assume are likely to lean Democratic.

Nearly every state uses the "total population" number. In 2014, a conservative activist brought a lawsuit asserting that the Constitution *required* Texas to abandon that number in favor of the "eligible-voter population" one — again, because of the very premise of the one-person, one-vote rule. The Supreme Court disagreed.[3]

The case's most interesting feature wasn't the result but the difference between the arguments Texas made and those the U.S. government made supporting the state's choice. The Obama administration argued that rather than requiring the "eligible-voter population" number, the Constitution actually required the "total population" one. Texas, with a Republican governor and attorney general, made a narrower argument — that it could choose between the two numbers. That's the argument the Court accepted.

Significantly, however, Justice Alito wrote a separate opinion that came close to rejecting the Obama administration's position. If in the future a red state — perhaps Texas — switched from "total population" to "eligible voter," liberal activists would turn the earlier challenge on its head and say that the Obama administration was correct — states had to use the "total population" number. Alito's opinion provides the basis for rejecting that challenge, and liberates red states to adopt the more restrictive counting method.

In our federal system, even after a conservative constitutional regime takes hold there will be blue states that resist the national trend. Congress could enact statutes bringing these states to heel by denying them federal benefits—directing infrastructure investment to red states, for example. But sometimes, the issues aren't serious enough to get on a congressional agenda preoccupied with cutting taxes and reducing regulation. And sometimes, if addressing a problem would generate more controversy than politicians like, the courts can do the work. They can mop up problems that Congress doesn't have the time to deal with, or take the blame for solving an overly contentious issue, allowing politicians to blame the courts and to devise solutions because the courts told them they had to. The courts become collaborators with the political branches.

One obvious target for a reconstructed Supreme Court is campaign finance regulations. Many of the rules aimed at getting campaign finance under control have been held unconstitutional or made ineffective. One set of rules remains in place—those limiting the amounts people can contribute to candidates.

Justice Thomas and other conservatives have forcefully argued that these limitations are unconstitutional. To them, "contributors obviously like the message they are hearing … and want to add their voices to that message" by giving candidates money to spread the message more widely.

The Court has paved the way for finding contribution limits unconstitutional by holding that the only good reason for regulating such contributions is preventing *quid pro quo* corruption. The doctrinal move is to say that while there might be real problems of *quid pro quo* corruption resulting from contributions to politicians' personal bank accounts, there's no demonstrated problem of such corruption resulting from contributions to campaigns. And if there is such a problem, bribery statutes already deal with it. Limits on campaign contributions aren't "narrowly tailored" to address a compelling problem.

What else might a conservative Supreme Court do to entrench the new conservative constitutional order? Blue states might try to expand rather than restrict voting. Allowing people convicted of felonies to vote is a good example of a liberal-leaning policy aimed at partisan entrenchment because of the disproportionate effect of felon disfranchisement laws on African Americans.

Conservatives will challenge these partisan-motivated expansions. State law, rather than the Constitution, will almost certainly be a more promising vehicle for such challenges. An attempt by Virginia's Democratic governor to give ex-felons the right to vote was held up when Republicans persuaded a judge that the way the governor proceeded wasn't authorized by state law. Republicans in Florida tried to limit the effect of a voter-approved initiative restoring votes to felons who had served their sentences. It's difficult to come up with obvious constitutional arguments against expanding the voter base, but under pressure, conservatives will undoubtedly do so.

Arguments that the Constitution *requires* restricting the franchise in ways that disadvantage Democrats are available, and they illustrate how the Court can be an active collaborator in sustaining a partisan regime. The Court rejected one such attempt in the Texas census case, but others remain possible—including some not even on today's radar screen.

The Texas census case showed that even when districts have the same number of people, who the people are matters to politicians. If one district with 100,000 people has 80,000 people who vote and another has only 40,000 who do, each voter in the second district has twice as much clout. Republicans will like that if the non-voters trend blue and the voters trend red. The example of felon disfranchisement shows that Republicans benefit if they can get lots of prisoners into a district. And they can, by saying that a prisoner should be counted for districting purposes as residing not where their home is but where the prison is located, even though the prisoner can't vote. Most prisons are located in rural areas that vote heavily Republican, and most prisoners come from urban areas—so this shift increases rural voting power and funding at the expense of urban (mostly Democratic) areas.

Democrats have responded by trying to assign prisoners to the districts where they came from—their long-term homes. I can imagine creative arguments that this strategy is unconstitutional because of a combination of the Constitution's requirement that congressional districts be determined by an "actual Enumeration" of the population with some account of the basis for the one-person, one-vote rule.

Another example: Arizona tried to eliminate partisan gerrymandering by creating a commission to draw district lines. Republicans said that was inconsistent with the Constitution's provision that rules for elections within each state be provided by "the Legislature thereof." With Anthony Kennedy joining the Court's liberals, the Supreme Court disagreed, in an opinion by Justice Ginsburg saying that by amending the state constitution to create the commission, Arizona's people had effectively made the commission part of the legislature.[4]

Blue states such as California and red ones such as Iowa have found nonpartisan districting commissions—used in many modern democracies—an attractive response to partisan gerrymandering. The Supreme Court's decision about Arizona's commission leaves the door open to additional constitutional claims if Republicans want to bring them. Here are a few:

- Arizona's voters amended the state constitution to create their commission. That they amended the constitution provided a hook for saying that the commission was part of Arizona's legislative process. But only twenty-four states have initiative processes. Would the case be different if the *legislature* created the commission?

- Republicans have been skeptical about the claimed nonpartisanship of Arizona's and California's commissions. That skepticism can be translated into constitutional challenges invoking ideas of free speech and equal protection.
- Maybe a nonpartisan commission created out of concerns about balance between Republicans and Democrats violates the free speech rights of independent voters.

We can't know what new forms of partisan entrenchment conservatives might devise, because we can't see in advance where a threat to conservative political control might emerge. We can be pretty confident, though, that when those threats emerge and conservatives respond to them, their Supreme Court will either uphold conservative legislative responses or develop constitutional doctrines explaining why those threats take an unconstitutional form.

Still, it's important to keep in mind what it means to say that a constitutional regime has become consolidated. The courts don't have to do much to enhance partisan entrenchment once a constitutional regime has taken hold, because that fact *means* that one party has become entrenched (until the regime starts to decay).

Fulfilling Campaign Promises

Constitutional orders have a unifying ideology: the social safety net for the New Deal/Great Society order, "government is the problem" for the Reagan order. Those ideologies bring voters to the polls to kick out the dying order and support the new one. In today's world, that's not enough. Political parties have to mobilize support by promising to adopt specific policies: for example, to keep some pristine environment closed to development, or to open it up.

These policies, of course, have to be consistent with the order's guiding ideology, but they don't have to be linked to it by any rigorous logic. Their logic is political. Past constitutional orders have embedded interest groups in the system's operation. Guiding ideologies typically speak in terms of a general national or public interest. Interest groups' continuing role means that ideology can only damp down, not eradicate, an order's need to satisfy interest group demands — to fulfill campaign promises. Abortion, gun rights, and religious liberty are instructive.

We could construct an ideology unifying all these matters under some broad "conservative" label, but doing so might be artificial. Gun rights and appeals to Christianity might fit into a narrative of American nationalism, but bans on abortion could be squeezed into that narrative only with some effort. Libertarianism might fit gun rights but would also have difficulty with bans on abortion. We do better to see the conservative constitutional order as having a vague animating ideology accompanied by appeals to politically significant interest groups.

The Court's role in dealing with policy pledges varies with the different pledges. On abortion, the Court must remove an obstacle, left over from a prior era, blocking legislatures' ability to enact outright bans on abortion. On gun rights, the Court can invalidate restrictions adopted by blue states that Congress can't muster the votes to preempt. On religious liberty, the Court can force legislatures to adopt religion-favoring policies that blue states might not favor and red states (and Congress) might find politically difficult to adopt.

Abortion

The fight over Brett Kavanaugh's nomination was so intense because it would lead to conservative control over the Supreme Court for what could be decades—and because it portended overruling *Roe v. Wade.* Judge Kavanaugh accurately said that *Roe* was settled law, but that was meaningless: A case is settled until the Supreme Court overrules it.

Dissenting from a 2019 decision overruling a case handed down in 1979, Justice Breyer asked, "Today's decision can only cause one to wonder which cases the Court will overrule next."[5] Observers thought they knew what he meant: That *Roe* would be overruled seemed certain. How and when is less clear. In 1992, the Supreme Court reaffirmed *Roe*'s holding that states could not prohibit abortion completely. It also said that the standard for determining when a regulation of abortion was unconstitutional was whether it imposed an "undue burden" on the woman's right to choose. Pro-life legislatures responded by prohibiting specific abortion procedures. The Court struck down one such statute from Nebraska, then upheld exactly the same prohibition when Congress enacted it.[6] Another set of responses were what pro-choice advocates called "targeted regulation of abortion providers" (TRAP) statutes. These set out elaborate requirements that abortion providers had to satisfy, purportedly to ensure that their abortions were medically appropriate and safe. Satisfying the requirements was typically so costly that only a handful of providers in any state with a TRAP law could remain open.

The Supreme Court dealt with Texas's version in its last major abortion decision before Justice Kennedy retired. Ruling five-to-three (after Justice Scalia's death), the Court found that Texas's statute did impose an undue burden. Texas required doctors who performed abortions to have admitting privileges at nearby hospitals so that, Texas asserted, they could easily transfer a patient to a hospital if something went wrong; it required that facilities where abortions were performed conform to requirements typically used in outpatient surgical centers, including rules about how large the corridors and operating rooms had to be. The statute would have dramatically reduced the number of clinics able to perform abortions.[7]

In applying the "undue burden" test, Justice Breyer relied heavily on "record evidence," that is, evidence that had been introduced in the lower courts. According to Breyer, the trial judge who had held the statutes unconstitutional had properly evaluated the evidence. Some of it was specific to Texas, and some dealt with general matters such as the rate of complications in routine abortions.

The Court's emphasis on the record and on the trial judge's decision provides a wedge for finding other TRAP statutes constitutional. Lower-court judges can look at the record and say that there's more evidence showing that the statutes do address some medical problems associated with abortions than there was in the Texas case. Or, as in one case, they can suggest the possibility that for some reason — maybe it's the water — abortions in Missouri might not be as safe as those in Texas. Or they can find a smaller effect on the availability of abortions — making the burden not an "undue" one.[8]

The Supreme Court could let decisions on Texas-like laws accumulate in the lower courts; in insiders' jargon, it could let the issues "percolate" for a while. Then it could step in and "resolve" the issue by overruling *Roe*.

The alternative path is obvious, though perhaps less likely. A pro-life state could enact a complete ban on abortions, what Canadians call an "in your face" response to a constitutional court's decision. Or the state could ban abortions after a fetal heartbeat is detectable, a criterion that is functionally the same as repudiating *Roe*. Or a pro-life prosecutor could bring a case under some old abortion statute, not repealed but unenforceable after *Roe,* and dare the courts to prevent the prosecution. Perhaps the lower courts where these cases were brought would follow *Roe*. Perhaps one or two would be equally "in your face" and treat *Roe* as bad law. Such decisions would directly present the question of whether *Roe* should be overruled, and the court might accept the invitation.

It's worth pausing here to note that neither path leads the Court to overrule *Roe* right away. State legislatures and prosecutors have to decide to press challenges, lower courts have to decide cases, and the Court itself can choose when or even whether to take up the question of overruling *Roe*. The most likely path: A lower court strikes down a state statute that pretty clearly doesn't place an undue burden on the right to choose, relying solely on *Roe*'s "core holding." The state asks the Supreme Court to review that decision, and the Court agrees. By the time this happens, the justices may have a lot more information about the political environment in which *Roe* would be overruled than they do now. And that information might incline them to overrule it.

How would the justices do this? The case involving public employee unions (chapter 3) provides a roadmap.

- The initial decision was "poorly reasoned." Check as to *Roe*.
- Its reasoning was "recast" by later decisions, which "undermine" its authority. Check as to *Roe* in light of the Court's 1993 "undue burden" decision.
- It turned out to be unworkable. Check for the "undue burden" standard.
- Factual "developments" "eroded" the decision's "underpinnings." Justice O'Connor persistently made this point about the technology associated with birth and abortion. She argued that medical technology would push the point at which a fetus was viable outside the womb earlier and earlier, which turned out to be wrong— there seems to be a limit to what technology can do. But, claim

pro-life advocates, medical developments have made it increasingly clear that fetuses share such human traits as the ability to feel pain.

- Legal "developments" have had the same effect. Just as requiring public employees to pay to support political positions they disagreed with was an anomaly in First Amendment doctrine, *Roe* was—or became—anomalous in connection with Supreme Court decisions allowing the government to limit people's rights to make medically important decisions. The Court held that the government can prevent patients from using experimental medications even when all other courses of treatment have failed, and that it can prevent people from seeking assistance from physicians when they want to end their lives.[9]

- People haven't made irrevocable decisions relying on *Roe* to be overruled. In 1992 the Court did say that women had relied on *Roe* in thinking about their life courses, for instance in choosing jobs and careers. That's not the kind of reliance usually involved when the Court talks about overruling earlier decisions. Exactly how a woman might have relied upon *Roe* and the availability of abortion in deciding to become a lawyer or office manager was never clear. *Roe* might affect the decisions a woman makes about when (and with whom) to have intercourse, but she can easily recalculate.

All the building blocks are in place for overruling *Roe*. The last step will come when the Court decides to put the blocks together.

Or perhaps the next-to-last step. Pro-life activists have begun to push an argument that had gone dormant after *Roe:* Fetuses are persons within the meaning of the Fourteenth Amendment, which implies—in their eyes—that the Constitution *requires* that abortion be prohibited. This isn't a knock-down argument—yet. The underlying legal theory would raise questions about the widespread practice of punishing infanticide less severely than murder, for example.

But with a consolidated conservative Court these now-extreme arguments might gain some traction.

The Second Amendment

The Court's holding that the Second Amendment gives people a right to own guns for self-protection was an originalist triumph. After that it's been downhill in the courts for gun-rights advocates.

The *Heller* case involved a complete ban on gun ownership, and since it was decided, gun-rights advocates used it in their legislative fights, directly and indirectly, by threatening to rely on it unless legislatures removed existing restrictions on gun ownership. They were thus able to give weight to legislative proposals that went beyond *Heller*'s narrow holding.

In the courts, gun-rights advocates have been less successful. After holding that states couldn't completely ban gun ownership any more than the District of Columbia could, the Supreme Court regularly ducked substantial claims that some state law violated the Second Amendment. Most lower federal courts have upheld significant limits on gun owners' rights, while occasionally finding unconstitutional some limits that affected a handful of people.

One part of the reason for these outcomes has been *Heller* itself. The decision actually pointed in two directions. It elevated the individual right to gun ownership to constitutional stature. As gun-rights advocates liked to put it, the Second Amendment became like the First. And, they argued, just as the government had to provide very strong reasons for limiting speech, so should it have to provide strong reasons for limiting gun rights. The jargon here is "strict scrutiny": Limits on speech rights get strict scrutiny, and so should limits on Second Amendment rights.

The payoff comes in connection with many rules gun-rights advocates target: in particular, bans on carrying weapons openly and strict rules on getting permits to buy guns. Gun-rights advocates support strict scrutiny of these rules and assert that they aren't narrowly tailored to promote the important goal of limiting gun violence: If you're responsible enough to get a permit to buy a gun, for example, you can be trusted to act responsibly when carrying it in public.

The very framing of the Second Amendment as an individual right, then, points toward strict limits on the regulations governments can impose. Many advocates for "common-sense" gun regulations seem to agree that the regulations they favor wouldn't survive strict scrutiny. At least they devote a lot of effort to arguing that their favored regulations should get only intermediate scrutiny, meaning that the government's justifications have to be good but not overwhelming.

The lower courts have mostly applied intermediate scrutiny, over some notable objections by well-known conservative judges—objections that may foreshadow what a conservative Supreme Court would do. But how can the courts apply intermediate scrutiny if *Heller* says that the Second Amendment protects an individual right? By distinguishing the Second Amendment from the First.

There's no general rule that restrictions on individual rights always receive strict scrutiny. Statutes that authorize administrative searches don't get strict scrutiny. The First Amendment and rights to racial equality are special in triggering strict scrutiny, the lower courts argue, because of their special role in allowing our democracy to operate. When you look at other individual rights the Constitution protects, most often you find that the courts uphold regulations that they find reasonable or, sometimes, pretty well justified—that satisfy intermediate scrutiny.

That's the second direction in which *Heller* points. Justice Scalia's opinion for the Court, after all its elaborate analysis of original understanding, contains a paragraph that scholars find puzzling. Beginning with the acknowledgment that Second Amendment rights are "not unlimited," the paragraph says that nothing in the opinion "should be taken to cast doubt on longstanding prohibitions on the possession of firearms by felons and the mentally ill, or laws forbidding the carrying of firearms in sensitive places such as schools and government buildings, or laws imposing conditions and qualifications on the commercial sale of arms."

The puzzle here is the word "longstanding." Many of the prohibitions Scalia describes don't go back very far, certainly not to the Founding era. They can't be justified directly by original understandings. Maybe they fall into the domain of construction. This is where proponents of "common-sense" regulation pounce. What they want, they say, are exactly the kinds of reasonable regulations that have grown up over the past century. Even new regulations of new problems should be upheld, in their view, if they are reasonable extensions of past forms of regulation.

Maybe *Heller* was nothing more than a win in the culture wars, not to be taken all that seriously as legal doctrine. Yet gun-rights advocates, as supporters of a conservative political order, would be disappointed if that were all they got out of the Supreme Court. Conservative justices can readily find in *Heller* the resources to provide such advocates with the interest-group victories they seek.

Religious Liberty

The Roberts Court has already done a great deal that activists on the Christian Right like. As with partisan entrenchment, so with religious liberty: The Court can do a bit of mopping up, and it can require governments to accommodate religious liberty more than they already do.

The mopping up would involve overruling some cases that limit symbolic interactions between religion and government. There's essentially no chance that the Court would flatly overrule its decisions banning schools from requiring that the school day open with a spoken prayer. No superintendent of a school system in a decently sized city wants the headache of satisfying every religious group in the city. And there's some evidence, though it tends to be overstated, that mandatory prayers continue in small, especially rural school districts. Overall, though, a conservative constitutional order doesn't need to restore morning prayers to public schools, in the few districts where parents might favor them, to keep its support from the Christian Right.

Almost everything else is on the table. The Court barred schools from having religious benedictions at graduation ceremonies and from having prayers before football games. Questionable on their own terms, those decisions are open for overruling, through the same moves that would lead to overruling *Roe:* saying that prayers at basketball games aren't the same as those at football games because students feel less pressure to attend basketball games, or allowing a public school valedictorian to begin graduation ceremonies with a prayer she chose.*

The Court has decided some cases involving displays of crosses and other religious symbols on public land. The results have been inconsistent. Similar cases have rattled around in the lower courts, with a reasonably strong trend against allowing such displays. The Bladensburg cross case strengthened the position that symbolic interactions between religion and government rarely present a constitutional problem. And the next step is obvious—finding no constitutional problem with public prayers that are explicitly and exclusively Christian.

---

* Some courts have already allowed this practice.

Symbolic interactions don't cost anything. Providing financial support to religion does. As we saw in chapter 5, the Court has held that programs giving parents vouchers they can use to pay tuition and other costs associated with attending religiously affiliated schools did not violate the "no establishment" clause. It has also held that *excluding* religious institutions from programs that promote safety by providing recipients with money to improve playground conditions was unconstitutional.

That poses an obvious question: What about programs that give private recipients money to do what the legislature thinks are good works, but that exclude churches? A common example is a historic preservation program that gives recipients money to repair historic buildings damaged by fire, winds, or general decay. Suppose hurricane winds break a stained glass window with religious imagery in a historically significant church. Can the state refuse money for restoring the window? The playground repair case pretty strongly implies that excluding churches would violate the principle that the government must treat religion and nonreligion the same.[10]

The big issue here, of course, is school voucher programs. Can states require that vouchers be used only at schools that aren't affiliated with religious institutions? In allowing states to include such schools in voucher programs the Court mentioned, perhaps even emphasized, that parents, not governments, were deciding where to use the vouchers. It's not clear why that matters for "no establishment" purposes, but it almost certainly doesn't matter when the question is equal treatment of religion and nonreligion.

Chief Justice Roberts's footnote to the playground case, saying that the opinion does not "address religious uses of funding or other forms of discrimination," simply pushes the issue off to the future. It's difficult to see why the logic of equality doesn't apply to "religious uses of funding" that's available to nonreligious institutions, whether for repairing damaged windows or for attending schools. As Justice Gorsuch correctly put it in declining to join the footnote, "the general principle" the Court invoked does "not permit discrimination against religious exercise—whether on the playground or anywhere else."

Extending this nondiscrimination logic might give the Christian Right a short-term victory but a long-term defeat. Supporters of voucher programs have faced substantial political obstacles, mostly because of the programs' effects on the taxes paid by parents who moved to districts with good public schools. States can choose to have such programs or not. Anything that would increase their costs—like a rule requiring that they include religious institutions—only decreases the chances that they would be enacted, or continued.

Finally, how far must a government go to accommodate religious objections against complying with laws everyone else must follow? The Trump administration did its part by extending accommodations based on conscience—not necessarily religious—quite broadly, though the extensions have been challenged as improper under several statutes. What can the Court do?

Masterpiece Cakeshop relied on pretty thin evidence of hostility to religion as the basis for overruling a government agency's finding that a baker had discriminated against customers on the basis of their sexual orientation. Maybe the Court will find equally thin evidence of religious hostility in other cases.

Or perhaps the Court will overrule *Smith* and reinstate some sort of balancing test, weighing the government's interest against the religious objector's. That in itself might not help the Christian Right in cases involving claims of discrimination on the basis of sexual orientation. In *Masterpiece Cakeshop,* Justice Kennedy came close to saying that preventing sexual-orientation discrimination was a compelling interest but ultimately took the case in a different direction. The

Court could easily treat that discussion as dictum, and *then* strike the balance in favor of the religious objectors.

Nothing can be ruled out, of course. Perhaps the Court will come up with a broader requirement of accommodation of religion than present law, modestly extended, would support. At this point, though, we are back to the culture wars. For LGBTQ activists, a Court decision broadening religious exemptions from complying with antidiscrimination laws will be a slap in the face. Other groups protected by antidiscrimination laws will worry that religious accommodations will apply against them as well—a white supremacist restaurant denying service to African Americans, in the usual example. (In 2019 owners of an "event space" refused to rent it for an interracial wedding, citing their religious beliefs. After a public uproar, they retreated.)[11] The worries will be misplaced, because racist discrimination based on religion isn't part of any foreseeable culture war.

Perhaps most important, the symbolic significance of these extensions, were they to occur, would far exceed their practical import. That might be why the Court would be willing to go only so far: A symbolic payoff to an important interest group that has relatively little real-world impact is about as good as it can get.

Helping Congress Out

The Supreme Court is a regular player in maintaining a consolidated constitutional regime. It can take up some of the slack created by heavy demands on politicians' time, and it can sometimes absorb political heat politicians would rather avoid. Overall, though, the Court is usually a bench-warmer brought in to play only when something has gone wrong.

We have to abandon the baseball metaphor, though, to fully understand the Court's role in a consolidated regime. It resolves problems by writing opinions whose rhetorical nuggets sometimes encapsulate the principles that broadly guide the regime. Justice William O. Douglas's opinion in *Griswold v. Connecticut,* holding unconstitutional a state's ban on selling contraceptives, is an example. Douglas wrote: "We deal with a right of privacy older than the Bill of Rights—older than our political parties, older than our school system. Marriage . . . is an association that promotes a way of life, not causes; a harmony in living, not political faiths; a bilateral loyalty, not commercial or social projects. Yet it is an association for as noble a purpose as any involved in our prior decisions." This resonates strongly with New Deal/Great Society ideas about the government's role in ensuring the foundation of individual autonomy.

Douglas also offered an account of constitutional interpretation, writing that "specific guarantees in the Bill of Rights have penumbras, formed by emanations from those guarantees that help give them life and substance." Here he links living constitutionalism to the Constitution's text.

Griswold was a "mopping up" decision: When it was decided, only Connecticut and Massachusetts regulated contraceptive sales so heavily. It became iconic because it explicitly identified important principles that guided legislation and executive action during the New Deal/Great Society period. That sort of articulation often occurs when the Court comes off the bench to help an established constitutional order.

8

The Business Agenda

Within weeks of his inauguration, President Trump announced an ambitious plan for reducing the reach of federal regulation. For every new rule a federal agency proposed, it would have to eliminate two. The administration also dramatically reduced the budget for enforcing existing regulations.

Congress played its part too. A statute enacted as part of Newt Gingrich's Contract with America (and signed by Bill Clinton in 1996) gives Congress the power to repeal new regulations on a fast-track basis. Before 2017 it had been used only once, to set aside a rule dealing with workplace safety, but in 2017 Congress relied on it fifteen times, repealing regulations dealing with environmental protection, securities, and education.

Rolling back the administrative state is largely a task for the president and Congress. The courts' role is limited, at least in making large-scale changes. When administrative agencies revoke existing regulations, they have to go through a song-and-dance required by the Administrative Procedure Act. Such repeals are almost always challenged in the courts, and the courts can give the repeals their approval.

Courts can also set aside proposed regulations as unauthorized by Congress or as having been adopted without adequate procedural safeguards. But in a consolidated conservative order, that's likely to happen only in connection with regulations hanging over from an earlier period.

Even in such a regime, though, there will be holdouts. Some people, having lost the ability to get agencies or Congress to adopt new regulations, will look to the courts, including the state courts. Blue states will try to take up the regulatory slack, and the Supreme Court will do its best to thwart such efforts. Strikingly, the judicial ideologies that conservative justices say they adhere to will sometimes stand in the way of doing businesses' deregulatory bidding. And sometimes it will be quite unclear what legal rule is "good for business." The justices will often rightly see themselves as simply trying to figure out what the legal materials require—as calling balls and strikes.

Blocking Access to the Courts

Suppose the Occupational Safety and Health Administration tells employers that they can provide a lower standard of protective equipment to their workers; the Environmental Protection Agency decides to allow power plants to increase their emissions of sulfur dioxide; the Fish and Wildlife Service takes a small frog off the endangered species list; the Securities and Exchange Commission tells companies that they don't have to disclose information about some of their riskier projects when they try to sell stock.

What can workers, environmentalists, and investors do about this deregulatory agenda? They might think the new rules are unlawful—that is, the statutes the agencies rely on require them to stick with the old rules. Or they might believe the agencies didn't go through the correct steps before revoking the old rules—didn't get the expert evidence the statutes say they must have before acting.

The Administrative Procedure Act says that anyone "aggrieved" by an agency action can challenge it as either unlawful or procedurally improper. Sometimes it's easy to see who is aggrieved—workers exposed to greater risk, people who have to breathe polluted air. Sometimes it's more difficult: the frog might be aggrieved by being taken off the list, but is any person aggrieved?

The Supreme Court's rules on this topic are quite generous. Technically, you have to be within the "zone of interests" arguably protected by the statute. Eco-tourists who plan to look at the frog in its natural habitat probably are aggrieved; a herpetologist who specializes in studying the frog almost certainly is.

Layered on to that statutory requirement is a constitutional requirement, that you have "standing." The Court's doctrine here is often confusing. For now, what matters is that to have standing you have to run the risk of suffering what the Court calls a "constitutionally cognizable injury." This sounds very much like being aggrieved, but in practice it's more complicated.

The range of constitutionally cognizable injuries is pretty wide. They include environmental damage and the like, but only when they affect you personally. The Court said that eco-tourists who wanted to view an endangered elephant in its native habitat didn't have standing because they didn't have concrete plans to go there, but it strongly suggested that they would have had standing if only they had bought airplane tickets.[1]

Looking only at Supreme Court cases on standing gives a misleading impression. When the Court deals with standing it quite frequently finds that the plaintiffs haven't shown that they would suffer harm. Sometimes that's because the plaintiffs were trying to push the envelope and get the Court to broaden the rules about standing; sometimes it's because the Court sandbags the plaintiffs by tightening up standing rules, but in a way that allows the next set of plaintiffs to show that they were indeed harmed; and sometimes it's because the vagaries of litigation reshape the case from one in which some plaintiff unquestionably had standing into one where standing was problematic. And, of course, quite often the Court decides cases on the merits without even addressing standing, because everyone agrees that the plaintiffs did have standing.

People who want to overturn deregulatory initiatives can almost always move their cases forward by selecting plaintiffs carefully.[2] A Court bent on sharply cutting back on the ability to challenge deregulation could of course change the law of standing, but it doesn't have to. It's easy enough to reject challenges on their merits—to find that the Clean Air Act gave the EPA free choice between the old restrictive rule on sulfur dioxide and the new more generous one, or to find that the Fish and Wildlife Service had gotten as much expert advice as the Endangered Species Act requires.

There's another route into court. Instead of suing the government, you can sue the employer or the power plant or the company issuing stock. To do this you have to say that the underlying statute—the Occupational Safety and Health Act or the Securities Act—does more than authorize the government to create and enforce rules. It creates a "private right of action."

The theory behind such rights is simple: Congress passes a lot of laws imposing duties on corporations, but there are lots of violations and Congress doesn't give the executive branch enough money to catch and punish violators. The private right of action enlists injured workers, investors, or consumers to ensure effective enforcement of the duties Congress imposed.

That's the theory. The reality is that the Supreme Court has been eating away at it for thirty years. Now the rule is that you don't have a private right of action unless Congress has expressly given you one. By now we know that according to the Court, Congress hasn't done that in more than a handful of statutes—because plaintiffs and their lawyers have searched creatively to find new private rights of action, and the Court has batted down nearly every effort.

In short, it's relatively easy to challenge deregulatory moves under the Administrative Procedure Act, but it's also easy for the Court to uphold deregulation. It's basically impossible to claim a private right of action against the regulated business.

Only by substantially revising standing doctrine could the Court really scale back on consumer and environmental challenges to deregulation. Upholding deregulatory initiatives on their merits is much easier. And the Court has already done most of the heavy lifting in stopping consumers from suing businesses by invoking federal regulatory statutes that don't expressly give them a right to sue. The Court's contribution to the deregulatory agenda of a consolidated conservative regime is likely to be small.

Blocking States from Regulating

In 2015 the Federal Communications Commission, with a majority appointed by President Obama, issued an order requiring "net neutrality," a policy strongly favored by internet users and opposed by internet providers. In 2017 the FCC, now with a Trump-appointed majority, effectively abandoned the rule.

So far, a standard story of deregulation. But net-neutrality supporters didn't give up. They got the state of California to adopt its own net-neutrality law.

The next move was into court: The Trump administration sued California to force it to suspend its law under the doctrine of "preemption." That doctrine says that federal law—here, the Federal Communications Act and related statutes—prevails over conflicting state law.

Preemption is the main tool by which the national government may bring holdouts on the state level into line. The business perspective on preemption is complicated. When the federal government is deregulating, big business likes preemption of state regulations. Even in a world with a fair amount of national regulation, big businesses operating on a national scale often like preemption because it means that they have to comply with only one set of rules, not fifty.

Small business owners tend to take deregulation wherever they can get it. Sometimes, though, they understand that they are at a disadvantage competing with large businesses: the mom-and-pop pharmacy against CVS, the corner grocery store against Wal-Mart. And the owners of small local businesses, who are often politically active at the community level where state senators' and assembly members' fates are decided, may have more clout in the state legislature than the big interstate companies. A patchwork of different state rules can work to local businesses' advantage, and when it does, they may oppose preemption.

Consumers are divided as well. Regulations generally raise prices; some do so for good reason, while others simply protect businesses from competition. Consumers would like to have the former preserved and the latter preempted.

Expansive uses of preemption conflict with some of the ideological premises of modern conservatism. As a nationalizing doctrine, preemption is in tension with modern conservatism's purported commitment to decentralization and federalism. And some of its doctrinal formulations require courts to go beyond a statute's text and rely upon the law's purposes, which is in some tension with "textualism," the theory of statutory interpretation favored by originalists.

Individual justices feel the pull of these forces differently, some favoring the deregulatory agenda, others feeling bound by jurisprudential commitments. The upshot is something of a mish-mash— cases that look a lot alike may come out differently because of small differences in the national and state statutes involved. Preemption can be part of a business agenda, but exactly how it plays out almost always defies simple categorization as "pro-business" or "pro-consumer."

Preemption comes in three flavors: express, implied, and field preemption. Express preemption might seem the simplest. It occurs when Congress enacts a statute with a provision saying that specific state statutes are preempted while other statutes are "saved." The difficulty is that the courts have to decide whether the state statute being challenged is one of those expressly preempted or saved.

An example: federal automobile safety law says that you can't recover damages from car makers for negligently designing their cars if the cars are "in compliance with" federal regulations. When Alexis Geier was severely injured in a car crash because her car had seat belts but not airbags, the Supreme Court held that state law was preempted, because federal law at the time authorized car makers to choose to have or omit airbags. When Thanh Williamson was killed in a car crash even though she was wearing the seat belt provided for the rear middle seat, the Court held that she *could* recover because the car maker hadn't installed a stronger seat-and-shoulder belt. The difference was that Congress hadn't said anything about rear seats. Justice Breyer wrote both opinions, the first seemingly pro-business and the second seemingly pro-consumer. And Justice Thomas dissented from the first, citing his belief that modern preemption doctrine fit uneasily with federalism.

The Court had to interpret the words "in compliance with" to decide these cases. In the airbag case, the question turned out to be whether Congress had prescribed the safety measures car makers had to take. Nothing in the statutes said, "Use airbags or not, up to you." The Court found, though, that the statutes implicitly gave car makers that choice.

Implicit preemption isn't that different from express preemption. The justices examine the ordinary materials for interpreting a statute — its words, its legislative history, and whatever else they think appropriate, which for some of them includes the statute's overall purposes. They then ask whether the statute, properly interpreted, bars states from adopting regulations that conflict with the statute's words as they have been interpreted. Again, expansive preemption rules are in tension with federalism.

Field preemption is different. The name comes from the image of federal law completely occupying the field being regulated. The formal doctrine is this: if the state law stands as an impediment to the full accomplishment of the federal statute's goals, then it is invalid and the federal law prevails. Arizona's notorious "show me your papers" law, which allowed police officers to demand that people they arrested produce documents showing that they were lawfully present in the United States, fell to this doctrine. Modern conservatives don't like field preemption because it rests entirely on what judges say the national statute's purposes are, and not at all on the statute's words. As Justice Thomas put it in the Arizona case, field preemption "invites courts to engage in freewheeling speculation about congressional purpose that roams well beyond statutory text."[3]

How does all this play out in the net-neutrality example? A 1996 statute gives the FCC the power to make rules regulating the internet. The FCC says that its rule barring states from adopting their own net-neutrality rules is necessary to ensure that there will be one national policy, not fifty state policies. California relies on administrative law principles to say that the FCC's rule isn't authorized by the 1996 act. And it might argue that *Congress* can preempt state laws, but a mere agency can't — an argument typically favored by conservatives.

Overall, in the hands of modern conservatives, preemption doctrine will tilt in favor of businesses operating on a national scale, but the tilt will be modest. We can't be sure how the net-neutrality case will come out because preemption doctrine pulls together so many strands of judicial philosophy—views on the merits of regulation and deregulation, and about federalism and interpretive methodology. In 2019 the Court upheld Virginia's ban on uranium mining against a preemption challenge. The lineups indicate the issue's complexity. Justice Gorsuch wrote a textualist opinion joined by Justices Thomas and Kavanaugh holding that the relevant congressional statutes clearly indicated that Congress allowed states to regulate uranium *mining* but not later phases in nuclear power production. Along the way he discussed the difficulty of inferring congressional purposes: "It is our duty to respect not only what Congress wrote, but, as importantly, what it didn't write." Justice Ginsburg's opinion for herself and Justices Sotomayor and Kagan, agreed with the thrust of Gorsuch's opinion but objected to his discussion of purposes because it swept "well beyond the confines of this case." And the Chief Justice wrote an opinion joined by the remaining two justices finding that Congress did preempt state laws even against mining if their purpose was to reduce the risks to public health from mining's aftermath.[4]

A betting person would probably favor "the national government wins," but might have some sleepless nights before any specific bet paid off. But a betting strategy of always going with the national government would probably make you some money.

The Ambiguities of a "Pro-Business" Agenda

The pattern we see—or more accurately, the pattern we find difficult to see—in preemption cases is reproduced in other areas of business regulation. Over the past decade the Supreme Court has taken an interest in the law of intellectual property (IP law)—trademark, copyright, and patents. That's not surprising in an economy now driven more by technology than by manufacturing.

What results favor "business" is often unclear. Many cases pit one group of businesses against another, with each side saying that the rule it favors will benefit consumers. Some content-producers, mostly large businesses, want strong intellectual property protection; they say that strong protection encourages people to generate more material for consumers to use. Others want weak IP protection, saying that this allows them to innovate and (aha!) generate more material for consumers to use.

Many of the Court's IP cases are highly technical. In one, Justice Thomas set out the facts dealing with a complicated patent for a DNA test meant to determine whether a woman had a genetic predisposition to breast cancer. Justice Scalia concurred in the result, but not in the part "going into fine details of molecular biology," because he was "unable to affirm those details on my own knowledge or even my own belief."[5]

It's not just the underlying technology that's complicated; the doctrines themselves are riddled with complex terms that only lawyers deeply embedded in the field understand: the "reverse doctrine of equivalents," for example, or "file wrapper estoppel" (now known as "prosecution history estoppel," if that's any help).

In some cases, you can tell which outcome is likely to favor big businesses against smaller ones, or consumers against businesses. A decision saying that a buyer of a copyrighted item is free to resell it favors consumers over publishers—though depending on the details of the market, the outcome might lead to higher prices for similar items, or fewer of them being produced. Overall, though, whatever intuitions a judge has about who benefits from a decision are likely to be overwhelmed by the judge's feel for what seems like a sensible interpretation of IP statutes and doctrine. What outcomes are pro-business are unclear, and even a pro-business Court will rest its decisions mostly on the justices' view of whether the pitch was a ball or a strike.

Favoring Really Small Businesses

The Institute for Justice (IJ) is a libertarian public interest law firm initially funded by the Koch brothers. It has taken up the cause of small business owners blocked from operating by state licensing requirements. Some of those requirements are burdensome and silly: requiring that people who want to braid hair go through a long and expensive process of qualifying to become licensed cosmetologists, weird restrictions on who can make coffins, requirements that interior decorators know something about what makes a building structurally sound. The Obama administration issued a long report criticizing many state licensing requirements because they interfered with people's ability to set up their own businesses, and with the ability of people licensed in one state to relocate elsewhere.[6]

The New Deal/Great Society order had no problem with licensing requirements. It treated the states' power to regulate economic activity as basically unlimited unless you could point to some specific constitutional provision limiting that power. Hair braiders and coffin makers couldn't.

The IJ regularly argues for what it calls "judicial engagement." In its modest form, judicial engagement asks judges to apply the laugh test with some attention to real-world facts. Why do states make cosmetologists go through an extensive training program? Because they sometimes use chemicals that can injure their clients. Hair braiders don't, so it's silly to require them to take the cosmetology courses. Proponents of judicial engagement argue that applying the laugh test to restrictions on making coffins and on being an interior decorator would lead judges to find them unconstitutional.[7]

Indeed it might. A conservative majority on the Supreme Court might find judicial engagement attractive in cases like the IJ's,* but it might have two misgivings. One is theoretical. Judicial engagement is decidedly non-textual: it relies on a general background principle of freedom rather than any specific constitutional text. Or, when a text is brought into the discussion, it is the substantive Due Process Clause—the same text used to justify *Roe v. Wade.* Some conservatives might be uncomfortable in doing that.

The second problem with judicial engagement is that it doesn't come in a modest version only requiring application of the laugh test. The IJ clearly hopes that the cases it has pursued so far will open the way to others dealing with more substantial regulation of economic activity—such as workplace safety rules. Robust judicial engagement might question whether a particular rule about wearing goggles or thick boots really makes sense.

Some conservatives might be fine with cutting back regulation, yet think that judicial engagement is not the best way to do it. Still, we might expect a Court committed to a consolidated conservative regime to strike some minor regulations where the state's justifications might raise a smile, even if they didn't lead the judges to burst out laughing.

A Modest Tilt Toward Big Business

We might expect the Supreme Court in a consolidated conservative constitutional order to be pro-business. And it probably will be, a bit. It certainly can support pro-business initiatives by the president

---

* The Obama administration report suggests that some liberals might as well.

and Congress, most notably by upholding deregulatory innovations against legal challenges. And it can help insulate those innovations from legal challenge by making it more difficult for people to bring lawsuits against them.

Often, though, we cannot immediately tell whether a decision is pro-business, pro-consumer, or pro-some-businesses-but-not-others. When the Supreme Court overruled a decision dating from the era before e-commerce and allowed states to require that e-sellers collect sales taxes on purchases by local residents, Chief Justice Roberts dissented. Contesting the image that big sellers like Amazon enjoyed an unfair advantage, he wrote that the burden of collecting the taxes "will fall disproportionately on small businesses." For him, e-commerce connected "small, even 'micro' businesses to potential buyers across the Nation. People starting a business selling their embroidered pillowcases or carved decoys can offer their wares throughout the country—but probably not if they have to figure out the tax due on every sale." The chief justice didn't see the possibilities the free market opened: there are now low-cost web-based services, regularly updated to take into account changes in state and city laws, that do the calculation for small retailers.[8]

The lineup in the e-commerce case is suggestive. Justice Kennedy wrote the opinion, which was joined by Justices Thomas, Ginsburg, Alito, and Gorsuch. The chief justice's dissent was joined by Justices Breyer, Sotomayor, and Kagan. Ideas about federalism and constitutional interpretation drove the alignment far more than intuitions about who would benefit.

Progressives are likely to look at bottom-line results and say, "Business won this one, so the Court must be pro-business." Libertarians might look at the same bottom line and say, "Big business won this one, so the Court must be against the small business owner." Both perspectives might capture something about the Court's work, but both—and others that simply assess the bottom-line results—are quite likely to miss the point. In many areas of law dealing with businesses, neither we nor the Court really know what produces the best results for the U.S. economy. We and the Court can only work with the legal materials as best we can. Here it does seem fair to say that the Court is mostly calling balls and strikes.[9]

9

Deconstructing the Administrative State

A month after Donald Trump took office, his then adviser Steve Bannon gave a speech to conservative activists in which he called for the "deconstruction of the administrative state." Perhaps puzzled by Bannon's appropriation of the term "deconstruction," the *Washington Post* said that Bannon was talking about "the system of taxes, regulations and trade pacts that the president says have stymied economic growth."[1] In Bannon's circles, "the administrative state" had a lot to do with economic growth and regulations, a little to do with taxes, and almost nothing to do with trade pacts.*

Two leading academic conservatives offered an over-the-top version of their constitutional program:

> [T]he bad ideas of the 1930s that specifically drove the construction of certain parts of the modern administrative state—belief in omnipotent government by socially superior experts under broad subdelegations of legislative power, with a formal (or rote) separation of powers seen as an anachro-

---

* Constitutional law and the Supreme Court have almost nothing to say about the major effects of taxes on the administrative state, but they do have an important place in conservative thinking about that state. Lowering taxes will "starve the beast." Then, according to Grover Norquist, a leading low-tax advocate, the administrative state could be drowned in a bathtub.

nistic hindrance to modern scientific management of people, who are not ends in themselves but simply means to the accomplishment of collective nationalist or tribalist ends—are at the intellectual core of just about everything bad that occurred during that decade.

For them, "massive subdelegations of legislative and judicial power to appointed technocrats who are not directly accountable to the President are unconstitutional through numerous violations of the separation of powers, that they violate Magna Carta and the Due Process of Law Clause of the Fifth Amendment." Further, "all of the so-called 'independent' regulatory agencies should be recognized as fully a part of the executive department. The United States of America is a democratic republic in which everyone is born free and equal. There should be no 'experts' who can wield power that is not directly controlled by the President, Congress, and the federal courts." Now *that* is deconstructing the administrative state.[2]

Start with regulations. Every Republican president from Ronald Reagan on wanted to "deregulate"—get rid of regulations that, they believed, interfered with private enterprise as an engine of economic growth.

The problem with deregulation is that it's not permanent. Reagan and George H. W. Bush deregulated, Bill Clinton re-regulated; George W. Bush deregulated, Barack Obama re-regulated. And deregulation takes time. A federal statute, the Administrative Procedure Act (APA), requires regulators to go through an elaborate procedure to adopt a new regulation. They have to send out a notice saying that they're planning to regulate, propose a regulation, get public comments on it, respond to the comments, adopt the regulation—and then face court challenges. The challengers will say that the regulator botched the procedures: The regulation it adopted wasn't enough like the one it first proposed, so it should have started over and sought a new round of comments; somebody made a significant objection to the proposal and the regulator didn't answer it adequately; and much more. The Supreme Court says that regulators have to go through exactly the same procedure when they want to repeal a regulation.

If you think there's too much regulation, a simple program of deregulation won't cut it. Toward the end of the Reagan administration and through the next Republican presidencies, conservative lawyers groped their way to such a solution. Their first effort got the label "the unitary executive."

Understanding this theory requires learning a small part of modern administrative law. Regulations get proposed by two kinds of agencies. The first are "presidential" agencies. Organization charts show presidential agencies with lines of responsibility that ultimately end in the White House. The Environmental Protection Agency's head is a cabinet-level official who reports directly to the president; the administrator of the Food and Drug Administration reports to the secretary of health and human services, who reports to the president; the Occupational Safety and Health Administration (OSHA) is located in the Department of Labor. The president hires the heads of presidential agencies, and may fire them for any reason at all.

The other agencies are "independent." They include the Federal Communications Commission (FCC), the Securities and Exchange Commission (SEC), and the National Labor Relations Board (NLRB). Typically, independent agencies have several members, not just a single head, and more important, the statutes that create them say—or, in the case of the SEC, are understood to say—that the president's power to fire the members is limited. Typically, they can be fired only for misconduct and similar offenses, not merely because the president disagrees with the actions they've taken.

The unitary presidency theory holds that independent agencies are probably unconstitutional. The Constitution says that the president has to take care that the laws be "faithfully executed," and a president can't do that unless he or she is able to tell the people charged with executing the laws—agencies, in short—what to do. This theory has made a little progress in the courts. The Supreme Court held that an obscure agency that regulates stock brokers and similar companies violated the principle of presidential control because it was two levels removed from the president: its members were appointed by the independent SEC and could be removed by the SEC only for misconduct. As a court of appeals judge, Brett Kavanaugh wrote an opinion holding unconstitutional the structure of the Consumer Financial Protection Bureau (CFPB—Elizabeth Warren's signature piece of legislation) because its head was too independent.[3]

The CFPB example is instructive because by the time Kavanaugh was on the Supreme Court, the agency was headed by someone President Trump appointed. Like deregulation, though, that's not a permanent solution. If a Democrat becomes president, he or she will appoint a pro-regulatory head of the CFPB.

Notice how little the unitary-executive theory actually accomplishes. Republicans think that the SEC and the FCC have sometimes overreached, as when the FCC briefly required net neutrality from internet service providers, but their real concerns are the "big" regulators like the EPA, the FDA, and OSHA. Those agencies are *already* under the president's control—and Republicans don't think that formal, legal control has gotten them much permanent deregulation.

Aside from its inherently limited reach, the unitary-presidency theory ran into trouble on several fronts. Probably most important, lawyers for President George W. Bush overextended the theory in their efforts to defend torture and other extreme actions taken in response to the terrorist attacks of September 11, 2001. They asserted that the Constitution placed no limits on what the president could do as commander in chief of the armed forces, and prevented Congress from trying to impose statutory limits on the president's choices. Perhaps defensible in principle, that position was politically untenable, and it discredited more moderate versions of the theory that focused on presidential control over administrative agencies.

But, almost as important, the unitary-presidency theory was about the *legal* relations between the president and administrative agencies. Politics told a different story. Several generations ago, Harry Truman reportedly told his friends that Dwight Eisenhower was going to get to the Oval Office and, as a former general, would start issuing orders, only to discover that nothing happened. Things hadn't changed dramatically, even after the Reagan Revolution.

The unitary-presidency theory said that the president had to have the legal power to control what agencies did—and had the power to fire any administrator who resisted the president's directives. The legal theory ran up against political reality. President George W. Bush had enormous difficulty getting his EPA administrator, Stephen Johnson, to go along with the administration's position on regulations aimed at addressing climate change. Politics prevented Bush from firing Johnson and replacing him with a more compliant administrator. And that's just one example.

The unitary-presidency theory has some implications about the president's control over criminal prosecutions—implications that are important for President Trump but have little to do with deconstructing the administrative state. Under the theory—and indeed under almost any coherent account of presidential power—the president has the power to hire and fire the attorney general and the local U.S. attorneys who enforce federal criminal law. That gives the president the power to direct those officials to bring or drop criminal prosecutions. In ordinary circumstances, that's entirely sensible. Suppose the president thinks that bringing a criminal action against someone who seems to have spied on the United States for France would be a good thing, both for criminal enforcement and diplomatic reasons. The U.S. attorney says, "We think there's only a 50 percent chance we'll win, and our policies say, don't prosecute unless there's a 75 percent chance of conviction." The president certainly has the power to say, Bring the prosecution anyway.* Similarly for dropping a prosecution for policy reasons, if the president thinks these are more important than enforcing the criminal law in a specific case.† If a prosecutor refuses to go along, the president can fire her.

Though sensible in ordinary circumstances, this aspect of presidential power was troublesome with respect to President Trump, precisely because many people were concerned that his reasons for bringing or (more important) dropping prosecutions wouldn't be reasonable. Here too, the theory bumps up against political reality. Through much of 2018, President Trump clearly wanted to fire Robert Mueller and shut down his investigation of Russian influence on the 2016 election, but he simply couldn't get away with it. Even more bizarre from the point of view of any theory of presidential power, Trump regularly railed against decisions made by ordinary Department of Justice prosecutors, somehow seeing them not as his subordinates—which they were, as a matter of law—but as hostile forces (which some may have been) that he couldn't get rid of, which was true as a matter of politics.

This detour offers another example of how politics interacts with constitutional theory, but has relatively little to do with the primary

---

* Maybe the president couldn't direct the prosecution to go ahead if there were no reasonable chance of obtaining a conviction. The reason would be that bringing the case would then violate the defendant's rights.

† And again there might be a limit if the president's reasons were corrupt.

long-term concern here, deconstructing the administrative state. Political scientists explain the law-politics interaction in the administrative state as an "iron triangle." Agency heads are one point of the triangle, Washington interest groups another, and congressional committees the third. The president may appoint the agency head, but after that, Congress and the interest groups kick in, pressuring the agency head to do what *they* wanted, which wasn't always what the president wanted.[4]

It turned out to be really difficult to break the triangle even when Republicans took control of Congress. Some Republican-controlled committees had chairs who weren't entirely in tune with the president. And even when they were, the interest groups still pressured agency heads.

Conservative constitutional theorists came to see that the only permanent solution to overregulation was through legislation itself: they had to stop Congress from giving agencies the power to adopt regulations, and they had to stop agencies from using statutes already on the books to press forward with new regulations using, as two scholars put it, old statutes to solve new problems.

In one sense, it was easy to stop Congress from regulating or giving agencies the power to adopt new regulations. Gridlock did that automatically. The real problem was with statutes already on the books.

And here we need another lesson in administrative law. The regulations Republicans dislike have what administrative law calls "force of law." If OSHA says that companies digging deep trenches have to line them with wooden "trench boxes" to prevent the sides from caving in, a company that doesn't do it can be fined. If the EPA says that a power plant has to use a "scrubber" to reduce emissions of pollutants from its smokestacks, a company operating a plant without scrubbers faces penalties.

A non-lawyer might wonder, "Why are OSHA and the EPA making up these rules, rather than Congress?" More formally: The Constitution gives Congress "the legislative power," which means that Congress—and maybe only Congress—makes laws. And yet here are agencies located in the executive branch doing something that looks a lot like making laws—requiring trench boxes and scrubbers, backed up by the threat of fines.

For traditional constitutional law, the answer lies in distinguishing between enacting laws—legislating—and executing or applying those laws. From the beginning, people involved in governing knew that laws would be written in fairly general terms, leaving details to be filled in later as executive officials applied the laws. In the Occupational Safety and Health Act, Congress created a general duty that employers maintain safe working conditions. The trench-box requirement fills in one detail of what it means to have safe working conditions at a deep excavation.

The key is to figure out how we can tell when an administrative agency is filling in the details of a general statute Congress has enacted, and when it's making law on its own. The Supreme Court doctrine that describes this distinction is the "non-delegation" doctrine: Congress can't delegate its own power to make law to anyone else.

That doesn't get very far, of course, because it doesn't tell us when Congress has impermissibly delegated legislative power. The non-delegation doctrine is a bit more precise: when Congress gives an agency an "intelligible principle" to guide its actions, that doesn't count as delegating power.

So, what counts as an intelligible principle? The only way to figure that out is to look at what the Court has said are intelligible principles, because it's been seventy years since the Court found a violation of the non-delegation doctrine. The Clean Air Act requires the EPA administrator to set certain air quality standards that are "requisite to protect the public health" with an "adequate margin of safety." According to a unanimous Supreme Court, that was good enough — an intelligible principle. Justice Scalia's opinion in the case listed a slew of other standards that the Court had found "intelligible": price setting that "will be generally fair and equitable," for example, or regulation "in the public interest."[5]

If those are good enough, it's hard to see what wouldn't be. Justice Rehnquist once hinted that a provision in the OSHA statute might violate the non-delegation doctrine: standards to ensure safe and healthful workplaces must "most adequately assure . . . , to the extent feasible, on the best available evidence, that no employee will suffer material impairment of health or functional capacity." He suggested that "to the extent feasible" gave the agency no guidance whatever. But even he didn't think the statute was an unconstitutional delegation; he used his concern about delegation as the basis for interpreting the statute to require that OSHA's regulation address a demonstrable, "significant" risk of harm.[6]

What's the payoff of all this? The non-delegation doctrine in its current form doesn't limit what agencies can do. But a post-Trump Supreme Court could revitalize the doctrine by coming up with a more robust distinction between making law — for Congress — and the more limited task of filling in details.

The Court heard *Gundy v. United States* on the first day of its 2018–19 term, and decided it a week before the term ended. The reason was that, Justice Kavanaugh not having taken his seat yet, the rest of the Court was evenly divided for a long time about what to do about the non-delegation doctrine. In the end the Court upheld a delegation of authority to the attorney general to decide how quickly to make previously convicted sex offenders register with state authorities. The result was unremarkable. Justice Gorsuch's dissent foreshadowed what might become of the non-delegation doctrine, though. He proposed tightening up on the "intelligible principle" standard, though he didn't offer much to substitute. And Justice Alito concurred in the result, writing that though the outcome was consistent with the standard the Court had been applying, he was willing to reconsider it: "If a majority of this Court were willing to reconsider the approach we have taken for the past 84 years, I would support that effort. But because a majority is not willing to do that, it would be freakish to single out the provision at issue here for special treatment."

Finding the occasion for that reconsideration might be difficult. Progressives interested in turning conservatives' favored doctrines against conservative outcomes—constitutional jiu-jitsu—point to President Trump's declaration of a national emergency so he could get the money to pay for a border wall and his invocation of his power to raise tariffs as good candidates. But Justice Gorsuch's dissent in *Gundy* anticipated that. He wrote that broad delegations might be fine in areas associated with the president's Article II powers, and tariffs and border security probably fall within that category.

The real candidates for a revived non-delegation doctrine are environmental and health and safety regulations. Really tightening up the doctrine would be a nearly permanent solution to what Republicans see as the problem of overregulation. Congress would have to develop the regulations itself. In principle, of course, Congress could enact a statute requiring that deep excavations have trench boxes, with elaborate definitions of what "deep" means and descriptions of a trench box's characteristics. In the early twentieth century, Congress did enact statutes laying out detailed requirements for coupling railroad cars to avoid injuries to workers. No one thinks today's Congress would ever be able to do anything like that. Even if we did not require that degree of detail, a revitalized non-delegation doctrine in a world of congressional gridlock is a powerfully deregulatory move.

One element of deconstructing the administrative state, then, is a stronger non-delegation doctrine. Conservative constitutional theorists have begun to lay the foundations for such a doctrine. Experience suggests that the Supreme Court may find one or two delegations unconstitutional, but also find itself struggling to articulate why the statutes required some agency to legislate beyond filling in the details. Such decisions might free up some lower courts to hold a few additional statutes unconstitutional as well. A revitalized non-delegation doctrine might knock a few bricks out of the administrative state, but it's unlikely to dismantle large parts.

The unitary-executive theory and the non-delegation doctrine are the primary constitutional components of the project of deconstructing the administrative state. Even if fully implemented, they aren't likely to accomplish much.

Far more promising (or threatening, depending on your point of view) is the so-called *Chevron* doctrine, virtually unknown to the general public but central to the operation of the modern administrative state. The *Chevron* case is among the most cited Supreme Court decisions ever, and its doctrine is what greases the operation of the modern administrative state. Eliminating this doctrine has become part of the project of deconstructing the regulatory state, as it would help break the cycle of deregulation and re-regulation as Republican and Democratic presidents alternately come into office. According to one report, Judge Neil Gorsuch's criticism of the doctrine played an important part in his nomination to the Supreme Court.[7]

Everyone who tries to explain the *Chevron* doctrine begins by noting two ironies: The case that gave the doctrine its name upheld a Reagan administration deregulatory effort, yet today's conservatives want to get rid of the doctrine to bolster deregulation; and Justice Scalia, the iconic conservative justice, was an enthusiastic supporter of the doctrine, which his acolytes now want to repudiate.

Here's a short version of the *Chevron* case. The Clean Air Act divides the country into regions, some with air of acceptable quality, others with low-quality air. Companies that operate plants in the low-air-quality areas have to get permits to modify them. To get a permit, the applicant has to show that the modification won't increase air pollution. The statute says that the permit requirement applies to "stationary sources." Some manufacturing operations have several buildings at a single location—perhaps a building where energy to run the plant is generated, one with part of a production line and another with the rest of the line, yet another where completed products are tested, and so on. The Carter administration's EPA adopted a regulation that defined each building in a plant's complex as a stationary source. The Reagan administration changed the definition, adopting what it called the "bubble" concept: You put all the plant's buildings under a bubble and see whether the modification would lead to an increase in air pollution from the bubble.

Consider a two-part project. One part would modify the production line, the other the energy-producing building. Suppose the project's first part would increase air pollution but the second would decrease it even more, so that the two-part project improved air quality overall. Under the Carter EPA's definition, the company could get a permit to modify the energy building but couldn't get one for the production line. Under the bubble concept, the company could get a permit for the entire project. The justification for the bubble concept is that companies might not do the second part of the project, which improved air quality, unless they could do the first part at the same time.

Justice John Paul Stevens wrote the Supreme Court's opinion. The question before the Court was one of pure statutory interpretation: What did the words "stationary source" in the Clean Air Act mean? Looking at all the standard materials used in statutory interpretation, Stevens said that a reasonable interpreter could go either way. In such circumstances, he wrote—where, after looking at the ordinary sources for statutory interpretation, courts couldn't say that Congress had resolved the precise question—courts should accept the agency's interpretation if it was a reasonable one. That became the *Chevron* doctrine.

A huge body of law and scholarship now envelops this doctrine. Its critics observe, accurately, that it tells courts to accept an administrative agency's interpretation of a statute's words, but ordinarily we think statutory interpretation is the province of the courts. Why do agencies get to take over what looks like a purely legal task?

Justice Stevens said that agencies were politically more responsive than courts, as the shift from the Carter EPA's interpretation to the more deregulatory Reagan EPA interpretation suggested. That's part of the reason Justice Scalia liked the *Chevron* doctrine: It gave power to politically accountable agencies and took it away from judges who, he thought, too often interpreted statutes in line with their policy preferences. If policy determined a statute's meaning, better that the policy be made by people who reported to the president than by judges who reported to no one.

Stevens also wrote that agencies sometimes had expertise that was relevant to interpreting statutes. It's not that easy to see that point in *Chevron* itself, but maybe the EPA would be better than the courts in assessing a company's claim that it would do the project, thereby improving air quality, only if it could do both parts. Whatever the case for *Chevron* itself, it does seem true that for highly technical judgments, agency expertise is often helpful in figuring out the best interpretation of a statute.

Cass Sunstein, a strong defender of the modern administrative state, uses this example: A statute says that the secretary of labor can require mine operators to maintain records that will help the secretary carry out his or her duty to ensure safe working conditions in mines.

The secretary issues a regulation telling mine operators to report a "diagnosis" of silicosis or similar occupational disease within ten days. What's a diagnosis? The secretary interprets the term to mean "chest X-rays" showing a specific level of obstruction.* Of course, courts *could* come up with their own definition of "diagnosis," but an agency that deals with silicosis all the time probably can do better than judges.[8]

There's an important but subtle point about the *Chevron* doctrine's foundations. The Administrative Procedure Act says that courts should decide for themselves "all relevant questions of law." It's hard to see how the *Chevron* doctrine is consistent with the APA. Making sense of the doctrine seems to require you to say that when Congress enacted the Clean Air Act—and every other statute that comes within the doctrine's scope—it wanted reasonable agency interpretations to prevail unless Congress itself had clearly defined the words in question. Even more subtly, because Congress almost never expressly says things like that, the doctrine's best justification is that every statute giving agencies some authority implicitly gives them the authority to interpret unclear statutory words as well. A background assumption of the administrative state is that unless Congress says something different, agencies get to put a pretty strong thumb on the scales when dealing with unclear statutory words.[9]

At this point, the connection between the *Chevron* doctrine and deconstructing the administrative state begins to emerge. *Chevron*'s critics say that regulators—"bureaucrats"—like to regulate, and the *Chevron* doctrine gives them more latitude to do so. As the cycle of

---

* Technically, the example doesn't involve *Chevron* because the agency is interpreting its own regulation rather than a statute. The underlying concern conservatives have with *Chevron*—agencies acting in their own self-interest—applies to this doctrine too, though Chief Justice Roberts has asserted otherwise.

regulation and deregulation shows, that's not the complete story. The *Chevron* doctrine helps regulators who want to regulate, but it also helps those who want to deregulate. Still, the difficulties Republicans have had in fully breaking the iron triangle suggest that to succeed, they may need to get rid of the *Chevron* doctrine.

How much this might help depends in part on who you think is going to control the courts over the next several decades—which is why getting rid of *Chevron* is part of a post-Trump vision of the U.S. government. We have to think about two institutions, agencies and courts. Start with a world in which Republicans control administrative agencies, maybe because the unitary-executive theory has really taken hold, maybe because that's just what happens after you elect Republican presidents. But, in this first world, most of the judges on the federal courts have been appointed by Democrats. This is pretty much the world as it was in 2017–18. In that world, people interested in deregulation should really like *Chevron*. The agencies will push the boundaries of statutory interpretation to support aggressive deregulation, and judges faithfully applying *Chevron* will let them do it.[10]

Now imagine a world in which Republicans control agencies, and most judges have been appointed by Republicans. In *that* world—maybe the world we'll have for the next few years and even beyond—*Chevron* won't matter much. With *Chevron,* the judges will defer to deregulatory Republican agencies; without it, they will interpret the statutes themselves to have a deregulatory or antiregulatory meaning.

The final world is where the cycle of deregulation and re-regulation kicks in. We have agencies headed by pro-regulatory Democrats and courts with a majority of judges appointed by Republicans—like the world that might exist after the 2020 elections. If this is a world without *Chevron*, the cycle can be broken. Administrative agencies will try to regulate by adopting expansive definitions of statutory terms, but courts not bound by *Chevron* will slap them down, finding that

Congress hadn't authorized them to interpret the statutes on their own, and that the regulations rest on an interpretation of the statute's words that's inconsistent with the judges' own interpretation.

Eliminating *Chevron* interacts with the practical reality of the non-delegation doctrine as well. That reality is gridlock, which makes new statutes impossible. Facing new problems, agencies try to shoehorn what they want to do into old statutes. Agency lawyers will scour the statute books trying to find some statutory language that they can ("reasonably") interpret to authorize regulations that deal with the new problems. On the other side, agency heads who are forced to implement regulations that their predecessors thought were required by Congress will have their lawyers scour the statute books for something they can ("reasonably") interpret to say that the prior regulations weren't mandated and so can be repealed.[11]

Getting rid of *Chevron* blocks those moves. In theory, of course, Congress could enact new statutes to deal with the new problems, but gridlock prevents it. The result is that corporations and consumers, not the government, have to figure out whether there's anything they want to do about the problem. On the deregulatory side, Republican-appointed judges will say that, properly interpreted (by them), the statutes that earlier regulators thought required regulation actually only permitted it—or, even more aggressively, actually prohibited what prior agencies tried to do. Again, judges who oppose regulation don't need the *Chevron* doctrine to work that opposition into law. From their point of view, the doctrine is a major benefit when the cycle turns to re-regulation, and only a small benefit when the cycle turns to deregulation. On balance, abandoning the doctrine helps deconstruct the administrative state.

Understanding all this, though, I think we can be skeptical about the prospect of truly deconstructing the administrative state. Suppose the Supreme Court did everything it could: enthusiastically endorsed the unitary-executive theory, gave the non-delegation doctrine some real bite, and got rid of *Chevron*. That would make it easier to shrink the administrative state, but these actions in themselves wouldn't dismantle it. We'd still have a Federal Communications Commission, formally reporting to the president but still enmeshed with interest groups and congressional committees, and an Environmental Protection Agency filling in many truly technical details about clean air and water.

To succeed, Bannon's project would require sustained political pressure, not merely litigation and favorable court decisions. Even if the Supreme Court in a post-Trump world is strongly conservative, for the Trump presidency to bring forth a new conservative order would require reasonably sustained control of Congress and the presidency by conservatives as well.

10

Possibilities Thwarted and Revived

In the mid-2010s, Supreme Court watchers saw signs that the Court might be reconsidering its position on capital punishment. The first step would pay close attention to solitary confinement, and the second would then be a return to the short-lived constitutional rule that the death penalty was cruel and unusual punishment. Justice Kennedy's retirement ended that speculation.

In the 1990s Supreme Court watchers talked—fearfully or enthusiastically—about a "federalism revolution" and a "property rights revolution." By the mid-2010s they were trying to explain why those revolutions had petered out.

At any moment the Court has multiple paths before it, marked out by precedents that suggest lines of development. Sometimes it follows those paths, sometimes it doesn't—because the justices don't see the cases they could use to move down the path, or because individual justices have stronger or weaker commitments to the path (or strongly or weakly oppose moving forward). Justice Scalia was more enthusiastic about property rights than Chief Justice Rehnquist, and Justice O'Connor more enthusiastic about federalism than Justice Kennedy.

A conservative Court in a consolidated conservative regime may start down paths already visible—or find new ones to explore. Much will depend on how the justices understand the constitutional vision animating the regime, and that won't be clear for a while. Three thwarted initiatives suggest how this exploration occurs, even if they don't predict what the Court will do.

Capital Punishment

The easiest example is capital punishment. The Supreme Court struck down capital punishment in 1972, then upheld new death penalty statutes in 1976. Over the next decades, as the crime rate dropped, so did juries' willingness to sentence defendants to death. Several states got rid of their death penalty systems, most by legislative repeal, a few by court decisions that found the systems unconstitutional under state law. Death penalty abolitionists showed that death sentences were concentrated in a handful of counties, often because the prosecutors there were particularly aggressive in seeking death sentences. Some of those prosecutors were then defeated by reformers who promised to bring capital charges less frequently.

The Supreme Court chipped away at the new statutes by limiting the categories of cases in which the death penalty could be imposed: not for "simple" rape, not on people with significant mental disabilities, not on people who were young when they murdered others, not for child rape.* The Court regularly considered defendants' challenges to the death sentences and tended to rule in their favor. In Justice Kennedy's last two terms, the Court decided eleven death penalty cases and ruled for the defendant in eight. Two of the state victories didn't even involve whether the death sentence had been properly imposed. They came in cases involving the statute regulating how defendants can challenge their sentences in federal court.[1]

---

* In a case also dealing with the Cruel and Unusual Punishment Clause the Court held it unconstitutional for states to impose mandatory life sentences on people who were young when they committed their crimes.

Most of the cases involved individual injustices—a prosecutor who failed to disclose evidence favoring the defendant, a juror's racial bias—although some decisions had broader significance, such as one basically invalidating Florida's death penalty system because it didn't give juries the final say on the sentence. The cases favoring defendants weren't typically five-to-four, either. With one exception, Chief Justice Roberts—who had represented capital defendants pro bono while he was in private practice—joined the decisions vacating death sentences.[2]

All this gave death penalty abolitionists some hope. They were especially encouraged when Justice Breyer invited renewal of a frontal attack on capital punishment—because, they thought, he probably wouldn't have done so without some belief that the challenge might succeed.

That hope disappeared with Justice Kennedy's departure. In 2019 the Court rejected a challenge to Missouri's method of administering lethal injections to criminals sentenced to death, and along the way expressed real impatience at what the majority saw as legalistic efforts to throw obstacles in the way of carrying out lawful death sentences. With no obvious additional categories to be carved out of death penalty schemes, only the "individual injustice" cases remained. The Court will almost certainly continue to hear a fair number of these. It takes only four justices to grant review in a death penalty case. The liberals have no strategic reasons for refusing to grant review in cases of individual injustice, precisely because any losses they and the defendants suffer have no broad implications.[3]

And they have reasons to think they might actually prevail. True, Justices Thomas, Alito, and Gorsuch regularly dissented in individual-injustice cases, and so might Justice Kavanaugh. But they would need only Roberts's vote to flip the outcomes.

Perhaps the chief justice voted with the liberals for strategic reasons: Why bother to alienate them by dissenting in a case with no long-term consequences? Court-watchers call this a "suppressed dissent"—when a justice disagrees with the outcome but doesn't care enough to register that disagreement. Suppressed dissents used to be common, but most scholars today think they are rare. A less cynical view is that the chief justice actually agreed with the decisions.

The door to death penalty abolition via the Supreme Court seems closed, although the waning enthusiasm for imposing the death penalty suggests that the Court's categorical exclusions may stick. It may require a more severe mental disability in order to disqualify a person from eligibility for the death penalty, but finding legislatures, prosecutors, and state courts willing to revisit the other categorical exclusions is likely to be difficult.

The Court will likely continue to hear individual-injustice cases and suspend executions. The states usually get a do-over in these cases, but as time passes, enthusiasm for retrying the defendants usually wanes. One case at a time, the Court might continue to erode the death penalty.

Property Rights

Rehnquist Court decisions about the Constitution and private property led some observers to see an imminent property rights revolution. The Court seemed ready to use the Constitution's Takings Clause as a weapon against the modern regulatory state. Then it stopped.

The Takings Clause says that governments can take private property, but only for a public use and after paying the owner "just compensation." The "public use" requirement has been toothless for generations. Historically, the classic example of something that wasn't a public use involved a "naked" property transfer: Anne owned a piece of property, then the government took the property and gave it to Betty. Urban renewal programs in the 1950s put pressure on the public-use requirement, and economic development programs later pushed it to the breaking point.

In 2005 the Court upheld something no more than an inch or two away from a naked property transfer. The city of New London, Connecticut, wanted to lure the Pfizer pharmaceutical company's headquarters to promote investment in the city. Part of its plan involved assembling land to give Pfizer by offering to buy parcels from homeowners and forcing reluctant homeowners to accept the offers. A sharply divided Supreme Court held that the city's economic development plan was a public use. The opinion generated a backlash in the states, with voters and legislatures approving limits on taking property for economic development. The most important result was that city planners became more careful in designing economic development programs, making them less vulnerable to both public and legal disapproval.[4]

The property rights revolution focused on the heart of Takings Clause doctrine: What *is* a taking? Clearly, forcing a property owner to turn over some property—no matter how small—is a taking: New York had to offer compensation when it required apartment owners to install equipment to let tenants receive cable television programming.[5]

What city planners call "exactions" present a different takings problem. This is the scenario: You want to build an addition to your house or expand your store's showroom. You need a building permit to do so. The city says, "You can get the permit but only if you do something for us"—build a bike trail nearby, or allow people to walk through your property to get to the beach. The Court said these exactions were permissible only if they had some reasonably close relation to the action for which the permit was needed: You could be required to build bike stands near the expanded showroom, or expand your parking lot, but you couldn't be required to build an entire bike path in a park across town. In these cases the Court invoked the Constitution to promote "best practices" principles of urban planning.[6]

The biggest piece of the property rights revolution dealt with what were known as regulatory takings. The idea here is simple. Generations of lawyers have learned that property is a "bundle of sticks" — that is, not a single thing but a bunch of things that you are allowed to do with your property. Regulation keeps you from using one of those sticks as you want to: You want to build a modernist addition to your house, but the city says no because you live in a district covered by a historic preservation ordinance. Or you don't mind the risk of carbon monoxide poisoning in your house, but the city says you have to install a carbon monoxide detector.

Regulations limit what you can do with your property. The modern state would look very different, though, if every regulation were considered a taking of one of the sticks in the bundle, for which the government had to pay. Long-standing doctrine limited the doctrine. Regulation is a taking if it "goes too far" — yes, that's the doctrinal rule, not an informal paraphrase of it.

That doctrine proved completely unworkable. The "bundle of sticks" metaphor explains why. How many sticks are in the bundle? The answer determines whether a regulation goes too far. This came to be known as the "denominator" problem. If there are only a few sticks in the bundle — say, five — a regulation that takes away two might go too far. If there are five hundred sticks in the bundle, taking away two certainly doesn't go too far. Unfortunately for the doctrine, the Court discovered that it couldn't count up the number of sticks in any analytically defensible way. A city says that because your house is in a historic preservation district the addition you want to build has to look as if it's been there for decades. There would be no taking if the stick is your house, and maybe a taking if the stick is the addition. Similar problems of drawing arbitrary lines arose even when the Court wasn't employing the "bundle of sticks" metaphor.

The property rights revolution "stalled" or was "thwarted." It was one thing to find unconstitutional the relatively rare occasions on which governments actually converted physical property to its own use without paying for it. It was another to say that the government didn't have a public purpose for what it did, and still another to say that government regulations "went too far." Constructing a "regulatory takings" doctrine that didn't disturb well-settled forms of regulation was incredibly difficult.[7]

Yet in a new era, that might be the point of reviving regulatory takings doctrine. The first steps might involve blue-state regulations that, from the perspective of the new constitutional regime, go too far. Here the Court would be playing its standard role, bringing dissenters from the new regime into line. The next steps, however, might involve revisiting well-settled regulations to see whether they comport with the new understanding of regulatory takings.

Hints of such a revival are already available in mutterings about how restrictions on the reach of intellectual property, such as patents and trademarks, might amount to takings of IP rights. The doctrinal difficulties here are substantial, but a post-Trump Court might consider them worth confronting.

Federalism Again

Just as observers thought the Rehnquist Court was engaged in a property rights revolution, so they thought it might be engaging in a federalism revolution. Between 1937 and 1995, the Supreme Court basically gave up on trying to enforce the doctrine that the Constitution gave Congress a limited set of powers, leaving everything else to the states. But in 1995, it struck down a statute prohibiting possession of guns near schools, holding that this fell outside Congress's power to regulate commerce among the states.

This revived doctrine killed a few other statutes, the most important of which was a provision in the Violence Against Women Act that allowed victims of sexual assaults to sue their assailants in federal as well as state court. The Court also invoked the Eleventh Amendment, which prohibits people from suing state governments in federal court, to limit the remedies available under major civil rights statutes.[8]

Then the federalism revolution petered out. In a major setback to that revolution, the Court upheld a federal statute making it a crime to grow marijuana for personal consumption even in states where doing so was legal.[9]

Even the Court's Obamacare decision didn't obviously herald the revolution's revival. A majority found that Congress exceeded its power to regulate commerce when it required people to buy health insurance. One reason, though, was that the requirement was so unusual, and the majority's explanation of why the mandate was unconstitutional made it clear that the doctrine in itself would not cast doubt on any other existing statute. The holding was further defanged by Chief Justice Roberts's conclusion that the mandate *was* constitutional under Congress's power to impose taxes.

A second part of the Obamacare decision might foreshadow a revived federalism revolution. A majority that included Justices Breyer and Kagan held that Congress couldn't force states to expand their Medicaid programs by threatening them with the loss of federal Medicaid funding if they didn't. That, the Court held, unconstitutionally coerced the states.

Many other statutes threaten states with losing federal funds if they don't do what the national government wants. For example,

Congress sends money to states with strings attached for transportation and education programs. Colleges get federal money but only if they comply with federal regulations about dealing with allegations of sexual harassment. A revived federalism revolution might take on these conditional spending programs. A flurry of scholarly commentary immediately after the Obamacare decision looked at its implications for civil rights. Most authors concluded that the Court's "coercion" doctrine didn't threaten these programs.[10]

That was then—a Roberts Court with Justice Kennedy on it. Today there is a real possibility of renewed attention to conditional spending programs. The possibility is enhanced by coercion's interaction with "political correctness" and some well-founded concerns that some procedures for addressing sexual harassment charges are badly designed. Yet, once again illustrating how the Court might play a smaller role after a constitutional transformation, these regulations were put on hold while the Department of Education considered and then adopted regulations giving colleges more leeway.

If a new conservative constitutional regime takes hold, the Court might not get a chance to revive the federalism revolution. The statutes at risk are hangovers from the New Deal/Great Society regime. In a new conservative order, Congress isn't likely to enact new ones. More important, the statutes "coerce" only when the administration is willing to withhold funds from states that don't comply with what the states regard as unreasonable demands. A conservative administration isn't likely to make such demands. Anyway, it's difficult to come up with a version of Trumpist conservatism that has a deep commitment to federalism.

New Initiatives?

The Supreme Court was able to start down the three paths I've described because lawyers and legal scholars, supported by interest groups and social movements, had prepared the way. Offering legal analyses that were speculative, even "off the wall" when published, these lawyers made arguments available for the Court to adopt and tweak when the justices wanted to.

Maybe we'll see a revival of the property rights and federalism revolutions. But maybe the Court will strike out on an entirely new path—one that fits into the new conservative vision of the Constitution, perhaps in ways we can't see yet.

Somewhere in the files of a conservative think tank or public interest law firm there are dozens of memos offering creative approaches to some now-obscure doctrine that would dramatically push forward a conservative agenda. Buried now because their adoption seems completely unrealistic, one or two of these memos might be dug up when the occasion presents itself. But which "wacky" proposal will one day seem serious is completely unknowable to us.

11

The Weaponized First Amendment

Concerned that excessive consumption of sugary sodas harmed the public health, San Francisco's city council overcame heavy lobbying from the beverage industry and adopted an ordinance requiring that most advertisements for "sugar-sweetened beverages" include a warning: "Drinking beverages with added sugar(s) contributes to obesity, diabetes, and tooth decay. This is a message from the City and County of San Francisco." The warning had to occupy at least 20 percent of the advertisement.

The Court of Appeals for the Ninth Circuit—notorious among conservatives as overly liberal—held the ordinance unconstitutional. The problem was that the city hadn't shown that a warning that large was necessary. The court noted that some rules requiring drug and tobacco warnings did use the 20 percent figure, and the city presented a study showing that a warning covering 10 percent of an advertisement was "associated [with] an improved understanding of health harms associated with overconsumption of SSBs and may reduce the purchase of SSBs." But if 10 percent could get the job done, 20 percent was too much.[1]

Several judges would have gone further. They relied on Supreme Court cases saying that merchants can be required to make disclosures and post warnings containing "purely factual and uncontroversial information." But San Francisco's warning was, for these judges, neither purely factual nor uncontroversial. Sugar might cause Type II (adult-onset) diabetes, but it doesn't cause Type I (juvenile) diabetes, so the warning was inaccurate. And the FDA says that sugars "can be part of a healthy dietary pattern" if you don't consume too much. Even more, the statement was controversial—primarily because the beverage industry has engaged in a public relations campaign to cast doubt on physicians' claims about excessive sugar consumption.

This decision is founded on the First Amendment's protection of free expression. Say "First Amendment" and most people think about government trying to prevent political protests, campus speech controversies, and things like that—not commercials or health and safety warnings. But commercials and warnings use words, bringing the First Amendment into play.

The San Francisco case is an example of what Justice Kagan called the "weaponization" of the First Amendment. The First Amendment has become a tool for courts to micromanage—and thus discourage—ordinary economic regulation: 20 percent is too much, but maybe 10 percent is okay; the city should have said "Type II diabetes" instead of "diabetes." Another example is the union fees case we saw in chapter 3. The First Amendment is weaponized when what otherwise would seem to be ordinary regulation of economic relations—health regulations here, labor-management relations there—are said to be constitutionally problematic because of free speech concerns.

Weaponization is especially interesting because of developments in the way the government regulates the economy. Under the New Deal/Great Society regime, economic regulation was "command and control": The government might set the prices for soda, for example, or ban sodas with "too much" sugar. Command-and-control regulations came under attack, often justified, as being too rigid and as preventing people from figuring out better ways to achieve the government's goals, such as peaceful labor-management relations.

We now say that we live in an information society, in which

command-and-control regulation has been supplanted by regulation of information. There's no doubt that San Francisco could ban the sale of sugary sodas entirely—a classic command-and-control regulation. Saying to restaurants, "You can sell whatever sodas you want, but you have to tell your customers about some of the health risks they're taking" is an information-based regulation.

That regulation is arguably better for customers than a flat ban. They can vary in their personal evaluations of the risk of obesity and in how much they really like sugary sodas, and they can make their own decisions rather than having the city block their choice of soda.

The word "arguably" here does a tremendous amount of work. We have two competing economic accounts of which regulation is better for consumers. The New Deal/Great Society constitutional order told courts that when economists disagreed, legislatures, not courts, got to choose which side should prevail. Weaponizing the First Amendment lets courts override the legislature.

What Is Weaponization, and Who Benefits?

The weaponized First Amendment isn't completely new. A 1940 decision interpreting the National Labor Relations Act relied on the First Amendment to allow the Ford Motor Company to use tactics against labor organizing that the National Labor Relations Board had tried to ban. First Amendment concerns continued to restrict the NLRB's efforts to impose limits on union and management tactics in organizing campaigns.[2]

Modern versions of First Amendment weaponization occur in similar commercial contexts. They involve powerful economic actors, and apply a test that makes it more difficult for governments to defend their information-based regulations. Here's a short list of some information-based economic regulations that have come under First

Amendment attack.[3] Not all of these challenges succeeded, but the vulnerability of information-based regulations to these attacks means that governments may shy away from developing them.

- Vermont prohibited the sale of information, for commercial purposes, about which physicians prescribed which medications. The ban was a response to pharmaceutical companies' practice of using that information to target doctors in order to increase their willingness to prescribe specific medications. The Supreme Court held the statute unconstitutional.
- Congress required sellers of food products such as meat and nuts to label the products with their nation of origin. The lower courts have upheld the statute.
- Some states require food sellers to label foods that include genetically modified organisms (GMOs); other states prohibit sellers from labeling their products "GMO free." Both types of regulation have been challenged. Congress responded with a statute that told the Department of Agriculture to develop a national rule that would preempt state laws.
- Vermont required that ice cream made from milk from cows injected with bovine growth hormone (BGH) carry the label "made with BGH." Because the state couldn't show that BGH-milk was a greater risk to human health than non-BGH-milk (or even that it was possible to tell whether a milk product included milk from BGH-treated cows), the only justification for the regulation was "satisfaction of consumer curiosity." A lower court held the labeling requirement unconstitutional.
- Ohio *prohibited* sellers of milk products from labeling their products "BGH-free." If you're a consumer who worries about the health effects of BGH on humans (probably a mistake) or on cows

(probably real but small), what do you infer when you see one ice-cream carton with "BGH-free" on it, and the other with no label? A lower court held Ohio's prohibition unconstitutional. Sellers can decide on their own whether to label their milk "BGH-free."

- The National Labor Relations Board required that employers post a list of workers' legal rights. Two lower courts held the requirement invalid, relying on the employers' First Amendment rights as a reason to find that the National Labor Relations Act didn't authorize the board to impose the requirement.

Some of these regulations may be good policy, some bad. What's striking is how routine they are. They hardly seem to require rolling out the big guns of the First Amendment. The great cases we celebrate in our free speech tradition involve people prosecuted for criticizing the government—protesting U.S. involvement in the Vietnam War or organizing radical political parties. What do the rights of political dissidents and religious minorities like the Jehovah's Witnesses have to do with whether the nation's meat sellers should have to indicate their products' nation of origin?

The meat sellers are, in one sense, a minority. They were outvoted in Congress. That can't be the basis for giving them special concern, though, because every statute produces similar minorities. Republicans were a minority when Obamacare was enacted, but that doesn't give them any First Amendment argument against the statute—and although they've tried almost everything else, they haven't tried to say that Obamacare violates anyone's free speech rights (freedom of religion is another matter).

The weaponized First Amendment is used against routine information-based regulations, and on behalf of ordinary interest groups—sometimes large and well-organized ones—that happened to lose what appear to be fair fights in the legislature. How did we get to this point?

Why Weaponization?

Why use the First Amendment in this way? The easy and not entirely inaccurate answer is that weaponization gives businesses another tool against government regulation—and in an information economy, a particularly valuable tool.

But there's more to it than that. The best argument for weaponization is something like this: We really do want the First Amendment to protect political dissidents and the like. As David Cole of the ACLU puts it, "The targets of censorship are typically dissidents, outsiders, the marginalized," and they need a robust First Amendment to protect them. We have to figure out a way to ensure that, even under pressure, these dissidents' rights will be protected.[4]

Building our defenses against this pressure requires two related strategies. First, make sure that at least some people claiming First Amendment protection evoke judges' sympathy. That may help judges develop a mind-set open to taking *all* First Amendment claims seriously.

Second and more important, make sure that First Amendment doctrine is reasonably simple—hard-edged, some people say, or categorical. A categorical doctrine tells judges to focus on only one or two features of a case, and to disregard many of the features that might give pause to a person who took everything into account.

An overly simple example: The First Amendment, we might say, tells us to be extremely suspicious of government rules that punish people for the content of their speech. Again in Cole's words, "the amendment's core requirement is that the government must remain neutral regarding the content and viewpoint of speech." We look at a regulation and ask, "Does it impose penalties on people because of what they say?" It won't matter whether they are Nazis or Communists, labor organizers or management officials, proponents of organic farming or factory-farm corporations. If the regulation says, "You can't say this," or "You have to say this," we're going to worry, regardless of what "this" is. The rule washes away a judge's hostility to Nazi or Communist ideas. It also lets big corporations challenge content-based regulations, because the only thing that's relevant is whether the regulation is based on the content of what the speaker—dissident or corporation—says.

A hard-edged rule or a simple category is only the first step. We have to know what it means for a judge to be suspicious of a content-based rule. The formal doctrine for the weaponized First Amendment in our information-based cases is "intermediate" scrutiny. As with all doctrine, formal legal statements are less informative than simpler summaries, so: Intermediate scrutiny means that the government has to have pretty good reasons for its regulation, and the regulation has to do a pretty good job of satisfying those reasons.

What makes a pretty good reason? According to the lower court in the BGH case, protecting human health is a pretty good reason, but satisfying consumer curiosity isn't. In the pharmaceutical data-mining case, protecting patient privacy is a pretty good reason, but the Vermont statute didn't do a good enough job in protecting it.

What does it mean to do a pretty good job? Again according to the lower court in one of the BGH cases, requiring BGH-labeling didn't do a good job of protecting human health because there's no evidence that BGH milk is any more harmful to humans than non-BGH milk. For the Supreme Court, the ban on data-mining didn't do a good enough job of protecting privacy because the lists didn't include patient information, so selling the lists posed little risk to patient privacy.

The argument for weaponization, then, is that a hard-edged or categorical doctrine is needed to ensure that political dissidents and the like—the First Amendment's true beneficiaries—are protected. Protection of commercial speech is a side effect, worth accepting because of the hard-edged rule's benefits to political dissidents.

That's a pretty good argument for weaponization. Is it good enough?

Problems with Weaponization as Doctrine

It's not really good enough—because the Court hasn't been able to keep the rule system simple enough. Faced with problems that are difficult to fit into a simple system, the justices invent new categories or draw arbitrary lines.

We've already seen the first move. Formally the Court distinguishes between political and commercial speech, which is already a content-based distinction. The test for regulation of political speech is the "really good reasons and fit" one ("strict scrutiny," in the Court's terminology), while the test for commercial speech is "pretty good reasons and fit" ("intermediate scrutiny"). You'd be right to think that the Court's decisions about whether the reasons for regulating some political statement are good enough, or whether the reasons for regulating some commercial statement are good enough by the lower standard, can be influenced by the justices' approval or disapproval of the statements themselves.

The next move occurs within the category of commercial speech. The idea that some reason is good or not good is shot through with judgments that hard-edged rules are supposed to keep out of view. Some courts say that satisfying consumer curiosity about BGH in milk products isn't a good reason for a mandatory disclosure of uncontroversial factual information (there's no controversy about *whether* a particular food product is made with milk from BGH-treated cows in it, only controversy about whether such products are harmful)*—but then, what other reason is there for the "nation of origin" regulation? (It can't be that buyers will reasonably worry that meat slaughtered in Mexico is more likely to cause illness, because *that* concern is addressed directly by health and safety regulations applicable to all food products.)†

Even when the Supreme Court purports to operate within its hard-edged rules, the particulars of a case can lead it to introduce arbitrary distinctions. Here are three examples.

• *Animal crush videos.* Some people get sexual gratification from viewing small animals crushed by women's high-heeled shoes. Congress made it illegal to make or distribute portrayals of animals being maimed or tortured if doing so violated local animal cruelty laws. Long-standing precedent holds that governments can ban obscene materials if they have even a modest reason for doing so—such as the highly contested belief that viewing obscene works leads people to behave badly. The government defended the statute by analogizing animal crush videos to obscenity because they don't satisfy the definition the Court requires to find something obscene.[5]

Chief Justice Roberts, writing for the Court, rejected the analogy. Obscenity was one of a handful of types of speech that have a long pedigree of exclusion from the First Amendment. The Court refused to recognize any new excluded categories, particularly on the basis of

---

* The regulation will satisfy consumers' curiosity if most farmers are honest in saying that they do or don't treat their cows with BGH even if no one can tell whether a milk product comes from a BGH-treated cow.

† Maybe the regulations of food safety that apply to all products are too lax, but that doesn't mean products from Mexico that satisfy those regulations are more risky than products from Texas.

"startling and dangerous" arguments that material in the categories had little or no social value.

All well and good, except for one thing. The Court has upheld statutes banning child pornography, which, as the Court made clear, included material that wasn't obscene in the historical sense.[6] Child pornography was a "special case" because the ban helped dry up the market for material whose very creation involved child abuse, illegal everywhere. We might think that banning depictions of animal cruelty might also dry up the market for material whose creation involved animal cruelty, as defined by the law of the state in which it occurred.

One additional feature of the case requires mention. The government prosecuted somebody not for making an animal crush video but for distributing extremely graphic films of pit bulls fighting and, in one instance, attacking a pig. The chief justice wrote that the prosecution itself showed that we couldn't trust prosecutors to exercise good judgment about what cases to bring. Apparently, placing these films in a category with the crush videos was something like an abuse of prosecutorial discretion.

It's difficult to see anything operating here other than the justices' judgment that cruelty to animals, though bad, is not nearly as bad as cruelty to children. We might agree, but we might worry about the justices' writing into constitutional law their disagreement with Congress about the relative seriousness of child and animal abuse.

• *Disparaging trademarks.* Federal law allows people to submit trademarks for registration. A bunch of legal rights flow from registration, and those rights are worth something—literally, because registration lets you use the trademark to sell your products while forbidding others to use similar marks. The Slants are a rock band whose members, all Asian American, adopted the name to appropriate a term that historically had been used to disparage people of Asian origin—much as sexual and gender minorities have appropriated the word *queer*. When they tried to register the name so that they could sell swag at their concerts, they ran up against a provision of the trademark law that said "disparaging" trademarks couldn't be registered.[7]

The Court held that provision unconstitutional because it prevented registration of trademarks based on their content. In one line of defense, the government acknowledged that the regulation was indeed content-based, but observed that the Court had allowed the government to make content-based distinctions when it gave private parties benefits that it didn't have to. The government can set up a program to fund "Just Say No" programs to prevent drug abuse without also having to fund "Just Say Yes" programs.

So why can't the government say, "We'll give you the valuable right to a trademark, but only if your trademark isn't disparaging"? Maybe money is different from legal rights. Unfortunately for that line of argument, there are other cases, in which labor unions got what Justice Alito described as a valuable "non-cash benefit for the purpose of furthering activities that [the legislature] particularly desired to promote," but where the legislature did not "provide a similar benefit for the purpose of furthering other activities." Non-disparagement and disparagement seem to fit that description like a glove.

Justice Alito's response? Cases involving "cash subsidies or their equivalent" are "not instructive," because . . . Well, it's hard to tell why. Maybe because giving cash to private entities is different from giving them legal rights to services like police protection. It's not easy to see, though, why a legal right to exclude competitors from using a trademark is different from a legal entitlement to police protection.

Justice Alito is no slouch at legal analysis, but his analysis here is feeble. Again, the most natural explanations blend the facts and policy views. It's one thing to worry about denying a trademark to the Slants, and another to think about whether we really want to give valuable rights (that we don't have to give to anyone) to people whose trademarks incorporate the N-word or the K-word. On the policy level, it seems that Justice Alito and his colleagues don't think it's a big deal to allow trademarks for disparaging words—even though Congress apparently had a different view.

• *Material assistance to terrorism.* A final example is slightly different doctrinally, but it illustrates the point that you really can't control the courts by stating hard-edged rules. The Roberts Court upheld a statute that was interpreted to prohibit U.S. nongovernmental organizations from advising foreign groups on the national terrorism list about techniques for resolving conflicts without violence, including advising them of their rights under international law. By giving such advice, Chief Justice Roberts wrote, the NGOs were giving the terrorist groups "material assistance."[8]

Certain lines within the decision showed, by the arbitrary distinctions they made, that everyone understood the case to involve speech at the core of the tradition of protecting political dissent. The Court carefully refrained from saying that Congress could ban giving advice to domestic terrorist groups—doing so would almost literally put these groups outside the law because they couldn't get advice about their legal rights. And it limited the holding to advice that was "coordinated" with terrorist groups, which apparently would allow the NGOs to publish pamphlets about non-violent ways of solving conflicts and hope that they would fall into the right hands. The threat of terrorism was enough to overcome the barriers the hard-edged rules were supposed to erect.

It's important to understand the point of these examples. It's not that the Court got things right or wrong in any one of them. Rather, it's that when you look at the details of the Court's arguments, you find arbitrary distinctions being made on precisely the kinds of policy grounds that hard-edged rules are supposed to screen out of consideration.

Lawyers—here, specifically, government lawyers—are trained to spot a decision's weak points and use legal reasoning techniques to show how an apparently arbitrary exception is grounded in a deeper principle that—aha!—supports the constitutionality of the regulation they're defending. The effect is that the hard-edged categorical approach can't really keep governments from trying to punish people for their political or religious views: The government has to exploit the complex doctrinal structure, find weaknesses and loopholes within that structure, and then get five justices to go along.

What's the Alternative?

There's a plausible case for weaponization. Having hard-edged, categorical rules allows us to be confident that the First Amendment will protect political and religious dissidents.

Plausible, yes, but not realistic, given everything judges can do to soften the edges or create new categories when they feel the need. So what's the alternative? In the animal cruelty case, Chief Justice Roberts said that the Court couldn't assume "freewheeling authority to declare new categories of speech outside the scope of the First Amendment." What about a more structured authority?

The earliest weaponization cases did involve a relatively unstructured balancing test, and maybe balancing is too freewheeling. Justice Breyer has advocated adopting an approach—proportionality analysis—that constitutional courts around the world have found helpful. Put simply, proportionality analysis asks whether the challenged regulation is a proportionate response to the problem the government is trying to deal with. A key component is to ask whether there would

be some other way for the government to come close to the same result with less impairment to free speech. That component might get
the Court over its nervousness about the cases of animal cruelty and
the Slants.

But maybe proportionality analysis is also too freewheeling. Another possibility is to come up with a handful of additional categories.
The weaponization cases involve what the Court calls commercial
speech. Maybe we could sensibly divide up that category.

When the Court started down the road of using the First Amendment to limit regulation of commercial speech, it defined the category
narrowly. Regulation of speech that did no more than propose a commercial transaction had to be supported by pretty good reasons. The
Court has held that the First Amendment doesn't bar a government
from requiring disclosures of uncontroversial factual information that
helps consumers or patients or lawyers' clients make better informed
choices. But, as the San Francisco case shows, what counts as factual
or uncontroversial is sometimes itself controversial, particularly when
powerful interest groups want to create controversy.[9]

Weaponizing the First Amendment does address a real problem
associated with free expression — the temptation to succumb to immediate concerns and pressures when faced with political dissent. But
we probably could come up with a better way to address that threat.

That large corporations benefit from weaponization is a side
effect, perhaps a necessary one, of the best argument for weaponization.[10] Because there probably is a better way to protect political dissent than weaponization, we should use a political lens to see that the
benefits to corporations are a feature, not a bug, of the current phase
of weaponization.

To date the most important weaponization cases blocked the
government from implementing a congressional requirement that tobacco products have prominent and quite graphic disclosures about

the health dangers of smoking—warnings that are common in Europe and Australia. The government decided not to appeal those decisions to the Supreme Court because it was afraid that the Court would endorse weaponization. The union fees case described in chapter 3 is the most prominent Supreme Court case illustrating weaponization. But weaponizing makes the First Amendment an extremely useful tool for the powerful, who can piggyback on the cultural resonances that associate the First Amendment with the weak and powerless. A conservative Supreme Court will almost certainly continue to weaponize the First Amendment.

PART THREE
Progressive Alternatives— The Short Run

New policies, goes the adage, make new politics. A political party's actions while in office can of course satisfy the groups that pushed it into power, but they can also attract new supporters. And even before getting enough power actually to enact statutes, parties can develop an agenda that might help them get over the finish line. For Democrats, that means gaining control of the Senate and the presidency.

We can't know today what political agenda will emerge as parties and candidates assess their prospects, including the party's hopes for capturing the presidency and for some candidates their hopes of becoming president. Voters might reject the path of consolidated conservative rule without definitively choosing a different path. The interregnum between the end of the Reagan revolution and the emergence of its successor might be extended for another few years.

If so, we can expect to see aggressive assertions of untrammeled presidential power, intermittently but unsystematically constrained by whichever party isn't in the White House, and equally unsystematically endorsed by the Supreme Court when the president is a Republican and rejected by it when the president is a Democrat.

But suppose voters choose an alternative path to the one offered by conservatives. What new policies might they pursue to create and consolidate a new politics? Equally important for purposes of this book, what obstacles might they face from a Supreme Court controlled by conservatives in the first years of the new legislative majority?

12

Winning Elections, Enacting Statutes

The day after Democrats won back the House of Representatives in 2018, Ronald Klain, who had been chief of staff for Vice Presidents Al Gore and Joe Biden, set out "the first five things the Democrats should do." A week later, liberal columnist E. J. Dionne wrote about "what House Democrats need to do." The lists overlapped: on Klain's list were "reverse Republican voter-suppression efforts" and expand Obamacare's coverage; on Dionne's, "expanding health coverage, reforming our democracy,... curbing gun violence."[1]

We'll return to some of these proposals soon enough, but there's more that proponents of a progressive path can do. They can enact real laws—not federal laws, of course, because the Senate and the president won't go along—but state laws and city ordinances. States and cities can be, as Justice Louis Brandeis once put it, "laboratories of social experimentation." Local and statewide increases in the minimum wage, novel local supplements to a frayed national social safety net, a local version of Medicare for all, public pre-K education for all, provisions for paid maternity and paternity leave—and already on the agenda, "sanctuary cities" whose officials are directed not to cooperate with federal officials enforcing national immigration laws.

This book isn't what the next agenda for the Democratic Party should be, so I won't lay out details of any of these proposals. Instead, this chapter examines some underexplored avenues for advancing a new constitutional regime, some techniques liberals might use to defend their programs in court, and some obstacles the courts might place in their way.

State Courts

At the beginning of 2018, Republicans held thirteen of Pennsylvania's eighteen congressional seats. Relying on the state's constitution, the state supreme court found that the districting map, drawn by a Republican-controlled legislature, was an unconstitutional gerrymander. After the legislature failed to come up with an acceptable new map, the Pennsylvania Supreme Court drew one itself. The result: in November 2018, Democrats won ten seats, Republicans eight.

The press understandably devotes great attention to presidential nominations to the U.S. Supreme Court. That obscures the fact that most judges on state supreme courts are elected.* Judicial elections used to be sleepy, with lawyers and their families basically the only ones paying attention. That has changed. Large businesses and trial lawyers, concerned about the power of state courts to shape rules dealing with business's liability to consumers and workers, began to make campaigns for judicial office look a lot like campaigns for legislative office. "Down ballot" judicial races have become increasingly competitive.

What can state courts do? As the Pennsylvania gerrymandering decision shows, they can rely on their state's constitution to reach results the U.S. Supreme Court wouldn't. Sometimes that's because state constitutions are different from the U.S. Constitution. Chal-

---

* Governors usually have the power to fill vacancies when a justice dies or retires between elections, and typically the appointed judge has to run for a full term—though incumbents have a rather strong advantage in those elections.

lenges to the way public schools are financed are the best example. The U.S. Supreme Court rejected a challenge to inequalities in public school funding, framed as a violation of the national Constitution's guarantee of "equal protection of the laws." But many state constitutions specifically address public education, and some say it has to be "thorough and efficient" or "general and uniform." Some state supreme courts have used these provisions to require changes in public school financing.[2]

Even when state constitutions echo the words of the U.S. Constitution, state supreme courts are generally free to interpret them differently from the U.S. Supreme Court.* Decisions by the Alaska Supreme Court about searches are a nice example. Both the U.S. and Alaska Constitutions prohibit unreasonable searches. The Alaska Supreme Court has regularly found searches unreasonable in cases whose facts were identical to cases in which the U.S. Supreme Court had found the searches reasonable. The state court's rationale is that the people of Alaska simply care more about personal privacy than those in the rest of the country.[3] And nothing in the U.S. Constitution prevents them from putting that preference into their own law.†

---

* Some state constitutions explicitly bar their supreme courts from doing this, and some state supreme courts have adopted a rule that they will always interpret a state constitution to mean exactly what the U.S. Supreme Court says the same words mean when used in the U.S. Constitution.

† It's possible in theory for state courts to go "too far" in protecting constitutional rights. The U.S. Constitution generally puts a floor under our rights—states can't fall below the floor—but rarely puts a ceiling over them. It's quite difficult though not impossible to come up with plausible hypothetical cases where a state court might protect constitutional rights too much.

Using Conservative Constitutional Doctrine

For the past fifty years (and more), conservatives mounted constitutional challenges to liberal programs, and there's every reason to believe that they'll continue to do so. Now they'll have a conservative Supreme Court to hear them. That will pose strategic questions for liberals. Legal scholar Michael Dorf has urged progressives to use constitutional jiu-jitsu—conservative arguments to support liberal programs.[4]

• *Originalism.* The most obvious move in constitutional jiu-jitsu is to deploy originalist arguments for liberal outcomes. Unfortunately, such attempts have routinely—though not uniformly—failed. The Court offered one response in the public employee union fees case: it dismissed the arguments because the majority didn't think the advocates were sincere in offering the originalist evidence. As I observed in discussing that case, this response is irrelevant given originalism's premises. But precisely because originalism is a shibboleth for determining whether an argument is conservative, it's not a promising method for defending liberal policies.

The conservative position on affirmative action illustrates another response: ignoring originalist evidence rather than dismissing it. Or treating the evidence as relying on the now discarded method of "original expected applications originalism." Presented with evidence about what policies the Fourteenth Amendment's framers actually thought were consistent with what they had just enacted, conservative originalists say, "But that doesn't tell us enough about the original public meaning."

A third response is to apply the thinking that helps originalists resolve the "65–35" problem. This problem occurs when historical evidence shows that the original public understanding of a constitutional term was a matter of significant division and even controversy. The solution within originalism has been to say that the term's meaning was to be resolved by constitutional construction. In practice, that means relying on judicial doctrine in exactly the same way that living constitutionalists do—which licenses conservative interpretations of the relevant precedents.

And finally, there's precedent, the faint-hearted originalist's back-stop. As we saw in chapter 2, there's now significant evidence based on "corpus linguistics" that the Second Amendment was originally understood to protect weapons only in connection with organized state militias. Suppose the Court decides to review a state law restricting an individual right to keep and bear arms—a ban on concealed carry, a ban on open carry, strict licensing requirements, or a ban on the possession of semi-automatic weapons. Defenders of the restriction present the new originalist evidence. The Court might well respond, "Too bad. We already decided that the Second Amendment protects an individual right, and our task now is to work out the implications of our formulations. We're now concerned only with whether a regulation fits within the category 'traditional and long-standing limitations,' or deals with 'weapons in common use,' and other phrases we set out in *Heller*."

• *Federalism and anti-commandeering.* Another jiu-jitsu move occurs in cases involving blue-state legislation such as sanctuary city rules. The anti-commandeering doctrine (chapter 2) means that the national government can't force cities and states to use their own personnel to carry out national policy. On the face of things, the doctrine kicks in when a city says that its police officers won't help enforce federal immigration laws: If they arrest someone for a traffic violation and find out that the driver does not have permission to be in the country, they won't notify federal immigration officials; if they somehow find out that someone they've arrested is subject to an existing order requiring her removal from the country, they won't hold the person until federal immigration officials show up to take custody.

That's a decent argument, and so far it has prevailed. But there's a hitch. The Court has applied the anti-commandeering doctrine only when the national government has actually issued a command: Do gun background checks, make sports gambling illegal. What if the national government says, "Do what you want with your police officers, but if you want to get money from us, they're going to have to cooperate with our immigration enforcers." There's a decent argument that the anti-commandeering doctrine should apply here as well, so liberal litigators should of course try to use it. That an argument is decent, however, doesn't mean that it will prevail before a conservative Supreme Court.

Overall, conservative arguments may be deployed to defend liberal policies, and liberal lawyers trying to win their cases will use them. But we can question whether constitutional jiu-jitsu will work in cases conservatives care about.

Obstacles to Federal Policy Innovation: Congress

What about progressives' national policy priorities? Some seem invulnerable to constitutional challenge—now. That may change if a conservative Supreme Court starts to worry that new policies may create a new progressive constitutional regime.

Even if Democrats have majorities in the House and Senate, they are unlikely to have the sixty votes in the Senate needed to overcome a filibuster. They will have to change the rules if they are to enact the new policies they need to make a new politics. Changing the rules used to be called the "nuclear option," the suggestion being that changing the rules would raze the Senate to the ground. We now know that eliminating the filibuster for nominations didn't have that effect. If we wanted to pursue the metaphor, eliminating the filibuster for nominations was more like a tactical nuclear weapon than a "bunker buster" bomb.

Democratic senators will have to decide whether to preserve the filibuster in its current form and advance Democratic priorities through legislative vehicles that can't be filibustered, eliminate the filibuster for a list of high-priority items, or eliminate it altogether. Those are decisions about political tactics, on which I have no special insights. From a constitutional point of view, this is entirely a matter for the Senate majority to determine.

Now to the substance of policy. Take the "easiest" case: Congress enacts a law raising the national minimum wage to $15.00 an hour. We've had a national minimum wage statute for decades, and few today would take seriously an argument that it is unconstitutional, much less expect that the Supreme Court would support that view.

But conservatives have long railed against New Deal decisions holding that Congress's power to regulate interstate commerce gave it the power to regulate anything that affected interstate commerce. As we've seen, there's an originalist case for saying that the Commerce Power doesn't extend even to manufacturing, much less local retail sales. It's not beyond credibility to think that a conservative Court would buy these arguments, overrule precedents they say are discredited by originalist research and inconsistent with the proper scope of national power, and hold a national minimum wage unconstitutional.

I won't work through everything on the (still undecided) Democratic policy agenda, but a few additional examples will point the way.

Anticipating that the Supreme Court will overrule *Roe v. Wade,* some Democrats support adopting a national "right to choose" statute. If the Court says there's no constitutionally protected right to choose, Democrats can't rely on the Fourteenth Amendment's guarantee of individual rights against the states. So they've said that Congress has the power to protect the right to choose under the Commerce Clause—just as it protected the right of African Americans to get served at restaurants. How are abortions connected to interstate commerce? Doctors who perform them use implements that they got from out of state, and women who bear children often stay out of the workforce.

The connection between abortion and interstate commerce is strained. There are old cases, never formally repudiated, saying that Congress can't use its powers as a pretext for accomplishing goals that are otherwise beyond its power. The Court wouldn't have to overrule anything to find that Congress didn't have the power to enact a right-to-choose statute.

If Medicare for people over sixty-five is constitutional, how could Medicare for all be unconstitutional? Again, not today or next year, but later. Power companies challenged President Obama's Clean Power Plan in part because, they said, it was an unconstitutional regulatory taking. They had invested a lot of money in developing coal-based power, and the plan would send that money down the drain.[5] Health insurance companies could make a similar argument about Medicare for all.

There's more: some proposals for Medicare for all would require states to continue providing some services, such as long-term care. It's not difficult to cast this as commandeering the states.

And more: To make Medicare for all work, Congress might have to bar people from purchasing health insurance outside the nationalized system. Conservatives might easily characterize that as an unconstitutional limitation on people's right to use their money however they chose. Democrats would respond by saying that in *Lochner v. New York* the Court held a maximum hours law unconstitutional because it prevented people from working however long they chose. And conservatives might answer—with some justification and perhaps with the agreement of five justices—that *Lochner's* general principle of freedom of contract was correct even if, in that instance, it was misapplied on the facts.

Buried in Chief Justice Roberts's opinion in the Obamacare case is an analysis that suggests another line of attack. Roberts held that the ACA's expansion of Medicaid changed the program from one aimed at helping a vulnerable population of poor people into a general social welfare program. Medicare for all might be said to do the same—a program for vulnerable older people becomes a program for everyone. Why might that matter? Protecting vulnerable people from their own failings is a permissible form of paternalism, but extending this protection to everyone may take paternalism too far. If you want a citation to support anti-paternalism, *Obergefell v. Hodges*—a decision that placed much emphasis on dignity in authorizing same-sex marriage—will do: Acting paternalistically toward someone is inconsistent with recognizing her dignity.

I'm not saying that these are good arguments that the Supreme Court would accept today. With enough political will, though, conservatives could develop them—or other constitutional arguments against Medicare for all—publish policy papers and op-ed columns, and the arguments would become credible, then perhaps persuasive to the only audience that matters, five justices on the Supreme Court.

My final example involves Democratic proposals to prevent what they describe as voter suppression. Congress's power over elections depends on whether the elections are for state office—such as Georgia's gubernatorial election in 2018—or for national office, such as Florida's senatorial election that year. In elections for state offices, Congress's authority comes from the Fourteenth and Fifteenth Amendments. In elections for federal offices, it comes from the Elections Clause: "The Times, Places and Manner of holding Elections for Senators and Representatives, shall be prescribed in each State by the Legislature thereof, but the Congress may at any time by Law make or alter such Regulations."[6]

Let's take state elections first: Both the Fourteenth and Fifteenth Amendments give Congress the power to enforce their provisions "by appropriate legislation." The Fifteenth Amendment says that the right to vote can't be denied "on account of race." The Supreme Court has held that you don't have to intend to deny the right to vote because of race; all that's required is that a statute have the effect of denying the right to vote to significantly more members of one race than another. The Fourteenth Amendment, which deals with equality more generally, comes into play only if there is intentional selective deprivation of rights.

Suppose Congress set a mandatory national standard for state voter registration systems. Would that be "appropriate legislation" to address discrimination in voting? The Court considers legislation "appropriate" if it is "congruent and proportional" to the underlying constitutional violations. That criterion is so flexible that it could accommodate any holding: The problems associated with voter registration are substantial, and national standards are a congruent and proportional response to the problem's scope—or else, sure, there are problems, but national standards are a bomb used where a pea shooter would suffice.

We can deepen the problem. One proposal would require "automatic and portable registration through the [Department of Motor Vehicles] or other social service agencies." This looks a lot like Congress commandeering the states.

Now to elections for national offices: What falls into the categories of "time, place, and manner" that Congress can prescribe under the Elections Clause? Long-standing tradition and doctrine say that drawing district lines is part of the "manner" of conducting elections. Could Congress require states to set up nonpartisan districting commissions for congressional districts, or automatic voter registration through state DMVs? Yes under the Elections Clause but, again, maybe not because of the anti-commandeering principle.

That principle wouldn't block Congress from creating a national nonpartisan or bipartisan commission to draw congressional districts. The statute creating it would have to be pretty detailed about who is qualified to sit on the commission and the criteria it should use. Some of those provisions might themselves be unconstitutional. It's easy to see how defining what makes a person "nonpartisan" might raise First Amendment concerns, for example, and demanding that the commission be "bipartisan" might exclude political independents or supporters of minor parties. Although a national districting commission might be constitutional, the statute creating it would almost certainly be complicated, and complexity creates vulnerabilities.

What about a national voter ID law? There are a lot of proposals: requiring states to accept a wide range of photo-IDs, identification based upon utility bills and credit card bills, and many others. Would a national voter ID law deal with "time, place, and manner"? A natural translation of the phrase would be "when, where, and how." "Who" is not on the list. That is, the Elections Clause doesn't give Congress the power to determine who can vote—what's usually called voter qualifications. Most observers today describe a voter ID law as dealing with the manner of voting, a way of making sure that the person in front of the clerk is indeed the person on the voter rolls. It wouldn't be difficult to recast such a law as dealing with voter qualifications: You're not qualified to vote unless you have one of the approved forms of ID.

We could continue with the list of Democratic policies, and potential constitutional objections: statehood for the District of Columbia (what about the Twenty-Third Amendment, which gives "[t]he District constituting the seat of Government of the United

States" three votes in the electoral college?); a wealth tax (what about the requirement that "direct" taxes be allocated to the states in proportion to their populations?).

The point isn't that these constitutional objections would prevail today or tomorrow; they probably wouldn't. Rather, the point is that Democrats have to think forward. Were Congress to enact these laws and the Supreme Court to consider their constitutionality, Democrats shouldn't be confident that the Court would dismiss these arguments as silly. They should take seriously the possibility that the Court would find the arguments correct.

There's a final point. Any statute enacting Medicare for all, or dealing with voting reform, is going to be complicated. It will inevitably have gaps and internal inconsistencies in how it uses terms. Without holding the law unconstitutional, a court can exploit that complexity to limit its ability to generate a new politics.

The Affordable Care Act provides two examples. The Court first addressed constitutional challenges to the ACA in 2012. The portion of its complicated decision that matters here dealt with the statute's requirement that states expand the coverage they provided under Medicaid. Seven members of the Court agreed that this requirement was unconstitutional. States could choose to expand Medicaid, but they didn't have to—and several red states refused to do so. The effect was to limit the statute's reach and deprive it of the political support it might have received in those states.

The ACA came back to the Court a few years later. This time the challenge was statutory. The ACA set up subsidized markets known as exchanges for consumers to buy health insurance, and it made subsidies available for exchanges established by the "States." If a state didn't create an exchange, the national government would step in and create an exchange in that state. The question the Court had to decide was whether subsidies were available to consumers who bought their policies on these federal exchanges. ACA opponents argued that "State" exchanges had to be established by states, not by the national government. So subsidies weren't available to people who bought their insurance on the federal exchanges. The ACA would have collapsed had that argument—more than plausible on its face—succeeded. Chief Justice Roberts saved the ACA by creatively interpreting "State" to mean "federal."[7]

The linguistic glitch in the ACA resulted from its complexity and the polarized political context in which it was drafted and enacted, which prevented Congress from cleaning up obvious mistakes when they were pointed out. We can be reasonably sure that similar glitches will infect any complex statute that's part of a Democratic policy agenda, and for exactly the same reasons.

Chief Justice Roberts rescued the ACA at a time when it was still unclear whether or how the decayed Reagan constitutional regime would be replaced. If Democrats looked like they were on a path to consolidating a liberal alternative regime, they shouldn't be confident that Chief Justice Roberts or anyone else would bail them out again.

Obstacles to State-Level Policy Innovation

Some sanctuary cities do more than direct their employees not to cooperate with federal immigration officials. They tell employers in the city that they can't tell immigration officials about any undocumented workers who apply for jobs. Everyone agrees that Congress can preempt state and local laws that are inconsistent with national policy. That follows from the principle that national law is supreme over state and local law. The anti-commandeering principle says that Congress can't tell states and cities that they have to enact specific laws, but it doesn't mean that Congress can't override state laws that deal with private parties.

The question in preemption cases is whether some national law overrides a state or local law. Most courts dealing with sanctuary city laws have found that national immigration laws do preempt much of what cities and states have tried to do.

Blue-state policy innovations might also run up against preemption problems. Innovations in health care policy, for example, might be preempted by the Affordable Care Act or by Medicare and Medicaid. As we've seen in chapter 8, the answer to preemption questions depends on the language Congress used. But as we also saw, it's fairly easy for the Court to find a conflict between national policy and local law, or to construe an express preemption provision to cover a specific state law.

Preemption law kicks in only if there's already a national statute on the books. That's seldom a hindrance, because national policy covers almost every topic that blue-state legislators might want to address. If conservatives who oppose state-level innovations scour the federal code for a statute that they can say preempts the innovation, they're quite likely to find one or more. The real issue is going to be whether the federal courts find preemption.

Another example—electing the president by a national majority (or plurality) rather than an Electoral College majority. The Constitution says we have to use the Electoral College. How can states get around that? The Constitution also says that the states get to say *how* electors get chosen. Supporters of electing the president by majority vote have come up with the National Popular Vote interstate compact. Several states have enacted a statute saying that all of their electors will cast their votes for the winner of the national popular vote, regardless of the statewide result—but this statute won't take effect until enough states have enacted it to account for 270 electoral votes (a majority). If enough states do so by 2022, then in 2024 a national popular majority will elect the president.

This is pretty ingenious. There are two big objections. We can't be confident that the statute will "stick" if a Republican wins a large majority of Florida's votes but the Democrat wins the national popular majority. Floridians might well pressure their electors to vote for the Republican. The electors would be "breaking" Florida's law, but maybe the law is unconstitutional. The argument is that the Constitution's framers intended the electors to be independent decision-makers selected for a national purpose, whose actions can't be controlled by state legislators.

The other big objection is that the National Popular Vote's proponents call it an interstate compact, and the Constitution says that agreements between states have to be approved by Congress. The Supreme Court has interpreted that provision to mean less than it says. Congress doesn't have to approve agreements that don't, as the Court puts it, diminish congressional sovereignty. The National Popular Vote doesn't do that, so maybe it doesn't require congressional approval. But a conservative Court might expand the doctrine to cover agreements that impair fundamental aspects of constitutional design or diminish the sovereignty of institutions, like the Electoral College, that were designed to be independent.

Now this chapter's general theme recurs: How will a conservative Supreme Court apply existing doctrine when blue states try to build a new progressive politics by adopting new policies? Maybe it will stand aside, but maybe it won't. That uncertainty means that even when blue-state Democrats have the power to enact statutes that advance their agenda, they have to worry about how the courts will respond.

Watching the Whole Board

This part began with the observation that new policies make a new politics. If progressives actually get a chance to start developing a new political regime, their first priority will be to enact new policies. Those policies will be in the foreground of their efforts, but the courts will be in the background. Once the statutes are enacted and conservatives challenge them, the courts will move to the foreground.

Champion chess players know that they have to pay attention to the whole chessboard, not just the area where the pieces have been moving most recently: An attack might be launched out of a remote corner of the board. The same goes for politics.

Liberals and progressives interested in substantive policies—Medicare for all, overcoming what they regard as voter suppression efforts, "common sense" gun regulations, and more—have to keep in mind what the courts can do to impede those policies. That means drafting statutes with an eye to how a hostile court might see them. Nancy Pelosi, when asked by a reporter about the possibility that the Affordable Care Act was unconstitutional, famously said, "Are you serious?" Her successors, as leaders of a new constitutional order, can't have that attitude.

Those leaders should have court reform on their minds as well—not because this is intrinsically a high priority in the new constitutional vision, but because it's strategically important if that vision is to be implemented.

13

Putting Courts on the Progressive Agenda

When it came to appointing judges, Donald Trump hit the ground running. During his campaign he had published a list of people he would consider for his first Supreme Court appointments. Understanding that he had to build his credibility with important segments of the Republican Party—conservatives who focused on the courts, and evangelical Christians who fervently desired to see *Roe v. Wade* overruled—he had had the list vetted by people closely associated with the Federalist Society, an organization of conservative lawyers whose meetings had become the go-to events for those auditioning for Republican judicial appointments. And when Trump became president, Leonard Leo, a Federalist Society employee, took a leave of absence to advise the administration on judicial appointments. With Leo's guidance, Trump rolled out nomination after nomination shortly after his inauguration.[1]

The contrast between Trump's vigor in making judicial appointments and the near indifference of Bill Clinton and Barack Obama, the two Democratic presidents who preceded him, could not have been more dramatic. Clinton and Obama made judicial nominations a low priority. Like Trump's, their reasons were rooted in party politics. Democratic policy priorities—for Clinton and Obama, health care, for Obama, recovery from financial collapse—couldn't be accomplished through the courts. And no important constituency in the Democratic coalition cared a great deal about the judiciary;

Democratic interest groups were focused on policies to push through Congress.[2]

If Democrats ever gain consolidated control of the presidency and Congress, they should be concerned about the courts, because they will face a judiciary—especially a Supreme Court—that will be the final redoubt of conservative political power. Suppose the interest groups within the Democratic coalition see that their policies are at risk from the courts, and donors to the party supplement their policy concerns with attention to the courts. What can they do?

Staffing

Having a list of potential nominees in hand is the first and easiest task—though not without its difficulties. Pundits trot out the Great Mentioner every campaign season, compiling lists of people whom candidates will "consider" for a Supreme Court appointment. About half of the mentions are serious, with the others slipped onto the list to show the pundit's creativity.

Compiling a real list of potential Supreme Court appointees will be more difficult for Democrats than it was for Trump. Trump had to satisfy a single organization, the Federalist Society, on the sensible assumption that everyone that group approved would want to overrule *Roe v. Wade*. No organization has a similar place in the Democratic Party. Democratic presidents have to satisfy a number of interest groups—African Americans, women, the disability community, and trial lawyers, among others. Those groups form a legal network roughly parallel to the Federalist Society. Instead of being able to get their list from one place, Democrats have to work each of the network's nodes to find out who is acceptable.[3]

Putting a list together might seem to ease the overall task by allowing the Democrats' judge-pickers to point to *someone* on the list who would satisfy each constituency—someone suggested by the groups at each node. That might work for the lower courts, although it might also provide targets for sniping as the groups maneuver for position. That the *list* satisfies all the groups won't matter when the time comes to make a Supreme Court appointment, because only one name can be chosen at a time, leaving the others hoping, without guarantees, that they'll be next. Again, this contrasts with the Republican strategy, where anyone on the list is pretty much as good as any other.

Of course, Democrats' opportunities (if they have them) will go beyond the Supreme Court. Lower court judges get ill and retire, change careers, or pass away. President Trump had many vacancies to fill as soon as he took office, in part because of the slow pace at which Obama nominated judges, and more because of the similarly slow pace at which the Senate processed them.

There will be some vacancies to be filled on January 21, 2021, though we can assume that in advance of any changeover from Republican control of the Senate and presidency to Democratic control, the lame-duck Senate will rush to fill every seat it can. A Democratic president can have a list of possibilities for whatever vacancies remain. The Democrats' relative lack of concern about judicial appointments has traditionally given senators a larger role in Democratic nominations than in Republican ones—but the explicitly ideological and results-oriented tone of Republican appointments might now change that attitude. In any event, coming up with serious candidates is the Democrats' least difficult task.

Size

Everyone agrees that Congress has an essentially free hand in creating new positions for judges in the federal trial and intermediate appeals courts. Congress has regularly increased the number of such judges in response to new demands on the courts: more cases involving immigration, for example, or appeals from administrative agencies dealing with social welfare programs.

Congress increased the number of federal judges in October 1978, when Jimmy Carter was president, in April 1982 and July 1984 under Ronald Reagan, and December 1990 under George H. W. Bush. Since then, it has added some new trial court judges but no new judgeships for the courts of appeals. Divided government almost certainly explains this inaction: Democratic Congresses didn't want to give Republican presidents a chance to appoint a bunch of new judges, and vice versa for Republicans.

Should Democrats control Congress and the presidency, they could make a decent case for increasing the number of federal judges. The good-government case would be the usual one—demands on the federal courts that have led to a decline in access to speedy justice. The partisan case is also straightforward—new appointments to the lower federal courts could "re-balance" them more quickly than waiting for vacancies.

Republicans might well describe increasing the number of lower court federal judges as "court packing." Historical practice with respect to those courts might weaken the sting of that charge. Expanding the Supreme Court, in contrast, would be highly controversial.

Term Limits

Democrats who focused on the Supreme Court talked a lot about how Senator Mitch McConnell "stole" a Supreme Court seat from Democrats by refusing to allow a hearing on the nomination of Merrick Garland to fill the seat opened up by Antonin Scalia's death.*

---

* This criticism assumed that had there been a hearing at least some Republicans would have voted in favor of Garland's confirmation. That assumption is probably correct, but it is not unassailable.

Neil Gorsuch's appointment didn't alter the Court's ideological composition, so the muttering quieted for a time.

That changed with Anthony Kennedy's retirement. Anyone on the Federalist Society list from which Trump took his nominees would shift the Court even further to the right. And the contentious hearings on Brett Kavanaugh's nomination revised talk among Democrats about doing *something* about the Court's composition. The language varied—"Court reform," "Court expansion," and, most honestly, "Court packing." The most prominent suggestion was to increase the Court's size by two—one to "take back" the seat McConnell "stole," and one to offset the votes cast by Justice Gorsuch, who "shouldn't" have been there in the first place.

Court-packing is controversial even among liberals. Maybe it's unconstitutional, though as we'll see the case for unconstitutionality is complex. Before I deal with it, it's worth addressing another suggestion for Court reform, to give us a sense of how constitutional arguments about Court composition go.* That suggestion is that we should limit the terms of Supreme Court justices. The Constitution says that federal judges "hold their Offices during good Behaviour," which everyone agrees means that they hold their offices for life (subject to the possibility of impeachment for misconduct). The most prominent suggestions for term limits assume that the Court's size is fixed at nine, and propose an eighteen-year term. If everything goes smoothly, that would give each president two nominations during a four-year term.† How can term limits be constitutional?

---

* I focus on two simple proposals; others, with more bells and whistles, have been floated, but in my judgment only the simple versions have even the barest chance of getting any political traction.

† You have to work out details to deal with unexpected resignations or deaths, but once you're over the big hurdles, those details aren't difficult to deal with.

Of course we could amend the Constitution, but that's really difficult. In 2005 Roger Cramton and Paul Carrington, two prominent law professors, both political centrists and both highly experienced in judicial administration, argued that term limits could be imposed by statute.[4] Their argument was simple: Federal judges hold their "offices" for life, but Congress can define the office to which a judge is appointed. So, they argued, Congress could define the following office: "Supreme Court justice for eighteen years, followed by service during good behavior on a federal court of appeals." When you're appointed to *that* office, you have life tenure as a federal judge but not a lifetime seat on the Supreme Court.*

This works going forward, but it doesn't do anything about the Court today. That's probably why the proposal didn't get anywhere: Politicians don't want to spend time advancing controversial proposals whose benefits won't appear until a decade or more in the future. Congress might try to apply this definitional move to judges already on the Supreme Court, but whatever one thinks of the Cramton-Carrington proposal for future appointments, it's far less persuasive applied to sitting judges. The Cramton-Carrington argument is essentially, "The office you hold is the thing described in that piece of paper you have hanging on your wall," and for sitting justices, the paper on the wall says they're there for life.

Surveys show that Americans like term limits in general, though the surveys haven't asked about applying them to federal judges. Term limits for elected officials may ensure that representatives keep in

---

* Another statutory possibility is to reduce the staffing available to Supreme Court justices. The Court has reduced its caseload by about half but has maintained the same number of law clerks for each justice. It wouldn't be difficult to justify cutting the clerk allocation in half as a good-government move. And doing so would at least send a real signal to the Court that Democrats think it's gotten out of hand.

touch with their constituents—something we don't expect from federal judges. Approaching the issue from the political right, Steven Calabresi, a co-founder of the Federalist Society, offered policy concerns about life tenure: "a Supreme Court divorced from democratic accountability," "increased politicization of the confirmation process," "an improper emphasis on the age of potential nominees," and "a rise in 'mental decrepitude' on the Court." The last two points are perhaps the strongest. Life tenure gives presidents an incentive to appoint younger judges, who may not have enough real-world experience. Anthony Kennedy, reflecting on his appointment to the court of appeals at age 39, suggested that he had been too young for the job. Lifetime tenure also allows some judges to stay on the courts after their capacities have declined. And at the Supreme Court level, it introduces a combination of randomness and strategy. Presidents' opportunities to make appointments depend on the vagaries of illness and death, and justices can time their retirements to ensure that their replacements will be named by a president likely to appoint someone they approve of.[5]

If we think term limits for Supreme Court justices is good policy, maybe we can do it by enacting a statute. But the Supreme Court would decide whether the statute is constitutional, and maybe the justices would hold that the Constitution defines "Justice of the Supreme Court" as a position distinct from "federal judge." That means that other ways of reforming the Court can't be taken off the table.

Calabresi's support for term limits, even if only through a constitutional amendment, brings out an important feature of discussions of "court reform": They are a sometime thing. Conservatives and liberals are happy to stick with existing court structures when these serve their ends, and want to change those structures when they don't. The politics of court reform are thus no different from the politics of any other aspect of political regimes—stable when a regime is stable, unstable when there's a real possibility of a regime shift. Court reform has not been on anyone's agenda during the interregnum between the end of the Reagan regime and whatever comes next. As the possibility of a regime shift becomes more substantial, it remains off the agenda for conservatives, who won't want to reform the Court whether the next regime is liberal or conservative. But it is on the progressive agenda because of concern that the courts would obstruct consolidation of a new progressive regime.

Court-Packing

The journalist Richard Neuberger heard from ordinary people that Franklin D. Roosevelt's court-packing plan "had to be put into effect by a Constitutional amendment because the Constitution specifies nine judges." It doesn't—but, though Neuberger's readers were wrong in 1937, perhaps today the Constitution, properly interpreted, would forbid Court-packing.[6]

The Constitution lets Congress set the Court's size. In 1789 there were six justices. Later it became five, six again, seven, nine, ten, seven, and nine again in 1869. It's stayed there ever since.

Most of the changes in the Court's size were done for good-government reasons, with a soupçon of politics. Until the late nineteenth century, Supreme Court justices "rode circuit," traveling around the country to sit on appeals courts. As the country grew, Congress created new circuit courts of appeal, and each time it did, it made sense to add a Supreme Court justice to ride the new circuit. Because each new circuit gave the president a chance to nominate a new justice, politics affected *when* Congress created a new circuit: it did so when it was in sync with the president politically.

But some changes in Court size were purely political. On their way out of power in 1800, the Federalists reduced the Court's size by one (to take effect when the next sitting justice left the Court) to deprive the incoming president, Thomas Jefferson, of the opportunity to name a new justice.* Once in office, though, Jefferson's Democrats promptly restored the Court's size to six. During the Civil War, Republicans concerned that the Court might be dominated by pro-southern Democrats added a new seat, which President Lincoln filled. When Andrew Johnson became president after Lincoln's assassination, Congress reduced the Court's size to seven so that Johnson, whom the Republican majority distrusted, couldn't make any new appointments.† After Ulysses S. Grant was elected, Congress restored the Court's size to nine, giving Grant two appointments. That was particularly timely because the Court had just held paper money unconstitutional by a five-to-three vote, and Republicans wanted to reverse the decision—which the Court did, the new appointees voting with the earlier case's dissenters.

In 1937, Roosevelt faced a Court he thought was hostile to the New Deal. It had struck down two major New Deal statutes and had criticized his actions in two other cases. Roosevelt feared that the Social Security Act and the National Labor Relations Act would fall next. Disingenuously claiming the Supreme Court's aging justices could not keep up with the Court's work, FDR asked Congress to allow him to appoint one new justice for every sitting justice over the age of seventy—a total of six. This was a good-government fig leaf for his desire to stack the Court with justices who would uphold key New Deal statutes. No one bought it.

---

* The reduction never took effect because no justice left the Court while its size was set at five.

† The reduction was to take place by attrition. As justices resigned or died their positions would not be filled. Only one justice had done so when the first Legal Tender (paper money) Case was heard.

The proposal, quickly labeled a Court-packing plan, faced little opposition in the House of Representatives. The Senate was a different matter. The proposal divided the Democratic Party almost down the middle, but Roosevelt, devoting massive political and personal capital to the proposal, almost managed to pull it off. The key was Senate majority leader Joseph Robinson, whom FDR had promised a Supreme Court seat. Robinson in turn drew upon his personal relations with other senators to accumulate what looked to be a narrow majority for the plan. But when Robinson died of a heart attack, the support collapsed and the plan failed.

Many observers then and since have taken the plan's defeat to show that we have an unwritten constitutional norm—a "convention"—against Court-packing. The convention can't be that the Court's size is forever fixed at nine; history shows that there are sometimes good reasons for changing its size, and such reasons might recur. Rather, the convention is that you can't change the Court's size simply to shift its political or ideological composition.

As we'll see in more detail in the next chapter, thinking about constitutional norms or conventions requires some care. Even showing that there *is* a norm is tricky.

How do we know there's a norm against changing the Court's size to shift its political composition? Here's how the argument against it would go. The only evidence we have is that FDR's plan failed, but one case does not a convention make. With a slight change in circumstances—had Robinson died a week after the vote on the plan rather than before the vote was taken—the precedent probably wouldn't exist.

What about the fact that no one has seriously tried to change the Court's size since 1937? There are many reasons things *don't* happen, and some of those reasons might give us a good account of why there's no convention.

An old joke points the way. Two parents were worried that their child hadn't said a word in the six years since birth. They consulted doctors and speech therapists, but nothing helped. One morning the child came to the breakfast table, tasted the cereal, and piped up, "This oatmeal is too lumpy." His astonished parents said, "So you can talk!" The child replied, "Of course I can." The parents—after replacing the cereal—asked, "So why haven't you said anything for six years?" The child replied, "Everything was fine until now."

So too with the Court's size: In a political world in which the Republican and Democratic parties were complex political coalitions, each containing conservative and liberal factions—in short, in the world of the New Deal/Great Society regime, and to a lesser extent the world of the Reagan Revolution—each side expected to, and did, get its fair share of nominations to the Supreme Court. The oatmeal was fine. There was no norm against changing the Court's size for political reasons, just no reason to try.

With the rise of political parties that are internally unified and sharply at odds ideologically, that has changed. Changing the Court's size would surely require capturing the presidency and the House of Representatives, and a supermajority in the Senate—or else veto-proof majorities in both houses. If either party achieved one of those goals, such a move would be in its interest: for Republicans, to further entrench their control of all three branches, and for Democrats, to overturn conservative control of the Court. Either way, reviving the idea of Court-packing wouldn't violate some already existing norm, because the practice of not changing the Court's size wasn't a norm in the first place.

If they gained both Congress and the presidency, Democrats would argue that Court-packing doesn't violate an existing norm, and Republicans would disagree. Surveys do suggest that the public is nervous about changing the Court's size for political reasons, though not for good-government ones. The difficulty for Democrats is that they can't really come up with decent good-government reasons for adding two justices to the Supreme Court (in contrast to their ability to come up with such reasons for expanding the lower courts).[7]

The political fight to expand the Court would be as divisive as anything we've yet seen, and Democrats shouldn't provoke that fight right away. But if they find a conservative-dominated Supreme Court impeding their ability to create a new politics, they should have already developed the argument that Court-packing is constitutionally permitted. The alternative, as one critic of Court-packing agrees, is "accepting a generation of legal defeats."[8] If they do suffer such defeats they can decide whether it makes sense politically to provoke a fight over Court expansion—a matter on which constitutional scholars can offer no advice.*

Judicial Legitimacy

Almost every critic of Court-packing proposals says that doing so would weaken the Court's legitimacy. What the critics don't explain is what they mean by "legitimacy," and why undermining it matters. Donald Trump and John Roberts did a better job.

President Trump signed an executive order saying that the government wouldn't process asylum applications from people who didn't present themselves at a designated port of arrival. A federal judge said that the order couldn't go into effect, citing a statute that

---

* Were they to control the House, the Senate, and the presidency Democrats might consider "seizing the day" immediately, concerned about the possibility that they might lose the House and/or the Senate in the next election. This might occur because they would still be in an interregnum. And, in such a case, the chance that Republicans could gain control of the House, Senate, and presidency and retaliate by expanding the Court in turn might be slim.

says any alien who arrives in the United States can apply for asylum "whether or not [the alien arrived] at a designated port of arrival." The statute's language seems pretty clear, though specialists in immigration law could perhaps develop arguments supporting the executive order. President Trump's reaction was not legalistic. He said that the decision was made "by an Obama judge," and "it's not going to happen like this anymore."

Roberts responded, "We do not have Obama judges or Trump judges, Bush judges or Clinton judges." Judges, for the chief justice, were "dedicated [people] doing their level best to do equal right to those appearing before them.... The independent judiciary is something we should all be thankful for." Trump then reiterated his position: "Sorry Chief Justice John Roberts, but you do indeed have 'Obama judges.'"

The disagreement was whether judges are mouthpieces for policies of the president who nominated them, or are doing their best to follow the law as they understand it. Put in those terms, the argument is silly. The question is not "whether or not" but "how much." In this conversation, judicial legitimacy depends on maintaining a distinction between decisions taken according to law and those taken according to politics. Everyone ought to agree that decisions on highly contentious matters blend law and politics, but, according to its devotees, judicial legitimacy requires that politics can't play "too large" a role.

Why does this matter? The same devotees point to cases in which the courts have interpreted the Constitution to protect unpopular people or causes, such as criminal defendants or political outsiders. If those outcomes result from a disinterested application of "the law," people who disagree with the results might swallow their disagreement and go along out of respect for the judges' knowledge and integrity. But, the argument goes, if the outcomes reflect only the judge's political views, people with different views have no reason to accept the decision.

Judicial legitimacy matters, then, because the distinction between law and politics gives people reasons to accept decisions they disagree with. But do people actually think that the courts really do follow the law and politics? Survey evidence suggests that people don't abandon their views about what results are good or bad simply because courts have other views, yet they still retain a general respect for the courts. Political scientists offer several possible explanations for this "diffuse support" for the Supreme Court. I believe the best is that everyone sees the courts taking their side often enough—sometimes conservative, sometimes liberal, but not sometimes Republican, sometimes Democratic. That explanation, though, rests on replacing a narrow understanding of the distinction between law and politics with a slightly broader one.[9]

We can fairly wonder how often someone says, "Well, I think the result in this case is wrong, but I'll go along because the judge tells me it's what the law requires." Sometimes, one can explain the reasoning behind a decision, and people accept that there were at least serious arguments on both sides. At other times, they might go along because they don't see any effective way to challenge the outcome, but still think that the decision was motivated by politics and can be overturned by political action, such as voting for a president who will appoint different judges.

More important, we can fairly wonder to what extent Court-packing would undermine judicial legitimacy. The role of Federalist Society officials in vetting Trump's judicial nominees shows what we already know: ideology is the first consideration when presidents make judicial appointments, and only if a candidate is ideologically acceptable do they look at factors like background or temperament. Trump's reference to "Obama judges" wasn't out of line with how most people think about the courts. And the cynic's view of Roberts's response is that he wanted to preempt criticisms he expects in future cases when the Court divides five-to-four along conservative-liberal lines. The law-politics distinction having already been substantially undermined, Court-packing can't add much more. And in the event that the Court does start to obstruct progressive policy initiatives, Court-packing might do some good, as Democrats will see things.

Once again, we should think about constitutional matters with constitutional regimes in mind. Sustaining the distinction between law and politics might make sense once a constitutional regime stabilizes. When conservatives actively sought to undermine judicial legitimacy by attacking the Warren Court, it was an indication that the New Deal/Great Society order was passing from the scene. When the Reagan Revolution began to fade, liberals returned the favor, though less enthusiastically because the courts were still doing some things they liked. Should that change, liberals will grow less protective of judicial legitimacy—and conservatives will try to use the old rhetoric about judicial legitimacy to show liberal hypocrisy.

Should Progressives Try to Preserve the Court's Legitimacy?

"But wait," liberal critics of Court-packing say, "we need to have a Supreme Court that's available to make decisions on behalf of unpopular minorities." There are trade-offs. A conservative Supreme Court will occasionally rule against petty local tyrants trying to stifle dissent, and will sometimes rule in favor of criminal defendants who were the victims of gross injustice. Liberals should look back to Part 1 of this book and think about what they lose from preserving the Court's legitimacy. The conservative Court has already ruled in favor of such oppressed minorities as Big Pharma, and against minorities such as Muslims and African Americans. The idea that on balance a conservative Court will promote progressive goals seems wildly mistaken.

Like the prospect of being hanged, the prospect of a liberal takeover of Congress and the presidency should concentrate the mind. Such a takeover would occur against a backdrop of conservative control of the lower courts and, more important, the Supreme Court. Presidents Clinton and Obama did not put a high priority on transforming the courts, for good reasons associated with the politics and policies of the Democratic Party. For equally good political and policy reasons, the next Democratic president should pay more attention to the courts. Staffing the lower courts won't be difficult as a matter of law, but the Supreme Court is both legally and politically trickier. Democrats should already be thinking about how they would handle the legal and political landscape.

14

Playing Constitutional Hardball

Wisconsin Democrat Tony Evers won the governorship from the incumbent Republican, Scott Walker, in 2018, but Republicans retained control of the state legislature. Taking advantage of the several-month gap between election day and inauguration day, and following a path Republicans had blazed a few years earlier in North Carolina, the Republican-dominated Wisconsin legislature enacted, and Walker signed, a package of bills transferring some of the governor's powers to the legislature—even though Republicans had previously done nothing to curb those powers when they were in Walker's hands. The Wisconsin legislature remained in Republican hands because the party benefited from a severe gerrymander that the U.S. Supreme Court had refused to overturn. No prominent Republicans criticized the Wisconsin Republicans' actions.

During the same post-election period, New Jersey Democrats proposed to amend the state constitution to set up a system of drawing district boundaries. Their proposal was widely characterized—unfairly, some said—as ensuring that Democrats would permanently hold a majority of legislative seats. After criticism from New Jersey's Democratic governor and former Obama attorney general Eric Holder, among others, Democrats in the state legislature pulled the amendment from the agenda.

These events unfolded at roughly the same time. They illustrate what commentators have started calling "constitutional hardball" in action. They also suggest that Republicans are better at playing hardball than Democrats. Of the court "reforms" discussed in the previous chapter, Court-packing is a prime candidate for hardball status.[1] What is constitutional hardball? Should we worry about it?

Defining Constitutional Hardball

Steven Levitsky and Daniel Ziblatt's book *How Democracies Die* identified the weakening of democratic norms as the murder weapon. Weeks after Donald Trump's inauguration, the liberal-oriented national security blog "Just Security" began posting an episodic "Norms Watch" with the subtitle "Tracking the Erosion of Democratic Traditions."[2] The first post dealt with the administration's efforts to get friendly media coverage "while blasting critics," and with "shock and confusion" over the administration's first "Muslim ban." One focus of the latter discussion was that "Trump's team 'did not follow the standard agency review process that's typically overseen by the National Security Council.'"

Constitutional hardball has to do with norms and traditions. The written Constitution and laws provide only some of the framework in which politics occurs. The rest comes from unwritten practices and values about how politicians should behave. "When you lose," for example, "you accept defeat and don't take advantage of whatever remaining power you have to stick it to the other side."

Because norms and traditions aren't found in the Constitution and statutes, our arguments about them are forced into a special but familiar frame.

Arguing About Constitutional Norms

When Democrats complained that Senator Mitch McConnell had broken the unstated rules of the game—had played hardball—by denying Merrick Garland a hearing and then an up-or-down vote on his nomination to the Supreme Court, Republicans had two answers. McConnell said that since 1940, the Senate had never taken a vote on a Supreme Court nomination made in a presidential election year, and it had been even longer since a Senate controlled by the party not holding the presidency did so. Democrats responded that the reason for that was simple: there hadn't been any such nominations.

Republicans also said that Democrats had started it all, sometimes pointing to what they saw as unfair attacks on Robert Bork when he was nominated in 1987, or to the Democrats' refusal to give Miguel Estrada a hearing on his nomination to the court of appeals in 2001. Democrats responded that at least Bork had received a hearing and an up-and-down vote (he lost by a substantial margin) and President Reagan got to fill the position anyway—and that there's a difference between nominations to courts of appeals and to the Supreme Court.

Hardball puts the unstated rules of the game into play. A background assumption is that hardball moves are constitutionally permissible. You can gin up an argument that the Senate has a constitutional duty to consider Supreme Court nominations on the merits, rooted perhaps in the word "shall" in the constitutional provision about the president's power to nominate Supreme Court justices. The argument is strained and in tension with the Senate's power under the Constitution to make its own rules. Mostly, though, arguments about hardball moves acknowledge that they are constitutionally permissible—but still breach existing norms.

Lawyers know how to argue about rules that are found in practices rather than in statutes or constitutions. It's what they do in "common law" reasoning. Courts decide cases about accidents and contracts relying on prior decisions by their predecessors, but those decisions often don't involve crisply stated rules. As we saw in chapter 1, lawyers use a set of standard moves to extract a rule from the case's facts and the reasons the court gives for its decision. They distinguish the case on the facts, or they find that the case stands for a broad principle, and so on. And those moves are still available even when the court purports to set out a broad rule. If you think the rule shouldn't be applied in the circumstances you face, for example, you say that the court's language was "dictum," meaning that it wasn't necessary to support the case's outcome.

That's exactly how arguments about constitutional hardball proceed. Republicans: "no confirmation votes during a presidential year"; Democrats: "distinguishable because no need." Republicans: "our rule is supported by the principle that the people should have a say on who gets to nominate"; Democrats: "they did have a say when they elected President Obama." Or, as we saw about Court-packing: Opponents: "FDR's failure to get Court-packing through in 1937 established a norm"; supporters: "no norm because no need until now." Opponents: "the norm against Court-packing simply to change anticipated outcomes is supported by the principle of judicial independence"; supporters: "you compromised independence by stealing one seat and making another blatantly political nomination of Brett Kavanaugh."

It's important to emphasize that I'm not endorsing any of these arguments, just pointing out that they are lawyers' arguments and, as I argued in chapter 1, arguments are all there is. Your political views, not your legal ones, will tell you which side you're on, and political power will determine which side wins.

Imagine that a Supreme Court justice retires or passes away in early 2020. One can fairly be skeptical that Senator McConnell would invoke the "rule" against considering nominations during a presidential year. I expect that he would distinguish the situations: "The rule is against considering nominations made in a presidential election year by a president who is barred from running for re-election. The people can express their opinion of Trump's nomination by voting for or against him in November; they couldn't do the equivalent in 2016." And, I stress, there's nothing wrong with recasting the argument in light of new facts and a more precise formulation of the underlying principle.

The Risks and Benefits of Changing Norms by Breaching Them

Norms and traditions change, and on the whole that's a good thing. We shouldn't be saddled with norms and traditions that have become outdated, and since they're unwritten, the only way to update norms and traditions is to violate them. That can provoke an argument, not about whether the norm has been violated but about whether it is worth following any more.

Broadly speaking, political norms help elected officials coordinate their actions to get things done or help them improve policy outcomes. An example of a coordination norm is this: The Senate would grind to a halt if senators insisted on strict compliance with every procedural rule. For example, the rules say (roughly) that committees can't meet when there's a floor debate going on; insisting that those rules be complied with would slow committee work to a crawl. The solution: a norm that senators won't insist on compliance with the rules, embodied in a practice of granting unanimous consent to waive them.

An example of a "good governance" norm is this. Some bills deal primarily with one topic—agriculture, for example—but have implications for other matters, such as welfare policy via food stamps. Nothing in the law prevents that sort of bill from emerging solely from the Department of Agriculture or the Senate and House committees on agriculture. But a norm of consultation across departments or committees developed to prevent such bills from having unintended consequences.

These reasons for norms also illuminate when people can reasonably breach the norms. Coordination norms help get things done, but if you think that things are fine—or that efforts to make things better generally make them worse—you're happy to see things grind to a halt. Good-governance norms are supposed to improve policy, but if you think that consultation just entrenches "group think" among the like-minded, you may want to drop your policy proposals fully formed.

This is all pretty general, but it plays out in real practices of norm-creation and norm-breaching.

• *The filibuster.* Senators used to reserve the filibuster—unlimited debate until terminated by sixty-seven (later sixty) votes—for what enough of them regarded as fundamental issues of deep principle. That changed in the last quarter of the twentieth century. Senators of both parties began to filibuster central elements of their opponents' platforms—important proposals, to be sure, but also the meat-and-potatoes of ordinary politics. A rule change in 1970, allowing other business to go forward while a filibuster is going on, reduced the cost of filibustering. As a result, the actual filibuster—epitomized as Jimmy Stewart standing in the Senate and speaking indefinitely—has disappeared almost entirely. Today, minority-party senators announce that they will filibuster a proposal if it comes to the floor and point out that they have enough votes to prevent the Senate from terminating the debate. The majority doesn't even seek a vote.[3]

Today newspapers routinely report that some proposal won't get through the Senate because it doesn't have sixty votes behind it—a filibuster-proof majority—as if this were a fundamental feature of Senate practices. And today it is, because the norm against routine filibusters has gone away.

One reason for the change is clear: increased polarization in the Senate. Each side thinks that many of their opponents' policy proposals are so bad that the country would suffer were they to be enacted. Another reason is that the Senate's workload has grown, making filibuster threats a more effective weapon.

There's also another reason. Senators, again from both parties, came to believe—or at least came to say—that *other* parts of the legislative process had changed. In their eyes, their opponents were ramming legislation through with narrow majorities, were not taking the opponents' objections or proposed compromises seriously (even if in the end they rejected the objections), and were generally failing to cooperate. The norm against routine filibusters made less sense in the new legislative process. It was breached, then abandoned, amid an atmosphere of general distrust.

Finally, both parties usually want to get stuff done, but Democrats, as a more pro-government party, are somewhat more likely to want to get stuff done than are Republicans, who favor less government. Making filibusters routine—or, equivalently, increasing the majority required to get stuff done—favors Republicans more than it does Democrats. Of course, Republicans figured this out.

• *Presidential consultation before acting.* In an important article, law professor Daphna Renan describes a norm within the executive branch: Before making important decisions, presidents should find out what relevant cabinet officers and what high-level permanent employees—career civil servants—think they should do. The norm rests on the mostly accurate view that consulting people with empirical knowledge and long experience will lead to better decisions. A president may have a vague sense that something ought to be done and come up with a policy that addresses the problem. Career civil servants can refine the proposal to eliminate parts that aren't likely to work well (or are illegal), or propose alternatives that are likely to get the job done better. These are tweaks to the basic idea, not attempts to undermine the president's initiative.[4]

Wide consultation within the executive branch is a "good government" norm that usually produces better policy than unilateral presidential decision-making. Are there conditions under which a president could reasonably think the consultation norm isn't worth following?

I'll lay out what I think is a decent argument for President Trump's disregard of this norm. He came to office envisioning a transition from the interregnum to a Trumpist regime—a substantial shift in prevailing policy. Career civil servants did indeed have empirical knowledge and deep experience, but their knowledge was about conditions that Trump wanted to change and their experience was with policies quite different from the ones he wanted to implement. From his point of view, the civil servants were bureaucratically "conservative."* The advice he'd get would not improve his policies but weaken them.

We might compare Trump to another president who came to office promising truly new policies, Franklin Roosevelt. Roosevelt assembled a group of close advisers—the Brains Trust—whom he consulted in devising policy. He didn't consult broadly with cabinet officers or civil servants; his managerial style often involved pitting cabinet members against each other, leaving him free to pursue the policies he preferred. Once the New Deal took hold, Roosevelt's practice changed, and he followed something like the consultation norm.

That suggests an important point: Some norms are characteristic of stable constitutional orders and may even be considered ways in which the order manifests itself. The consultation norm might be one: Presidents will consult broadly once the new regime gets control of

---

* This is a non-conspiratorial account of what conspiracy theorists describe as the "deep state."

the bureaucracy and shifts its orientation from old principles to new ones. Norm violations can help us see that the existing constitutional order is degenerating, or that we are in an interregnum, with something new on the horizon.

The mere act of breaching a norm, then, doesn't tell us that a politician is acting badly. We have to ask whether the norm is worth following under current conditions. The answer requires a close look at what's actually going on. Sometimes we'll conclude that the norm is worth following, and criticize politicians who breach it. But sometimes the politician has a decent argument against following the norm. We might disagree with the argument and the evaluation of current conditions on which it rests, but that's just an ordinary political disagreement, not a threat to democracy.

Levitsky and Ziblatt describe norms as the "guardrails" of democracy. In their view, norms are more important than constitutional and statutory provisions regulating politics. Not all, of course. Maybe President Trump breached a norm when he refused to make his tax returns public. The norm does have something to do with democracy: the tax returns might tell us how rich Trump actually is, whether he accurately described his wealth, whether he used "creative" strategies to avoid paying taxes, whether he did or did not have financial dealings "with" Russia—information that some people would take into account in deciding whether to vote for him. The norm about disclosing tax returns might be one small slat in democracy's guardrails, but it's hard to see the car careening off the mountain simply because that norm disappeared.

Other norms might be more consequential. Two interrelated ones figure prominently in current discussions. One is that attempting to achieve bipartisan compromises on important legislation is a good thing; the other is that you treat your opponents as people you disagree with, not as enemies.

On compromise: Democrats say that President Obama negotiated in good faith for quite a while over the details of his health-care proposals, incorporating into them the idea of requiring people to buy health-care insurance, which came from the Heritage Foundation and legislation sponsored by Mitt Romney. Republicans say that in the end, Democrats enacted a huge social program with—for the first time—no support whatever from Republicans. And people fall all over themselves to praise the bipartisanship that led to the First Step Act of 2018, a quite modest change in federal criminal justice policy that was accurately described as "the most far-reaching overhaul of the criminal justice system in a generation."

On enmity: Democrats point to Mitch McConnell's statement in 2009 that Republicans' first priority was to ensure that Barack Obama served only one term as president, and to Michelle Obama's assertion, "When they go low, we go high." Republicans point to Eric Holder's reformulation, "When they go low, we kick them," and to James Comey's statement, "All of us should use every breath we have to make sure the lies stop on January 20, 2021."[5]

Is *democracy* imperiled by refusal to compromise? Philosophers and legal scholars have written books about "rotten compromises" and "dealing with the devil." Their conclusion, in my view, is that sometimes circumstances force you to make rotten compromises. Importantly, though, they do not defend these compromises as valuable in themselves. When important matters are at stake, there's no value in the mere fact that the outcome is a compromise.[6]

Refusal to compromise across the board, on matters small and large, might indeed threaten democracy by supporting the thought that your opponents are enemies, to be defeated in every skirmish. If something you consider really important is at stake—broader access to health-care insurance, or tax cuts—it's not obvious that there's anything anti-democratic about a refusal to compromise. Hardball when the stakes are high makes sense.

The erosion of the norm against treating opponents as enemies might be more troubling, but also less enduring. An optimist might see it as a symptom not of *democratic* decay but of a transition to a new constitutional order. After the transition, the new regime will have no need to raise enthusiasm by threatening to throw its opponents into jail.

In a famous speech during the 1936 presidential campaign, Franklin Roosevelt said, "We had to struggle with the old enemies of peace—business and financial monopoly, speculation, reckless banking, class antagonism, sectionalism, war profiteering.... Never before in all our history have these forces been so united against one candidate as they stand today. They are unanimous in their hate for me—and I welcome their hatred." Roosevelt's opponents thought he was an authoritarian-in-waiting. They turned out to be wrong. Under the New Deal/Great Society order, Democrats sometimes sought Republican support, though always on the Democrats' terms, as with the adoption of civil rights statutes in the 1960s. The same was true, with the parties reversed, during the Reagan Revolution. The tax cuts of 1981 and 1986 required Democratic support, and even before the Reagan Revolution arrived, President Jimmy Carter and Senator Edward Kennedy promoted the deregulation of the airline industry.

The ideological homogeneity and polarization of the parties today may limit the degree to which something similar might occur in the new regime. Those same features, though, should make it easier for the dominant party simply to ignore rather than attack its opponents. It's not at all clear why that's something small-d democrats should worry about.

Hardball as a Political Strategy

Two observations show that hardball isn't a single move but a game with many innings. First: A political observer "who opposes hardball" worries that removing the guardrails will lead to a democratic "death spiral." For him, Democrats should "continue to allow themselves to get kicked in the face for the next 35 years" rather than risk the death of democracy in the United States.[7] Second: One important argument gets deployed almost every time hardball is played: "You started it," or, in a more cynical but probably more accurate version, "It all started when he hit me back."

The fact that hardball is a game with many innings has led many observers to analyze it using informal versions of what economists call game theory. The game is the Prisoners' Dilemma, and it goes like this. Republicans and Democrats have to choose in each round of play whether to compromise with the other party or to play hardball. If they both choose to cooperate, each party gets something on its policy agenda. If they both play hardball, the result is gridlock and neither party gets anything. The kicker is this: If Republicans play hardball and Democrats don't, the Republicans make out like bandits (and, of course, vice versa).

In any given round, Republicans and Democrats both gain more by playing hardball than they would if they cooperated. In economic-speak, playing hardball is individually rational but it results in the worst payoffs possible.

But the story is different if they play multiple rounds. Then, experiments show, the most successful strategy is called "tit-for-tat," in which a player cooperates in the first round. The other side compromises, both continue to compromise. But suppose that Democrats play hardball in the first inning and Republicans compromise. The Democrats win big. In the second inning Republicans play hardball—the "tit" for the Democrats' original "tat." Democrats, having gained a lot from playing hardball in the first inning, play hardball again—and then everybody, but most important the Democrats, loses. Tit-for-tat teaches Democrats a lesson, and in the third inning they compromise and so do the Republicans. And after that compromise reigns—until one side decides to play hardball again, and then faces the tit-for-tat reply.[8]

The suggestion is that each party should reply to hardball from the other side by playing hardball itself. Eventually—and one hopes soon—both sides will learn that cooperation leaves both better off.

The game-theory argument is neat, but politics doesn't fit the model perfectly. The economists have their experimental subjects play the same game over and over. Politics isn't like that. The players change. To adapt a famous phrase from political scientist Kenneth Schepsle, parties are a they, not an it. A dramatic example is the invocation of Robert Bork's failed nomination in discussion of Merrick Garland's nomination. Some Republicans said, "You did it to Bork, now we're playing tit-for-tat with Garland." Senator Amy Klobuchar (and every other Democrat in the Senate except Patrick Leahy) could say, "Who, me? I didn't have anything to do with the Bork nomination—I wasn't here then." Similarly, a Republican gerrymander in Pennsylvania isn't a tit-for-tat response to a Democratic gerrymander in Maryland.[9]

The issues change too. If Democrats say they're going to expand the size of the Supreme Court as a response to the Republican "theft" of Merrick Garland's seat, Republicans will describe the Democratic action as an escalation of the disagreement—a permanent change in the Court's size in response to a single controversial action.

Hardball as a purportedly temporary response to hardball—as tit-for-tat—does indeed open up the possibility of a "death spiral" in which both parties always play hardball, and neither side gets anything it wants.

Or maybe not. If one party thinks that gridlock isn't a bad thing, it will play hardball all the time. It wins a lot if the other party compromises, and it doesn't lose much if there's gridlock. That's one reason for what law professors Joey Fishkin and David Pozen call "asymmetric" hardball, in which Republicans play it more often and better than Democrats.

Achieving a New Political Equilibrium

Can we avoid a death spiral? Michelle Obama thought so, as reflected in her campaign statement, "When they go low, we go high." That didn't work in 2016. To quote our political consultant again, the Democrats got kicked in the face, and they might not like the prospect of that happening for thirty-five years.

Maybe, though, 2016 was a singular event that shouldn't be taken to indicate something deep about the game of American politics. Perhaps a party can gain strength by modeling good behavior. It will lose some elections in the short run, but eventually the American people will repudiate the party that seems always to be playing hardball. Or maybe the public will put up with hardball on both sides for a while, then look for politicians who promise to change things permanently.[10]

Another pretty obvious way the death spiral could stop is if one party wins so decisively that it's pointless for the other party to play hardball. Filibusters would disappear if one party could expect a Senate majority of sixty votes most of the time. Or if a party that expected to have more than fifty votes for the foreseeable future simply eliminated the filibuster entirely. The foreseeable future for politicians is undefined. It's longer than "until the next election," but probably not "for the next twenty years."

The death spiral happens when one party plays hardball because it has enough power to do so, but not enough to make it unnecessary. The other party retaliates or escalates when it has enough power. Democrats during the height of the New Deal/Great Society regime and Republicans during the height of the Reagan Revolution didn't play hardball because they didn't have to—they didn't see their regime being replaced in the foreseeable future.

Constitutional hardball on a large scale, then, may be a sign of a degenerating constitutional order or an interregnum—times when politicians see themselves being replaced in the foreseeable future. They don't like that prospect, and play hardball to postpone the inevitable loss of power.

If the interregnum ends with a new constitutional order, new norms will arise. Just like yesterday's norms, the new ones will provide non-constitutional guidance for good political behavior. They'll almost certainly be different from the ones political observers know today. Seasoned scholars and the people with ready access to op-ed pages will lament the loss of the virtues they grew up honoring. The new equilibrium will be different from the old one. Whether that's good or bad will depend on your view of the policies the new constitutional regime pursues.

The Nightmare and the Refreshing Dream

Through much of early 2019, Americans heard about President Trump's violations of norms: wholesale refusals to provide information to congressional committees, presidential rhetoric attacking the press as enemies of the people, control over the Republican Party so substantial as to squelch any support within the party for investigating apparent crimes committed by members of his administration. The president's opponents feared that the nation was about to experience a nightmare of authoritarian rule.

Some of President Trump's actions might not have been norm

violations at all. Such violations typically involve *doing* things rather than merely saying them. It is disturbing to hear chants of "lock her up" two years after Hillary Clinton's loss, but it would be far more disturbing were there any reason to think that the Trump Department of Justice was taking serious steps to bring criminal charges against her. Wholesale refusals to provide information to congressional committees can be the opening steps in an elaborate dance, some of which occurs off-stage, that ends with the administration turning over enough documents to satisfy the committees. Refusing a Supreme Court order to turn over the material would be something else again.

When other presidents have used rhetoric similar to Trump's and have taken initial steps like his, we could be confident that things would work out acceptably in the end. The nightmare is that Trump is different. His critics fear that he will use all the force at his disposal when push comes to shove—call his supporters on to the streets to use their Second Amendment remedies, for example.

There's another possibility, a refreshing dream instead of a nightmare. The refreshing dream is that there's nothing wrong with hardball as such. Every time it's played, the existing political arrangements are disrupted a little bit, and the more it's played, the more likely those arrangements are to collapse. Sometimes, though, the arrangements *should* collapse—or, perhaps more precisely, the arrangements place some group or political party at such a disadvantage that disrupting them is the only way of getting their policies adopted. Hardball is bad if those policies are bad, but not if they are good—which is why we can't condemn hardball in itself.

Hardball isn't necessary when a constitutional regime is flourishing. The regime itself sets expectations about politicians' behavior, and the regime's stability means that it is to nearly all politicians' advantage to meet those expectations. Hardball becomes an attractive strategy when a constitutional order begins to decay, and in the interregnum between orders. A new set of taken-for-granted political norms, different from those of the old order, will arise once a new regime is in place. We shouldn't be nostalgic about how nice things were when politicians from both parties sat down and had dinner with each other. Instead, we should get used to new arrangements that we probably can't even describe now. They might, for example, involve norms about how politicians refer to each other in their tweets (or whatever the next major social medium turns out to be).

One thing is almost certain. The transition from the interregnum to a new order will be painful—necessarily so for the losing side, but perhaps also for the winners, who will have to adjust to new ways of "doing" politics. Once a new constitutional regime stabilizes, the losers will have to get used to being on the losing side for quite a while. Republicans did that at the height of the New Deal/Great Society order, Democrats did during the Reagan Revolution (recall Bill Clinton's "the era of big government is over"). If the new constitutional regime is Trumpist, Democrats will have to do so again, and if it's the progressive alternative, Republicans will.

● ● ●

Parts 2 and 3 have explored some possibilities—in particular, the possibilities for the Supreme Court—that would open up if, to repeat Sam Wang's observation quoted in the Introduction, we go someplace new. We might not, though. The interregnum might go on and on.

Getting to the new place requires that a dynamic new political order gain control of both houses of Congress and the presidency for an extended period. Any other configuration—one party controlling two of these but not the third, or even a trifecta lasting only one election cycle—extends the interregnum. (During 2019 Democrats debated the extent to which they should or could develop strongly progressive policies that would reconfigure politics permanently and thereby end the interregnum by "permanently" installing a newly energized Democratic Party.)[11]

We know a lot about constitutional politics and policy during this particular interregnum: gridlock in Congress, expansive exercises of presidential authority by presidents who think something needs to be fixed and who believe, to quote Donald Trump's acceptance speech in the 2016 Republican convention, "I alone can fix it."

What about the Supreme Court? Without substantial changes in its political coloration, the Court will uphold expansion of presidential power by Republican presidents and slap down similarly expansive exercises of power by Democratic ones.

PART FOUR
Progressive Alternatives—
The Long Run

A democratic death spiral can't be ruled out. There are more optimistic possibilities, though. My text here is Leonard Cohen's anthem, "Democracy."

> Democracy is coming to the USA . . .
> It's coming from the sorrow in the street
> The holy places where the races meet
> From the homicidal bitchin'
> That goes down in every kitchen
> To determine who will serve and who will eat . . .
> It's coming to America first
> The cradle of the best and of the worst
> It's here they got the range
> And the machinery of change
> And it's here they got the spiritual thirst.[1]

I take Cohen here to be evoking ideas about popular constitutionalism, the topic of chapter 15, as well as ideas about "the machinery of chang[ing]" the Constitution by amending or replacing it, the topic of chapter 16.

15

Popular Constitutionalism Versus
Judicial Supremacy

Brett Kavanaugh's appointment to the Supreme Court brought about an interesting reversal in perspectives on the Court. For decades, conservatives had complained that the Court was a political body controlled by liberals. With Kavanaugh's appointment they see the prospect of a Court devoted to calling balls and strikes. They also expect to win most of the games because the Constitution is on their side.

Liberals celebrated the Court for vindicating fundamental rights (and complained that it sometimes didn't do so vigorously enough). They didn't like the balls-and-strikes metaphor but were just as committed as conservatives to the view that the Constitution told the Court what the right answers were. For them, the Court wasn't political in any pejorative sense.

Now things are different. Liberals rightly worry that a Court controlled by conservatives will be political. It will be not merely a conservative Court but a Republican one. Democrats expect to lose many ball games because the umpires are calling balls and strikes for their favored team.

Different as they are politically, both perspectives start from the same point—that interpreting the Constitution is a task almost exclusively reserved for the Supreme Court.* Judicial supremacy says that the courts, ultimately the Supreme Court, determine the Constitution's meaning.

In that tradition, the Court's interpretations are authoritative and dispositive—after it speaks, politicians have to accept what it has said. As Justices Kennedy, Souter, and O'Connor once put it, in a case involving abortion regulations, "the Court's interpretation of the Constitution calls the contending sides of a national controversy to end their national division by accepting a common mandate rooted in the Constitution." Politicians can disagree with the Court's interpretations but they shouldn't support new laws that they acknowledge are inconsistent with what the Court said.

There is another rich tradition that deserves our attention today, if only because it might lower the heat in our discussions of the Supreme Court.

That tradition is popular constitutionalism. Ordinary people act through politics, not through the courts, to articulate their understandings of the Constitution. They go into the streets with placards saying, "Health Care for All—A Constitutional Right," or "The only thing that stops a bad guy with a gun is a good guy with a gun."

This is not a new practice. Historical examples abound. Larry Kramer, formerly dean of Stanford Law School, wrote an important book describing how popular constitutionalism operated in the nation's early years. Many policies now considered ordinary had constitutional overtones at the time: Did Congress have the power to fund infrastructure projects (then called "internal improvements"), or cre-

---

* The Court has developed a "political questions" doctrine: Political questions are constitutional ones whose resolution is left entirely to Congress and the president. Today most conservatives and liberals believe that the doctrine's reach should be quite narrow.

ate a national bank? The contours of the new government's powers weren't well defined by the Constitution's terms, accepted practices—the constitutional constructions of today's originalism—or judicial decisions. Local political leaders brought people into the streets using slogans that explained what they thought the Constitution meant.[1]

Law professors William Forbath and Joey Fishkin brought the story closer to the present by showing how, from the late 1880s through the 1930s, labor organizers argued (and union members agreed) that the Constitution protected their right to organize and strike. Legal historians David Rabban and Laura Weinrib have shown that throughout U.S. history, political activists have defended their protests by saying that the constitutional right of free speech protected them even when the courts disagreed.[2]

Popular constitutionalism's most important feature may be that the people's interpretations are often different from—even inconsistent with—the views prevailing among elite lawyers.

- The NRA was pushing a popular constitutionalist interpretation of the Second Amendment when Chief Justice Warren Burger referred to that interpretation as one of the greatest frauds perpetrated on the American public.
- In the early twentieth century, courts routinely rejected arguments that workers had a constitutional right to organize and strike.
- When courts were mired in thinking that the right of free expression did no more than prevent "prior restraints"—pre-publication censorship—popular constitutionalists were vigorously asserting their constitutional right to say what they wanted where they wanted to say it.

The tradition of popular constitutionalism is not bothered by—indeed sometimes celebrates—the inconsistency between popular and elite constitutional interpretations. Why should we try to retrieve that tradition?

The answer is simple. Popular constitutionalism expresses democracy's core commitment to popular self-government, while judicial supremacy expresses a commitment to government by elites. Advocates for judicial supremacy say that the people had their say when they created the Constitution but have no continuing role in its interpretation except to go along with what judges tell them. Advocates for popular constitutionalism give the people an ongoing role—living constitutionalism by the people rather than Supreme Court justices.

Still, one might worry that popular constitutional interpretations are uninformed and determined by policy views rather than by neutral understanding of the Constitution's meaning. The argument that ordinary people are uninformed about the Constitution comes in several varieties. Public knowledge about much of the constitution's structure is indeed low. How many people know that the president has the power to declare Congress in recess when the House and Senate can't agree? (How many educated professionals know that?)[3]

All this is largely irrelevant if we are interested in popular constitutionalism understood as offering ways of organizing government's decision-making that work better than gridlock. Ordinary people work in organizations with others all the time, and many have good ideas about how to get a frozen operation into motion. Popular constitutionalism might give us better ideas about how to govern ourselves, although for popular constitutionalists, improving the quality of government is at most a side-effect. Once we get those ideas in hand, lawyers can do the technical work needed to fit them into the specifics set out in the Constitution.

What about the large number of surveys that show that people don't even understand their own constitutional rights? We have to look at those surveys carefully. Often what they show is that people don't understand their rights *as the courts have defined them*. For a popular constitutionalist, that shows disagreement, not ignorance. Some surveys, for example, count it as ignorance if a person answering the survey disagrees with what a majority of the Supreme Court held in cases where several justices dissented. If we don't want to call the dissenters ignorant about the Constitution's meaning, neither should we call the public ignorant in these instances.

Even if the Court had been unanimous, or a doctrine had been long established, we should be cautious about calling disagreement ignorance. Maybe the people who disagree have, or could have, a reasoned alternative take on the constitutional right.

Putting all that aside, there's a deeper difficulty with relying on surveys to show that the people can't responsibly interpret the Constitution. The surveys are taken outside the context of the politics that has always animated popular constitutionalism. Popular understandings of constitutional provisions take shape during political contests. Political leaders—party leaders in the early years of the nation, union activists later on, political "influencers" on Twitter today—talk to people and work out with them what rights the people want to claim.

What judges and other legal professionals have to say isn't irrelevant to popular constitutional understandings. Judges and lawyers may have thought a lot about the problems and may have insights that people with less experience can take advantage of. But for popular constitutionalists, judges' views aren't dispositive. People will hear and evaluate them on the merits, sometimes agreeing—"There's no constitutional right to health care"—and sometimes disagreeing—"There really is a constitutional right to organize and strike."

Nor should we forget that professional understandings aren't uniformly terrific. Anyone who watches legal experts on television knows that many of them simply clothe partisan talking points in the supposedly neutral language of legal analysis.

Progressives sometimes object to the idea of popular constitutionalism not because the people's views of the Constitution are uninformed but because they believe those views are too conservative. "The people" are said to think that the government should be able to punish speech that's mildly critical of the United States as a nation. They are said to think that those accused of crime should be processed into prison more quickly than they now are.

Put aside the possibility that these descriptions are wrong—that, for example, communities affected by the combination of crime and the Black Lives Matter movement might have sensible ideas about good ways of sorting criminals from other people.[4] If the people are "too" conservative from a progressive's point of view, progressives ought to ask why that's so.

Here are several possibilities.

- Popular constitutionalism is conservative today because it's been shaped by several generations of political regimes that were themselves conservative. Under the New Deal/Great Society constitutional order, popular support for universal health care and even a job guarantee was high, and might have been translated into constitutional terms. If a progressive constitutional order takes hold and persists, popular constitutionalism could once again become progressive.
- Popular constitutionalism is conservative today because progressives have spent too much time working within the framework of judicial supremacy. They thought a progressive constitutionalism could be embedded into law only by judicial decisions and neglected the possibility that a progressive popular constitutionalism might be more lasting.
- Some conservative strains of popular constitutionalism arise from a sense that even as we change course, we ought to maintain conti-

nuity with the pasts of our families, communities, and the nation. Progressive popular constitutionalism doesn't have to abandon that kind of conservatism, and might even benefit from embracing it.

All this suggests that popular constitutionalism isn't necessarily conservative in the sense that progressives often worry about. But it also suggests that if progressives want to embrace popular constitutionalism, they have serious political work to do.

The issue of felon disfranchisement shows what can happen when progressives engage in constitutional politics. The courts rejected nearly every effort to use the Constitution or federal statutes to overturn laws barring convicted felons from voting. First Virginia's governor revoked this rule, then the people of Florida did, showing that the people aren't always the reactionaries depicted by popular constitutionalism's opponents.

Popular constitutionalism takes constitutional interpretation away from legal elites and returns it to the domain of popular self-government. But, of course, popular constitutionalism is about constitutional *law,* and popular interpretations have to be translated into law. How does that happen?

As with the Second Amendment, sometimes it occurs when legal elites come to accept the popular interpretations—and then dress up their acceptance in legalistic terminology (originalism, in that example).[5] For this reason we can now recast the discussion of social movements in chapter 5 as a preview of the discussion in this chapter.

Sometimes the translation into law comes through statutes like the Social Security Act, Medicaid, and the Voting Rights Act of 1965. Academics have labeled these "super-statutes," meaning that the statute has received a deep enough public endorsement that politicians treat overturning it, or even the prospect of substantial alterations, as a "third rail," politically dangerous even to contemplate aloud much less attempt to enact.[6] Justice Scalia notoriously referred to this quality when justifying the Court's decision to hold unconstitutional the pre-clearance provision of the 1965 Voting Rights Act: "Even the name of it is wonderful: The Voting Rights Act. Who is going to vote against that in the future?"[7]

Politicians sometimes tinker with the details of super-statutes, and their ability to do so is what makes these things statutes rather than constitutional provisions. In practical political terms, though, super-statutes are as embedded in the constitutional order and as difficult to change as constitutional provisions themselves.

The difficulty of changing super-statutes comes from the political risks, which arise in part from the sentiment captured in the iconic "Keep your government hands off my Medicare." Super-statutes confer benefits that people will fight to retain. But that's only part of the story: No one thinks that the tax deduction for home mortgages is a super-statute, even though politicians don't dare propose repealing it because repeal would immediately lower the value of houses people have already bought.

For popular constitutionalists, the more important reason for the political weight of super-statutes is normative: The American people think they are good for the country.*

Many legal academics seem skeptical about the idea that the people's constitutional views can be written into super-statutes. They worry about drawing a line between tinkering with details—okay according to the theory of super-statutes—and modifying core elements, not okay. They worry that the category has blurry boundaries: Is the Clean Air Act a super-statute? The Endangered Species Act?

---

* Maybe some politicians think that having a nation of homeowners is a good thing, but most ordinary people like the deduction because it's good for them, and don't worry about whether it's good for the country.

What counts as a super-statute depends on whether you think the statute is a good thing. The category's boundaries are determined by policy preferences.

For popular constitutionalists, that's not an objection, simply a description. Policy preferences matter precisely because popular constitutionalism is about what the people think the Constitution means, and the people's views about constitutional meaning are shaped in political contests over specific policies.

The second problem with the idea of super-statutes is more serious. All the examples I've given are liberal super-statutes—the legacy of the New Deal/Great Society constitutional order. The "super-statute" version of popular constitutionalism seems flawed if it can't identify super-statutes enacted during the Reagan constitutional order.

But perhaps we shouldn't fetishize super-statutes. They are only one of the forms in which popular constitutional understandings work their way into a constitutional order. Another form is a transformation of politicians' mind-sets. In the Reagan era, for example, popular constitutionalism embedded the idea that cutting taxes is a central policy goal and that government regulation of the economy should be substantially cut back. For popular constitutionalists, one signal of their success is that Democratic as well as Republican politicians endorsed those ideas—though they may not continue to do so if we enter a new constitutional era after the 2020 elections.

The discussion so far suggests yet another problem. Popular constitutional views *can be* translated into law, but how do we know when they have been? We need some reasonably clear idea of what the law is, and popular constitutionalism may generate "views" that are too unclear to count as law.

Still, we shouldn't exaggerate how clear things must be, if we are to consider them law. At the most general level, we all agree that the

Constitution is law, but we disagree a lot over specific constitutional questions. That disagreement doesn't lead us to think that the Constitution isn't law. "Disagreement" is just another word for "uncertainty at this moment."

Popular constitutionalism might differ from judicial supremacy because the courts can eliminate uncertainty by giving us answers to the questions we disagree about. Popular constitutionalism has no formal way of providing these answers. That contrast, however, exaggerates the differences in two directions.

- It underestimates the degree of clarity we can get when political discussion focuses over several (or many) years on whether we have a constitutional right to health care, or to organize and strike. Medicare wasn't a super-statute in 1970, but it has gradually become one. Identifying the content of popular constitutional law means interpreting the culture rather than the Constitution's words.
- It overestimates the degree of clarity we get from the courts. The Court told us in 1992 what *Roe v. Wade*'s "core holding" was. As for whatever is outside that core, we know only that laws placing "undue burdens" on a woman's right to choose are unconstitutional. We don't know which laws fall into that category. The example can be multiplied indefinitely. Judicial supremacy allows courts to clarify the Constitution's meaning with respect to the specific question presented,* but lawyers and judges can deploy all the techniques in their toolkits to show how a single Court decision leaves essentially every related question unanswered.

* Many popular constitutionalists are comfortable with the proposition that the Supreme Court can indeed definitively resolve specific controversies, but dispute the proposition that decisions doing that necessarily set out principles that themselves resolve other questions, even closely related ones.

Maybe judicial supremacy has some advantage over popular constitutionalism along the dimension of certainty, but the advantage isn't large. Popular constitutionalism has other advantages — primarily, its direct connection to the ideas of democratic self-government that underlie the Constitution itself. That might allow us to live with the proposition that popular constitutionalism can give us *enough* certainty.

Popular constitutionalism is an alternative to judicial supremacy. As a program, it is in some tension with the idea of expanding the Court's size, discussed in chapter 13, which would simply shift the political valence of judicial supremacy from the conservative to the progressive side. Political movements are often coalitions shot through with internal tensions. The one between Court-packing and popular constitutionalism might be an example. And if "the people" end up endorsing judicial supremacy, it's hard to see how an advocate of popular constitutionalism could object.

In any case, super-statutes and value commitments associated with constitutional regimes show that popular constitutionalism never completely disappeared from our constitutional system. That's because popular constitutionalism and judicial supremacy each have a political logic that is the flip side of the other's.

This political logic is best introduced with historical examples. At the beginning of the twentieth century, political progressives were able to win elections and enact minimum wage laws, price controls for railroads, and other consumer protection laws. They had to deal with a Supreme Court still in the hands of the prior conservative regime. That Court sometimes interpreted progressive statutes narrowly, sometimes held them unconstitutional, and occasionally upheld them. Progressives responded by offering popular constitutionalism as a counter to judicial supremacy. They proposed to make it easier to remove judges from office, and to amend the Constitution to eliminate the provisions the courts invoked most often against them. These measures mostly failed in the short run, but they influenced elite and popular thinking about the courts and the Constitution.

Then came Franklin Roosevelt. Some of Roosevelt's supporters who thought about the Constitution retained their skepticism about judicial supremacy. But during the height of the New Deal/Great Society order, its supporters enthusiastically endorsed the Warren Court's assertion of judicial supremacy. Even decades after that order disappeared, liberals retained their affection for judicial supremacy because the Supreme Court managed to pull off some Warren Court–style decisions, most notably about abortion and gay rights.

As the New Deal/Great Society constitutional order began to decay, Republican challengers drew upon some aspects of the popular constitutionalist tradition. Most notably, Reagan's attorney general Edwin Meese III gave a widely reported speech, "The Law of the Constitution," in which he said, "constitutional interpretation is not the business of the Court only, but also properly the business of all branches of government." Academics labeled Meese's approach "departmentalism" rather than "popular constitutionalism." But once we understand that popular constitutionalism involves political leaders as well as ordinary people, we see that departmentalism is a version of popular constitutionalism.[8]

The political context of Meese's intervention is clear: The Reagan regime had just started and might not become fully consolidated, and the Supreme Court was a holdover from the New Deal/Great Society regime. Departmentalism offered a constitutional counterweight to the Court as constitutional interpreter.

Hints of popular constitutionalism can be found in conservative accounts of the Second Amendment and religious liberty, where activists proposed interpretations of the Constitution sometimes in strong tension with—or even inconsistent with—existing Supreme

Court doctrine. The right-to-life movement never accepted *Roe v. Wade* as authoritative, and continued to eat away at its "core holding" until today very little remains.

As Republican presidents nominated more and more Supreme Court justices, departmentalism became less attractive to conservatives and judicial supremacy more so. By the first decade of the twenty-first century, conservatives were once again advocates for judicial supremacy.

Here's the political logic more abstractly: When a constitutional regime is firmly established, the Court is simply one of its institutions. Judicial supremacy makes sense then because the Court can do some of the regime's work. It can mop up backwaters that aren't worth Congress's attention. More important, it can invoke the Constitution to get rid of policies enacted during the former regime, when a Congress hobbled by remnants of the prior regime cannot. Recall here the Court's decision in *Shelby County,* finding unconstitutional a statute that, according to Justice Scalia, simply couldn't be repealed.

As constitutional regimes decay, judicial supremacy becomes increasingly attractive to the adherents of the old order, who generally control the Court well after they have lost their grip on Congress and the presidency. Judicial supremacy allows the Court to protect the former regime's accomplishments and, if worse comes to worst, thwart the new regime's initiatives—at least until the new regime gets a firm grip on the government, including the Supreme Court. The only partly successful conservative judicial attack on the Affordable Care Act can be taken as an example.

Now think about the political logic of judicial supremacy and popular constitutionalism in connection with Merrick Garland's thwarted Supreme Court appointment, and the appointments of Neil Gorsuch and Brett Kavanaugh. All occurred when the Reagan constitutional order appeared to be on its last legs, with something new likely to arrive between 2016 and 2025. In the background was all sides' commitment to some modest version of judicial supremacy.

Conservatives hoped to consolidate a new constitutional regime in the Supreme Court—as liberals saw it, precisely when it appeared that the Reagan constitutional order was about to be replaced by a more progressive one. These competing hopes made the fight for control of the Court almost existential: If the Republican appointments succeeded, either a new conservative constitutional order would be fully consolidated over the next decade, or a new progressive one would find itself blocked by a conservative Supreme Court.

Thus the political logic of both sides: You like judicial supremacy when you think you're going to control the courts but maybe not the legislature, and you dislike it when you think that you're going to control legislatures but maybe not the courts. The logic of popular constitutionalism is just the reverse. You like it when you think you're going to win elections but not control the courts, at least for a while, and you dislike it when you control the courts but aren't sure you can win elections.

Consider a decaying constitutional order. Suppose someone who challenges that order happens to win the presidency, and has the opportunity to fill several seats on the Supreme Court. Defenders of the old order will find popular constitutionalism an attractive weapon to use against a Court now in unfriendly hands. Those who hope to institute a new constitutional order might see the possibility that they will win elections more quickly than Court seats open up. They too will find popular constitutionalism attractive—at least until they get control of the Court.

Now we can return to this chapter's starting point. Instead of—or better, in addition to—continuing to accept judicial supremacy and engage in intense fights over the Supreme Court, progressives might revive the popular constitutionalist tradition. As Kramer put it, "the people themselves" can be authoritative constitutional interpreters.

Losing control of the Supreme Court is unfortunate because, even for popular constitutionalists, what the Court says about the Constitution must be taken into account in determining the Constitution's meaning. But for a popular constitutionalist, there are many other paths to getting the Constitution's meaning right.

Progressives might find the political logic of popular constitutionalism kicking in over the next few years. And if their hope for a progressive constitutional order in the next decade or so is realized, they might then find the political logic of judicial supremacy kicking in. Like conservatives between the Reagan years and now, they might be popular constitutionalists now, judicial supremacists later.

Popular constitutionalism, though, is not merely something that comes and goes as political conditions change. It is also an attractive account of how ordinary people can govern themselves in a democratic constitutional system. Progressives would do well to start thinking more systematically about what popular constitutionalism should mean now and in a progressive constitutional order, should it come about. As Justice Felix Frankfurter put it, "Wisdom too often never comes, and so one ought not to reject it merely because it comes late"—or, I would add, because it comes as a result of changes in the political climate.

16

Amending the Constitution

Suppose Democrats do manage to pack the Court. What comes next? The answer is easy: a constitutional challenge to Court-packing. It's not hard to imagine the Supreme Court holding that there is a convention against changing the Court's size simply to affect outcomes—and that the convention can be enforced by the Court itself (despite its being an interested party).

Then "the people's" only recourse would be amending the Constitution.

Rexford Tugwell, a member of Roosevelt's Brains Trust, spent many years toward the end of his life writing a constitution for what he called the Newstates of America: six branches of government, twenty republics with equal population, and more. It was published in 1970 and of course went nowhere.

Richard Labunski, a journalism professor, called for a second constitutional convention in a book published in 2000, with a foreword by third-party presidential candidate John Anderson. It too went nowhere.

Sanford Levinson, a respected law professor, published *Our Undemocratic Constitution* in 2006, arguing that only a constitutional convention could change hard-wired provisions in the Constitution like the requirement that each state have the same number of senators. It too has gone nowhere, so far.

In 2016, Texas governor Greg Abbott presented what he called "the Texas plan" to "restore the rule of law" by adopting a group of statutes and constitutional amendments that would "reign [*sic*] in the federal government and restore the balance of power between the States and the United States." After presenting the plan, Governor Abbott appears to have done nothing to move it forward.[1]

As of 2018, twenty-eight state legislatures had called for a convention to consider adding a balanced-budget amendment to the Constitution. Four others passed such a call and then rescinded their resolutions. According to Article V of the Constitution, Congress "shall call a Convention for proposing Amendments" if two-thirds of the states (meaning, at present, thirty-four) ask it to do so.

Dissatisfaction with the Constitution is a persistent, maybe permanent feature of U.S. constitutional discussions.[2] Sometimes it arises from Supreme Court decisions that critics dislike. That particular form of dissatisfaction can be assuaged by the argument that you don't really need to amend the Constitution; you just have to elect presidents who will appoint justices who will in turn overrule the decisions you don't like. For progressives, this might be the response to proposals to amend the Constitution to allow more regulation of campaign finance than the Supreme Court currently allows. It's a standard response to efforts to revive the Equal Rights Amendment: The Supreme Court's already done almost everything the ERA would do, making a revival almost entirely symbolic.[3]

That response isn't available when the constitutional provisions you don't like are, in Levinson's term, hard-wired: so clear that they can't be "interpreted" away. There's no currently plausible way, for example, to interpret the Constitution to require that Congress enact only balanced budgets. On the other side of the aisle, there's no currently plausible way to bring representation in the Senate more in line with the distribution of population between big (mostly urban) states and small (mostly rural) ones.*

Even people who dislike particular hard-wired constitutional provisions, though, often worry about amending the Constitution. They worry about adding one or more discrete amendments to the Constitution, and worry even more about convening a new constitutional convention. Many of the concerns arise from unsettled and unsettling questions about how a constitutional convention would operate.

Popular constitutionalism offers a different take on the possibility of convening a constitutional convention. After dealing with some of the concerns about Article V conventions, I will turn to the possibility of amending the Constitution *outside* of Article V through an exercise of popular sovereignty.

Article V Conventions:
Problems and Possible Solutions

The Constitution sets out two routes for amending the Constitution. The one that's been used so far involves Congress and the states: Two-thirds of each house of Congress propose an amendment and send it to the states. If three-quarters of the states approve, the amendment goes into effect. The other route tries to cut Congress out of the process. State legislatures in two-thirds of the states "apply" to Congress to "call a Convention for proposing Amendments," and Congress "shall" do so. After that, three-quarters of the states (thirty-eight today) have to approve any proposed amendments before they go into effect.

---

* Similarly difficult is reading the existing Constitution to *require* term limits for members of Congress.

We've never followed the second route, and questions about it abound.[4]

- *Can a convention be confined to a single topic?* The applications for a convention to propose a balanced-budget amendment assume that it can. But Article V describes "a Convention for proposing Amendments," in the plural. And it makes sense to have one process for proposing discrete amendments, the route going through Congress, and another for rethinking the Constitution as a whole, the route that bypasses Congress.[5]
- *Can a single-topic convention "go rogue"?* Suppose Congress gets enough applications for a single-topic convention and calls one. Can the convention propose amendments beyond its assigned topic? The way the original Constitution was proposed suggests that the answer is "Yes." The 1787 Convention was called "to propose amendments" to the Articles of Confederation (the constitution then in place), but the delegates disregarded their instructions and wrote an entirely new constitution. The difference was widely noted at the time. And allowing a convention to go beyond its narrow charge might make sense. The drafters of a balanced-budget amendment, for example, might conclude that such an amendment could only be effective if the Senate were allowed to originate appropriations bills. (Article I, section 7 says, "All Bills for raising Revenue shall originate in the House of Representatives.") Or, more radically, that it could be effective only if we substantially changed how representatives and senators are elected, or changed the overall powers of the president.
- *Who sets the rules for electing delegates to the convention?* The candidates are Congress and the states. Letting Congress set the rules seems inconsistent with the idea that the convention bypasses Con-

gress. Why, though, direct Congress to call the convention un-less it's going to have some role in the process? Letting the states set them means that delegates might be chosen by widely varying rules. We would be setting up the possibility of severe conflict and possible collapse if California chose its delegates in a state-wide election and Texas had its legislature do it. Each state's delegates might challenge the legitimacy of the other's.

Scholars of constitutional conventions have come up with addi-tional uncertainties, but these are enough to show that we really don't know the mechanics of calling a constitutional convention. We would have to figure it out on the fly, with conditions changing as one, then another, state decides what to do. These uncertainties are offered as reasons for not even trying to have an Article V convention.

Looming over all this is a question of politics. Advocates for a constitutional convention generally think that we need it because our current political system isn't functioning well and needs to be by-passed. Suppose we actually did manage to get thirty-four states to de-mand a convention. The political concern is this: What do you think the politics—the elections of delegates, the maneuvering inside the convention—would look like?

Almost certainly, they would reproduce the pathologies of our ordinary politics. If you think the Koch brothers' money plays too big a role in electing senators, you'll see their money influencing the delegate elections. If you think interest-group lobbyists prevent Con-gress from enacting good laws, you'll see plenty of lobbyist activity at the convention.

This political concern is well-placed in one sense, misplaced in another. Were a convention to be called *today,* the entire process would indeed be infected by the pathologies of today's politics. (One indication is that some opponents of the balanced-budget call describe it as the "Charles Koch" convention.)[6] But a convention to re-think the entire Constitution isn't going to happen today or tomorrow. It will come about only after substantial political mobilization, in which advocates point out contemporary problems and propose a range of solutions that a convention might consider. That mobilization itself might change the way politics is conducted. It might replace some pathologies with a less diseased way of doing politics. Of course it could make them worse: A charismatic rabble-rouser might get control of the convention and produce a new constitution that entrenches him in power. Everything depends, then, on how you evaluate things today—how bad are they?—and how risk-averse you are.

Were the "good" version of mobilization over having a convention to happen, of course, we might not need a convention. We might have remedied our pathologies without one. From some points of view, including that of some proponents of substantial constitutional change, that would be a happy outcome. These proponents aren't interested in constitutional change just to adopt a constitutional design that conforms to some theories of good constitutional structure. They're interested in change because they think the current constitutional structure has produced a pathological politics. Transform that politics, and the need for formal constitutional change disappears.

This discussion of a new kind of politics emerging from discussions of calling a constitutional convention has been quite abstract. And because an Article V convention would occur within the framework of the existing Constitution, the idea that a new form of politics might emerge might be mistaken: Instead of focusing on what they believe needs to be done, proponents would have to swat away—and thereby be distracted by—the kinds of objections listed earlier.

The idea of changing politics through a new constitutional design can be made more concrete by thinking about a constitutional convention *outside* of Article V.

A Constitutional Convention Outside of Article V

The U.S. Constitution's framers agitated for replacing the Articles of Confederation through the means of communication they had at hand—newspapers and pamphlets. Today we have other ways of getting ideas across. Here are three innovations in governance made possible by modern methods of communication.

• *Internet town meetings.* Advised by some political scientists, a few members of Congress have conducted "internet town meetings." Instead of physically going to some city council room, the congress-member invites a randomly selected group of constituents to a virtual meeting over the internet. The format appears to foster substantially more thoughtful discussions of contentious issues than in-person town meetings do. Many more constituents can participate, since they don't have to travel to a town hall's physical location, and the congressmember can hold many more internet town meetings than physical ones because the logistics are much simpler.[7]

• *Deliberative polling.* Political scientist James Fishkin developed a technology he calls deliberative polling. In ordinary polling the pollster asks a large number of randomly selected people a series of relatively short questions, sometimes preceded by a tiny bit of information to set the context. A typical question might be, "Do you think President Trump's policies are helping the nation's economy, hurting the nation's economy, or aren't making much of a difference?" Answering such questions doesn't take much time.

Deliberative polling brings together a smaller group of randomly selected people for a longer period. A typical poll covers only a handful of issues, sometimes even just one issue. The pollsters give the respondents a packet of materials developed by experts describing the issues in some detail from a variety of political and policy perspectives. Then the respondents sit down to talk about the issues. Experience with deliberative polling strongly suggests that people who start out disagreeing with each other can hash out their differences and end up generally agreeing on how to deal with the policy questions they've been asked to consider.*

Deliberative polling has been used outside the United States to generate proposals on constitutional matters: Korean unification, schooling in Northern Ireland, whether Australia should become a republic. Perhaps because of the scope of the issues such polls have dealt with, their immediate impact on policy has been relatively small, though the results may have had some modest effect in shaping public debates.[8]

• *Drafting a new constitution for Iceland.* For about a decade, a "crowd-sourced" constitution has been on Iceland's political agenda. Outraged at the political elite's failures, which culminated in a disastrous financial crisis in 2008, Icelanders developed an innovative process for developing a new constitution.[9]

The first step was an assembly convened by a nongovernmental organization. The assembly brought together 1,200 people chosen at random from the national census list and 300 representatives of Icelandic companies and other groups, to discuss national problems. Ultimately the assembly recommended adoption of a new constitution. The national legislature set up elections for a "constitutional assembly." Anyone could nominate himself or herself to sit in the assembly, but people currently serving as political party officers or holding political office were disqualified from serving. More than five hundred people ran for the twenty-five seats.

---

* There is some evidence, though, that these deliberations can sometimes push people to polarized positions, apparently when there's a slight imbalance between those who support and oppose each other on issues that both sides care deeply about. Cass R. Sunstein, *Going to Extremes: How Like Minds Unite and Divide* (Oxford University Press, 2009).

The constitutional assembly operated as a standard constitutional convention, except that it was internet-accessible. Everything it did was almost immediately available on the internet, and it accepted suggestions from the public for constitutional provisions — the crowd-sourcing part of its design. Some of these suggestions were of course lunatic, and some bolstered ideas that were already on the agenda, but the assembly took some crowd-sourced suggestions seriously.

The public endorsed the constitution the assembly came up with, in a referendum that was technically only advisory to the legislature. The legislature in turn stifled the proposal, partly because Iceland had recovered well from the financial crisis and partly because the legislature's political parties had opposed rewriting the constitution from the beginning. Elections in 2017 revived the idea of adopting the new constitution, because of the new Pirate Party's electoral success. Though that party was ultimately left out of the coalition government, its advocacy of constitutional reform kept the issue alive. (Ireland has used a similar process, though one slightly more controlled by the government in place, to generate proposals for constitutional reform, including the removal from the constitution of a ban on abortion.)[10]

As solutions for our constitutional ills, all of these techniques have obvious drawbacks. People have questioned, for example, the neutrality of the expert briefing material presented in deliberative polling, and the possibility of getting a truly representative group of people to take the time to participate. The Icelandic constitutional process generated a document that, according to some constitutional experts, had some technical flaws (in my view, the flaws weren't serious). It hasn't yet been concluded because, by design, it bypassed the political parties whose support was important in moving the project forward. Notably, though, a new party saw political advantage in backing the proposal, and the new party's success has kept the project alive. No matter what, though, Iceland is an unusual case because the nation's population is under 350,000.

Internet town meetings and the development of a proposed new Icelandic constitution occur under the aegis of existing government institutions. Some deliberative polling has done so as well. But government sponsorship isn't essential to these techniques' effectiveness. Any of them might be sponsored by an NGO. That's just another way of saying that we the people could organize ourselves to propose an entirely new Constitution—not a one-person operation like Tugwell's, but popular constitutionalism in action.

Imagine that popular constitutionalism, working through NGOs and modern communication technologies, developed a new constitution for the United States. Imagine as well that the movement seemed to have some political traction. We might see mainstream politicians pushing for the adoption of specific components of the proposed constitution, either as legislation or through a more familiar route of constitutional amendment. That's a quite rough account of how Progressive-era constitutional amendments—changing the way senators are chosen, woman suffrage, the income tax (and less attractively, alcohol prohibition)—came about. Twenty-first-century amendments could address both hard-wired and soft-coded constitutional provisions.

So far I've described mechanics and politics that might be associated with a constitutional convention outside Article V. In my view, that amounts to what social theorist Erik Olin Wright called a realistic utopia—not something that will happen right away, but something that sensible people might take as a long-term project.

Now for the theory. Amending the Constitution without following one of Article V's routes is obviously *extra*legal. Is it *illegal?* Not in the sense that people could be thrown in jail for advocating such a process, for convening to develop and write a new constitution, or for holding polls to show that large majorities support it.*

We have to begin with a simple question: Why is Article V in the Constitution at all?† Pretty clearly because the drafters understood that no matter how hard they tried, they might not get it right the first time—and even if they came up with the best constitution for the United States as it was in 1787, the world might change in ways that required constitutional adaptation.

What, though, is the status of the specific amendment formula in Article V? Participants in the French Constitutional Convention of 1792 addressed this directly. The problem began, in their eyes, with their understanding that they were no more than representatives of the people of France as a whole—what constitutional theorists came to describe as the "constituent power." Like the drafters of the U.S. Constitution, they understood that they might not come up with a perfect constitution, and that amendments might be necessary. But they worried that they were not the ones to tell the people they were representing *how* to change the constitution. They could describe what they as representatives thought was the best formula, but they might be wrong about that, just as they might be wrong about anything else in the constitution. In the end, they concluded that they should include an amendment formula in their proposal, but they ex-

---

* The Spanish courts did hold these sorts of actions illegal in connection with the Catalonian independence movement. The judicial intervention doesn't seem to have helped in resolving the issue.

† Some framers argued against including an amendment formula because they believed that doing so would signal to the public that the drafters were not sure that they had designed the best constitution possible.

plicitly described it as a recommendation, not a legal rule. The people themselves were to decide how to change the constitution.

On this view, the constituent power can't be constrained by preexisting law. Citizens might find it wise or convenient to follow the drafters' amendment formula, but the decision to do so is entirely up to the citizens.

American colonists actually worked this out in practice before they defeated the British in the Revolutionary War. Patriots set up "Committees of Correspondence" that displaced local governments reporting to British authorities. They became local governments just by acting as local governments.[11]

Suppose a state's citizens become so dissatisfied with their current legislature that they decide to bypass it entirely. They set up "committees of governance" that come up with new rules, and tell the state's citizens that they should follow the committees' rules rather than those enacted by the legislature. The committees deregulate a swath of the local economy: They say that recreational marijuana use is not a crime, or that employing workers for more than forty hours is just fine.

Now comes the key step: Suppose those charged by the state legislature with enforcing marijuana or wage-and-hour laws simply stop doing so—they accept the committees' rules as binding. One prominent view of what "law" is takes it to be the rules regularly followed by (roughly) the officials charged with enforcing it. On that view, the committees' extralegal actions have determined the law for citizens simply because the relevant officials behave as if those actions were the law.

Replacing one constitution with another without following existing rules for amendment or replacement is a form of constitutional revolution. It can happen without violence: That's pretty much what happened when Americans replaced the Articles of Confederation with the Constitution. As I've noted, the Articles said that they could be amended only with unanimous agreement of the states, while the Constitution said it would go into effect when three-quarters of the states agreed. Rhode Island did not even send a delegation to the convention and did not ratify until 1790, but the Constitution was accepted when the three-fourths requirement was met two years earlier. And just as in my examples of the Committees of Correspondence and a new state constitution, the Constitution actually became effective because people obeyed the commands issued by the new Congress.

A constitutional convention outside of Article V, then, would have grounding in constitutional theory and U.S. constitutional history.

Revisiting Specific Constitutional Amendments

The current Supreme Court doesn't interpret the Constitution to allow legislatures to adopt reasonable campaign finance regulations. But as the dissenters in *Citizens United* showed, the Court *could* do so. That is a legally plausible interpretation.

The example of an individual right to own guns—once "fraudulent" to mainstream Republicans, now the prevailing interpretation of the Second Amendment—shows how legal arguments become plausible. The idea moved from being "off the wall," to use law professor Jack Balkin's useful phrase, to being on the table.* In general, ideas and legal arguments are on the table when—and because—they are

---

* In Balkin's formulation, the idea has moved from being "off the wall" to "on the wall." Although his wording preserves some parallelism, "on the wall" seems metaphorically inapt.

developed and promoted by a movement that gains enough political power to be heard.

What about the hard-wired rule that each state gets the same number of senators? The hard-wiring seems especially strong because that rule is itself protected by a rule in Article V, that "no State, without its consent, shall be deprived of its equal suffrage in the Senate."*

There are extremely creative arguments rattling around today to the effect that principles of equality reflected in the Fourteenth Amendment and in the amendments expanding suffrage (the Fifteenth [race], Nineteenth [sex], Twenty-Third [age], and Twenty-Seventh [District of Columbia]) have implicitly amended the "two senators for each state" rule and the "you can't amend the rule that each state gets two senators" rule. These arguments are off the wall today.[12]

A movement for a constitutional convention, either inside or outside Article V, that took as one of its goals changing the "two senators for every state" rule might put those arguments on the table. Supporters of the movement might be content if opponents said, "Look, we don't need a constitutional convention, with all the uncertainties associated with the possibility, to get us what you want. We've heard your argument that the rule violates principles of equality. And we know that there are equality-based legal arguments rattling around that would support interpreting the Constitution to allow Congress to apportion the Senate. Those arguments seemed weird and crazy last year. They don't seem quite so crazy any more. Let's see if the Supreme Court will buy them." And as with gun rights, maybe the Court would.

---

* We could amend the Constitution to give each state three or four senators (or only one), but we can't amend it to give big states more senators than small states have.

If it did, we wouldn't need a constitutional convention to decide that issue. But the movement to have one would have succeeded. That's one reason for discussing the possibility of a constitutional convention. It might put currently implausible legal arguments—including those that would convert hard-wired provisions into encoded and changeable ones—on the table.

2020 and After

Writing about the Constitution divides into two categories: breaking news, and overviews of the wide sweep of constitutional development. The two categories overlap a lot when we're in a period of constitutional stability, but they come apart when a new constitutional order appears on the scene.

Commentary about the Supreme Court in 2019 was dominated by unresolved questions about the extent to which the Court will come to reflect the conservatism of its Republican appointees. We know that Justice Kavanaugh is quite conservative, and from the evidence of his confirmation hearings, quite partisan. He hasn't yet had a chance to demonstrate those qualities on the bench, and the track record of nominees suggests that it takes several terms for their deepest commitments to emerge. According to one analysis, based on extremely thin evidence from Justice Kavanaugh's first weeks on the bench, "We should expect Kavanaugh to vote more moderately this term than he does in future terms."[1]

Speculation about Chief Justice Roberts—the new "swing vote" on the Court—focuses on his role as a strategic-minded leader of a Court for which he is said to have institutional as well as political concerns. How can he maneuver to maintain the Court's role in a constitutional system that might change dramatically within a few years? The obvious answer is to do his best to keep the Court from moving too far to the right too fast.[2]

Abortion provides the most obvious example. There's little doubt that five justices are prepared to overrule *Roe v. Wade,* but they need not do so at the first opportunity. Instead, they can find that increasingly strict regulations of abortion do not impose an undue burden on the (still) constitutionally protected right to choose. Similarly the chief justice can use his votes to signal—occasionally—that the Court is not yet committed to a full Trumpist constitutional agenda. A truly strategic chief justice, faced with a transition to a Democratic-dominated order after 2020, would do well to vote occasionally for the "liberal" side, thereby weakening Democrats' ability to support attacks on the Court as an institution.

Projecting the Court's behavior in 2019 into the indefinite future is almost certainly a mistake. We won't have a good sense of what the Supreme Court might do in the 2020s until after the 2020 election.

Seeing the Constitution and the Court through the lens of constitutional regimes is more productive. But the way we talk about the Constitution today is as gridlocked as our policy-making process. The lines of discussion have cut deep grooves into our thinking. We talk about originalism and living constitutionalism, whichever one we're for or against, in terms so familiar that they bore not only specialists but people in the general public who might otherwise be interested in thinking seriously about the Constitution. Whenever some new policy comes on the table, all the standard arguments are trotted out, with—shockingly—everything originalist pointing to the conservative view of the policy and everything living constitutionalist pointing to the liberal view.[3]

Political gridlock happens because an old order is dying and a new one is yet to be born. So too with the way we talk about the Constitution. Antonio Gramsci continued his observation about the old and the new, "in this interregnum a great variety of morbid symptoms appear." Perhaps we can't rid ourselves of the underlying disease until the new order emerges. Yet sometimes, treatment of symptoms can move a patient toward a cure.

What new modes of constitutional discussion might break us out of our current unproductive mode? How about a realistic utopianism on both the left and the right? Instead of taking for granted that our constitutional discussions have to be shaped by the Constitution of 1789 and 1868, we might start talking about constitutional design from the ground up. If someone comes up with something that seems sensible to some of us—a wealth tax or deconstructing the administrative state—the discussion shouldn't be stopped in its tracks by arguments that it can't be done under the existing Constitution. Instead, we might talk about how to get from here to there. This might involve breaching entrenched norms, coming up with exceptionally creative interpretations of the existing Constitution's terms to put off-the-wall arguments on the table, amending the Constitution, or even thinking about large-scale revisions.

Realistic utopianism—again, on the left and the right—won't resolve our disagreements about policy and politics. It might, though, support politicians as they develop appeals to the public that might lead to the birth of a new order. That order might not be the *novus ordo seclorum* imagined on our currency. But it might serve us well enough—until it doesn't, and another order will struggle to be born.

Appendix: Strategies of Supreme Court Decision-Making

The most important thing to keep in mind when thinking about the Supreme Court's place in the U.S. political system is that the justices have almost complete control over which cases they hear.* Any group of four justices can get a case heard by the entire Court.

The justices' votes to grant full consideration ("cert," in insiders' lingo) are typically based on several factors. Has the lower court held a federal statute unconstitutional? The chance that four justices will want to hear the case is quite high. What if the lower court held a state statute unconstitutional? Here the justices will consider how important the statute is, how many other states have statutes like this one, and whether four of them think the lower court might have been—or actually was—wrong.

A decent chunk of the Court's "plenary" docket—the cases in which the justices hear full argument—consists of cases where lower courts have offered conflicting interpretations of a federal statute (sometimes an important one, sometimes less so, like the "undersized fish" case in chapter 1). Here the justices vote to grant review just to clean things up—to make sure that the law applied in California is the same as the law applied in Nebraska.

The factors mentioned so far are fairly mundane and, mostly, objective. Put them together and you get roughly half of the Court's plenary docket. You also get a number of cases that don't attract wide public interest.

* Technically the Court is required to decide the merits of appeals in some cases involving voting rights, but it has developed a procedure that allows it to do so without hearing full argument.

The cases that matter are different. Here, strategic considerations play a larger role. That is, each justice decides whether to vote to grant review by making a guess about what would happen were the Court to hear the case—that is, about how the *other* justices would vote. If the guess is that there will be five votes for the position the justice favors, she will vote to grant review—and if her guess is that the "other side" would win, she will oppose review.

What's the basis for the guesses? Partly, experience—each justice knows how the others have voted before in similar cases. One important result: When a new justice arrives at the Court, the others can't use experience as a basis for guessing—and they sometimes hold off deciding important issues until the new justice gives stronger signals about how he or she would deal with them.

Even new justices, of course, provide *some* basis for guessing, particularly in important cases. Like the rest of us, justices have some feel for each other's general orientation—a judicial philosophy or a political inclination.

The guesses guide each justice's decision about whether to vote to hear the case. Mostly, a justice will vote to hear a case only if she or he guesses that, in the end, the position the justice prefers will prevail. So even though the formal rules say that the Court will grant review if *four* justices want to hear it, in practice, review occurs when five justices guess that the position they favor is going to prevail.

That's not always true, of course. Sometimes everyone will agree that a case is so important that the Court's public image compels it to decide the issue. Not always, though. The Court departed from this practice before agreeing to rule on whether states had to recognize same-sex marriages; the justices declined to hear several cases in which lower courts had found in favor of same-sex marriage, and took *Obergefell* only because the lower court there had gone the other way.

Each justice knows as well that his or her guesses can be wrong. Sometimes that doesn't matter. When a justice thinks some issue is really important, the justice might want to get the Court to decide the issue even if he or she probably won't like the outcome.

Sometimes the initial guesses turn out to be "wrong" because one or more justices change their minds. That can be annoying within the Court, but even though it's not that common—there's less real deliberation on the merits than one might hope—it happens often enough that the justices typically brush it off. Again, not always: Chief Justice Roberts's reported change of mind in the Obamacare case was (also reportedly) met with intense hostility by the Court's other conservatives.*

The fact that the initial guesses can be wrong sets up confounding situations. Sometimes both inside the Court and outside it, advocates for a particular position will hope against hope that their guesses are wrong. Advocates probably have to have that hope; otherwise they will find it difficult to get up the energy to argue the case as forcefully as they could. But even the justices have to figure out how to deal with disappointed expectations.

The Court's—or, again, four justices'—ability to shape the docket opens up several other strategic possibilities. The justices can shape the docket to control both the timing and the content of their decisions.

Suppose five justices believe that *Roe v. Wade* should be overruled. One state enacts a statute rather obviously inconsistent with *Roe v. Wade,* a lower court strikes it down, and the state seeks review. Another state seeks review of a decision striking down its abortion-regulating statute because, in the lower court's view, the statute imposes an undue burden on the woman's right to choose. The five justices can hear the second case and "hold" the first—that is, defer deciding what to do about it until they resolve the "undue burden" case. They then can reverse the "undue burden" holding without overruling *Roe v. Wade,* and vacate the other decision for reconsideration (suggesting, for example, that the inconsistency with *Roe* is not as dramatic as the lower court thought). Or they can simply overrule *Roe* right away.

Timing and substance are within the justices' control. Still, the five justices in the majority might disagree among themselves on the question of

---

* My own view is that the chief justice probably didn't change his mind, but rather ruled in favor of Obamacare on an issue that hadn't been the focus of extensive discussion within the Court beforehand—and on which no one should have thought that his guess about the chief justice's position had a firm foundation. Joan Biskupic, *The Chief: The Life and Turbulent Times of Chief Justice John Roberts* (Basic Books, 2019), describes the Obamacare case in detail.

timing: Two might want to overrule *Roe* immediately, while three want to tighten the "undue burden" standard for the moment, and then overrule *Roe* in a few years.

Here another feature of Supreme Court procedure comes into play. The chief justice, when he votes in the majority, has the power to assign an opinion to a justice. (Technically, justices can decline the assignment, but they rarely do.) That puts the chief justice in a position to make some strategic decisions. Suppose his initial analysis is that the plaintiff should win, but five justices vote for the defendant. Ordinarily the senior associate justice in the majority would assign the opinion—but the chief justice might fear that the assignment will go to someone who would write a broad opinion. He can join the already-formed majority for the very purpose of being able to assign the opinion, and then choose an author who, he hopes, will write a narrow one. Even without changing sides, the chief justice can make this kind of strategic choice. If he doesn't want to overrule *Roe v. Wade* right away, he can assign the opinion to someone who is also inclined to wait.

What goes into strategic decision-making? Many things, of course, including the intensity with which a justice feels about an issue. Perhaps the most important is a guess about how one or another decision will be received by the public—and in particular, whether the public might be upset about a decision today but might come to accept it a few years from now. Sometimes this is described as a concern for the Court's reputation, or—particularly in connection with Chief Justice Roberts—a concern that the Court be seen as "above politics."

These strategic decisions can always misfire. The justice who gets the assignment might change his or her mind, switch sides, and convert a victory (from the chief justice's point of view) into a defeat. Or the chief justice, preferring a narrow opinion, might assign it to someone who indeed writes one, only to find that the other members of the majority insist on a broader holding.* Or the public gets as upset about a narrow decision as it would have been about a broad one.

* This appears to have happened in a case striking down California's effort to regulate the sales of violent video games. Chief Justice Roberts apparently wanted a nar-

Noting the possibility that strategic choices may not pan out, and that initial guesses might turn out to be wrong, shouldn't obscure the fact that most of the time, most justices do a pretty good job of predicting and strategizing. When we think about what the Court is likely to do about a specific question and when it's likely to do it, we have to keep in mind both the merits (what the justices would be inclined to do if they had a free hand) and strategy.

---

row holding, that the statute was unconstitutionally vague, and assigned the opinion to Justice Alito. Justice Scalia, though, managed to get more justices to join a broader opinion dealing with core free speech questions, and Scalia's became the prevailing opinion. *Brown v. Entertainment Merchants Ass'n,* 564 U.S. 786 (2011).

Notes

Introduction

1. Steven Skowronek, The Politics Presidents Make: Leadership from John Adams to Bill Clinton (rev. ed., Harvard University Press, 1997). The idea of "interregnums" is loosely related to the concept of intercurrence developed in Karen Orren and Stephen Skowronek, The Search for American Political Development (Cambridge University Press, 2004).

2. I develop the idea of judicial time in more detail in Mark Tushnet, "After the Heroes Have Left the Scene: Temporality in the Study of Constitutional Court Judges," in Judicial Power: How Constitutional Courts Affect Political Transformation (Christine Landfried, ed., 2019)

3. Sam Wang, "Happy Thanksgiving," Princeton Election Consortium, Nov. 22, 2018, available at http://election.princeton.edu/page/2/, archived at https://perma .cc/HYR2-HKW9.

4. Mila Sohoni, "The Trump Administration and the Law of the Lochner Era," Georgetown Law Journal 107 (May 2019): 1324–91.

Chapter 1. Calling Balls and Strikes

1. Larry Gerlach, "Babe Pinelli," SABR, available at https://sabr.org/bioproj/person /8dbf8c1c, archived at https://perma.cc/9ECU-7RQW.

2. Louis Jacobson, "George Will says final pitch by Don Larsen in 1956 was foot-and-a-half from strike zone," Politifact, June 11, 2010, available at https://www .politifact.com/truth-o-meter/statements/2010/jun/11/george-will/george-will-says -final-pitch-don-larsen-1956-was-f/, archived at https://perma.cc/C9UF-EH9J.

3. Yates v. United States, 574 U.S. 528 (2015).

4. The references in this paragraph are to Joseph Hutcheson, "Judgment Intuitive: The Function of the Hunch in Judicial Decision," Cornell Law Review 14 (April 1929): 274–88; Karl Llewellyn, The Common Law Tradition: Deciding Ap-

peals (Little, Brown, 1960); Duncan Kennedy, Critique of Adjudication: Fin de Siècle (Harvard University Press, 1998).

5. Nevada Dep't of Human Resources v. Hibbs, 538 U.S. 721 (2003).

6. Neal Devins & Lawrence Baum, The Company They Keep: How Partisan Divisions Came to the Supreme Court (Oxford University Press, 2019), argue that "the orientation of Supreme Court Justices toward elite networks whose approval is important to them ... has also helped to create party-line divisions on the Court."

7. Karl Llewellyn, "Remarks on the Theory of Appellate Decision and the Rules or Canons About How Statutes Are to Be Construed," Vanderbilt Law Review 3 (April 1950): 395–406, uses the term "argument forms."

8. Lee v. Weisman, 505 U.S. 577 (1992). The account of Kennedy's "switch" in votes is in Mark Tushnet, A Court Divided: The Rehnquist Court and the Future of Constitutional Law (W.W. Norton, 2005), which quotes Linda Greenhouse, "Documents Reveal the Evolution of a Justice," New York Times, March 4, 2004, p. A1.

9. Jason Iuliano, "The Supreme Court's Noble Lie," UC Davis Law Review 51 (Feb. 2018): 911–77, at pp. 971–72.

Chapter 2. Originalisms

1. Robert Barnes, "Federalist Society, White House cooperation on judges paying benefits," Washington Post, Nov. 17, 2017.

2. The literature on originalism and its varieties is too large to summarize here. A recent critical account is Eric Segall, Originalism as Faith (Cambridge University Press, 2018). Still useful is Thomas B. Colby & Peter J. Smith, "'Living Originalism,'" Duke Law Journal 59 (Nov. 2009): 239–307. A sympathetic account of the intellectual and political background for originalism's development is described in Johnathan G. O'Neill, Originalism in American Law and Politics: A Constitutional History (Baltimore, Johns Hopkins University Press, 2005). For more critical perspectives, see Calvin TerBeek, "The Constitution as Political Program: The Republican Party and Originalism, 1977–1988," unpublished paper in my possession, and Kenneth Kersch, Conservatives and the Constitution: The Troubled Odyssey of the Modern American Right (New York, Cambridge University Press, 2019).

3. Marsh v. Chambers, 463 U.S. 783 (1983).

4. Printz v. United States, 521 U.S. 898 (1997).

5. Randy Barnett, "New Evidence of the Original Meaning of the Commerce Clause," Arkansas Law Review 55 (2003): 847–99.

6. Thomas R. Lee & Stephen C. Mouritsen, "Judging Ordinary Meaning," Yale Law Journal 127 (Feb. 2018): 788–879.

7. For another scholar's critical assessment, see Carissa Byrne Hessick, "Corpus Linguistics and the Criminal Law," Brigham Young University Law Review 2017 (Aug. 2017): 1503–30. For a sympathetic introduction to corpus linguistics analysis that carefully identifies the numerous places where judgment enters the analysis, see Neal Goldfarb, "A Lawyer's Introduction to Meaning in the Framework of Corpus Linguistics," Brigham Young University Law Review 2017 (Aug. 2017): 1359–1416.

8. An interesting experimental study of *contemporary* word-usage compared meanings found in dictionaries, a contemporary corpus of word usage, and judgments made by ordinary people, judges, and law students. The last set of judgments roughly corresponds to "original public meaning." The study showed that the meanings derived from dictionaries and the contemporary corpus differed from the meanings asserted by ordinary people, judges, and law students in somewhere between one-quarter and one-third of the cases. Kevin P. Tobia, "Testing Original Public Meaning: Are Dictionaries and Corpus Linguistics Reliable Measures of Meaning?" (February 26, 2019), available at https://ssrn.com/abstract=3266082. This is only one study, but it suggests some of the difficulties that are associated with corpus linguistics as a method of discovering original public meaning.

9. Josh Blackman & James C. Phillips, "Corpus Linguistics and the Second Amendment," Harvard Law Review Blog, Aug. 7, 2018, available at https://blog.harvardlawreview.org/corpus-linguistics-and-the-second-amendment/, archived at https://perma.cc/5YZC-3USG.

10. The distinction was introduced by Ronald Dworkin.

11. Rutan v. Republican Party of Ill., 497 U.S. 62, 95–96 n.1 (1990) (Scalia, J., dissenting).

12. Jack C. Balkin, Living Originalism (Harvard University Press, 2014). The survey is reported at Jack Balkin, "Fun with Citation Counts: My Multiple Names," https://balkin.blogspot.com/2018/08/fun-with-citation-counts-my-multiple.html, archived at https://perma.cc/4EPT-MTMQ.

13. Janus v. AFSCME, 138 S.Ct. 2448 (2018).

14. Caroline Mala Corbin, "Opportunistic Originalism and the Establishment Clause," Wake Forest Law Review 54 (forthcoming 2019), describes opportunistic originalism in contrasting two cases dealing with the Establishment Clause.

15. Eric Schnapper, "Affirmative Action and the Legislative History of the Fourteenth Amendment," Virginia Law Review 71 (June 1985): 753–98.

16. Grutter v. Bollinger, 539 U.S. 306, 349 (Thomas, J., dissenting).

17. Parents Involved in Community Schools v. Seattle Sch. Dist. No. 1, 551 U.S. 701 (2007).

18. Gamble v. United States, 139 S.Ct. 1960 (2019), contains instructive opinions by Justices Alito and Thomas dealing with the relation between originalism and stare decisis.

19. On amicus wrangling, see Allison Orr Larsen & Neal Devins, "The Amicus Machine," Virginia Law Review 102 (Dec. 2016): 1901–68.

20. NLRB v. Noel Canning, 134 S.Ct. 189 (2014).

21. Lucia v. SEC, 138 S.Ct. 2044 (2018); Jennifer Mascott, "Who Are 'Officers of the United States?,'" Stanford Law Review 70 (Feb. 2018): 443–564.

22. Obergefell v. Hodges, 135 S.Ct. 2584 (2015).

23. Michael Ramsay, "Is the Space Force Constitutional?," The Originalism Blog, Aug. 20, 2018, available at https://originalismblog.typepad.com/the-originalism-blog /2018/08/is-the-space-force-constitutionalmichael-ramsey.html, archived at https:// perma.cc/R4V3-PGAH. The best recent discussion of the "Who cares?" question is Louis Michael Seidman, On Constitutional Disobedience (Oxford University Press, 2013).

24. Ilya Somin, "Is Originalism a Theory? Is Living Constitutionalism?," The Volokh Conspiracy, Nov. 14, 2018, available at https://reason.com/volokh/2018/11/14 /is-originalism-a-theory-is-living-consti, archived at https://perma.cc/8ZGP-P4JN.

Chapter 3. Playing Politics

1. E. E. Schattschneider, Politics, Pressures and the Tariff (New York, Prentice-Hall, 1935).

2. For an analysis of the relation between the Second Amendment and the Republican Party, see Calvin TerBeek, "Gun Rights as Glue? The Contested (and Uncontested) Legal Policy Terrain of the Conservative Legal Movement," A House Divided blog, Jan. 24, 2019, available at https://ahousedividedapd.com/2019/01/24 /gun-rights-as-glue-the-contested-and-uncontested-legal-policy-terrain-of-the-con servative-legal-movement/, archived at https://perma.cc/74TR-5M2P.

3. For two reasonably dispassionate analyses that demonstrate how complex the question of partisan bias in campaign finance is, see Thomas E. Mann & Anthony Corrado, "Party Polarization and Campaign Finance," Brookings Institution, 2014, and Bipartisan Policy Center, "Campaign Finance in the United States: Assessing an Era of Fundamental Change," January 2018.

4. The Bipartisan Policy Center report states, "The expected influx of corporate treasury money into the federal campaign finance system, following the U.S. Supreme Court's decision in Citizens United v. FEC, has not happened.... [A] very small share of campaign financing comes from corporate treasury funds. If anything,

unions appear to have taken greater advantage of Citizens United, as they have spent more of their treasury money in this fashion."

5. Crawford v. Marion County Election Board, 553 U.S. 181 (2008).

6. Enrico Cantoni & Vincent Pons, "Strict ID Laws Don't Stop Voters: Evidence from a U.S. Nationwide Panel, 2008–2016," NBER Working Paper No. 25522 (Feb. 2019), available at https://www.nber.org/papers/w25522, archived at https://perma.cc/D8PZ-BSU4.

7. The Republican gerrymandering project is described in David Dailey, Ratf**ked: The True Story Behind the Secret Plan to Steal America's Democracy (Liveright, 2016).

8. Rucho v. Common Cause, 139 S.Ct. 2679 (2019).

9. The provision used an objective test based on registration and voting figures to determine its coverage. Applying that test, the provision later expanded to cover parts of California, Florida, New York, North Carolina, and North Dakota.

10. Northeast Austin Municipal Util. Dist. No. One v. Holder, 557 U.S. 193 (2009).

11. Coyle v. Smith, 221 U.S. 559 (1911).

12. State Farm Mutual Auto. Ins. Co. v. Campbell, 538 U.S. 408 (2003). The case reviews the line of development that led up to it.

13. Wal-Mart Stores, Inc. v. Dukes, 564 U.S. 338 (2011).

14. DIRECTV, Inc. v. Imburgia, 136 S.Ct. 463 (2015).

15. Janus v. AFSCME, 138 S.Ct. 2448 (2018).

16. Rebecca Rainey & Ian Kullgren, "1 year after Janus, unions are flush," Politico, May 17, 2019, available at https://www.politico.com/story/2019/05/17/janus-unions-employment-1447266, archived at https://perma.cc/P4HK-ZJBK (reporting that "a POLITICO review of 10 large public-employee unions indicates they lost a combined 309,612 fee payers in 2018. But paradoxically, all but one reported more money at the end of 2018. And collectively, the 10 unions reported a gain of 132,312 members," and attributing the outcome to "preemptive organizing").

Chapter 4. "We've Done Enough"

1. Buck v. Davis, 137 S.Ct. 759 (2017).

2. Parents Involved in Community Schools v. Seattle Sch. Dist. N. 1, 551 U.S. 701 (2007).

3. Green v. County School Bd. of New Kent County, 391 U.S. 430 (1968).

4. Hughes v. Superior Court, 339 U.S. 460 (1950), discussed in Mark Tushnet, "Change and Continuity in the Concept of Civil Rights: Thurgood Marshall and Affirmative Action," Social Philosophy & Policy 8 (Spring 1991): 150–71.

5. Grutter v. Bollinger, 539 U.S. 306 (2003); Gratz v. Bollinger, 539 U.S. 244 (2003).

6. Fisher v. University of Texas, 136 S.Ct. 2198 (2016).

7. Mullenix v. Luna, 136 S.Ct. 305 (2015).

8. Kisela v. Hughes, 138 S.Ct. 1148 (2018) (Sotomayor, J., dissenting). On the summary docket, see William Baude, "Foreword: The Supreme Court's Shadow Docket," NYU Journal of Law and Liberty 9 (2015): 1–47.

Chapter 5. The Court and Conservative Movements

1. Eugene Scott, "Amid Kavanaugh allegations, some evangelical leaders focus more on courts," Washington Post, Sept. 18, 2018; Maria Perez, NRA Spokesperson Dana Loesch on Brett Kavanaugh Allegations: 'Our Nation's Boys Are at Stake,'" Newsweek, Sept. 27, 2018.

2. The follow-up case is Mcdonald v. City of Chicago, 561 U.S. 742 (2010).

3. Congress responded to the Court's decision striking down RFRA as applied to state laws with a narrower statute requiring accommodations in connection with state prisons and local land use regulations (which many churches had run up against when they tried to expand). The Alabama prison case involved that new statute.

4. Burwell v. Hobby Lobby Stores, Inc., 573 U.S. 682 (2014).

5. Zubik v. Burwell, 136 S.Ct. 1557 (2016).

6. The Court seemed to envision a process by which the employers would notify the government of their objections, the government would search its own records to find out who provided health insurance to the employer, and the government would notify the insurer about its duty to swallow the contraceptives' cost. Some religious objectors might conclude that notifying the government also made them complicit in abortion, but as of this writing that possibility hasn't materialized in substantial litigation.

7. The computer case is Mitchell v. Helms, 530 U.S. 793 (2000).

8. Trinity Lutheran Church of Columbia, Inc. v. Comer, 137 S.Ct. 2012 (2016).

9. Van Orden v. Perry, 545 U.S. 677 (2005); McCreary County v. ACLU, 545 U.S. 844 (2005).

10. Lee v. Weisman, 505 U.S. 577 (1992); Santa Fe Ind. Sch. Dist. v. Doe, 530 U.S. 290 (2000); Marsh v. Chambers, 463 U.S. 783 (1983).

11. Town of Greece v. Galloway, 134 S.Ct. 1811 (2014).

12. American Legion v. American Humanist Ass'n, 139 S.Ct. 2067 (2019).

13. Susan Jacoby, "The White House Is Tearing Down the Wall Between Church and State," New York Times, July 5, 2018, available at https://www.nytimes.com/2018

/07/05/opinion/sunday/church-state-supreme-court-religion.html, archived at https://
perma.cc/AU9Q-X4WU. The Google search was performed on February 12, 2019.

Chapter 6. Culture Wars, Yesterday and Today

1. Romer v. Evans, 517 U.S. 620, 636 (1996) (Scalia, J., dissenting).

2. Jonathan Marks, "Embarrassing Persistence of Campus Speech Codes," Commentary, Feb. 20, 2018, available at https://www.commentarymagazine.com/culture
-civilization/education/embarrassing-persistence-campus-speech-codes/, archived at
https://perma.cc/K8YZ-WFCC.

3. For an overview from a temperate conservative, see Keith Whittington, Speak
Freely: Why Universities Must Defend Free Speech (Princeton University Press,
2018).

Part 2. Where a Modern Supreme Court Might Take Us

1. *Virginia House of Delegates v. Bethune-Hill,* a 2019 case denying a Republican
legislative house standing to challenge a racial gerrymandering decision, illustrates
all of these points. Justices Thomas and Gorsuch joined Justice Ginsburg's majority
opinion, and Justice Breyer joined Justice Alito's dissent. (The other votes were along
predictable partisan lines.) 139 S.Ct. 2715 (2019)

2. A good summary of the possibilities is Emily Bazelon, "When the Supreme
Court Lurches Right," New York Times Magazine, Aug. 22, 2018.

Chapter 7. Strengthening a New Constitutional Order

1. Husted v. A. Philip Randolph Institute, 138 S.Ct. 1833 (2018).

2. Department of Commerce v. New York, 139 S.Ct. 2551 (2019).

3. Evenwel v. Abbott, 136 S.Ct. 1120 (2016).

4. Arizona State Legislature v. Arizona Independent Redistrict Comm'n, 135 S.Ct.
2662 (2015).

5. Franchise Tax Board v. Hyatt, 139 S.Ct. 1485 (2019).

6. Stenberg v. Carhart, 530 U.S. 914 (2000); Gonzales v. Carhart, 550 U.S. 124
(2007).

7. Whole Woman's Health v. Hellerstedt, 136 S.Ct. 2292 (2016).

8. Comprehensive Health of Planned Parenthood v. Hawley, 903 F.3d 750 (8th
Cir. 2018).

9. United States v. Rutherford, 442 U.S. 544 (1979); Washington v. Glucksberg,
521 U.S. 702 (1997).

10. Justice Kavanaugh, joined by Justices Alito and Gorsuch, gave a strong hint that

he thought such exclusions were unconstitutional in concurring in a denial of review in a case that, he said, wasn't the right vehicle to address the issue. Morris County Board of Chosen Freeholders v. Freedom from Religion Foundation, 139 S.Ct. 909 (2019).

11. Katie Reilly, "A Mississippi Wedding Venue Refused to Serve Gay or Interracial Couples. Amid Backlash, Now the Owner Is Apologizing," Time Magazine, Sept. 4, 2019, available at https://time.com/5668444/mississippi-wedding-venue-gay-interracial-marriage/.

Chapter 8. The Business Agenda

1. Lujan v. Defenders of Wildlife, 504 U.S. 555 (1992).

2. Not always, though. The Court has made it quite difficult for people who think they are being subjected to unlawful but secret anti-terrorist and national security programs to show that they have been or are likely to be injured in a constitutionally cognizable sense. Clapper v. Amnesty International, Inc., 568 U.S. 398 (2013).

3. Arizona v. United States, 567 U.S. 387 (2012).

4. Virginia Uranium, Inc. v. Warren, 139 S.Ct. 2023 (2019).

5. Ass'n for Molecular Pathology v. Myriad Genetics, Inc., 569 U.S. 576 (2013).

6. Occupational Licensing: A Framework for available at https://obamawhitehouse.archives.gov/sites/default/files/docs/licensing_report_final_nonembargo.pdf, archived at https://perma.cc/L5TP-THTE.

7. Institute for Justice, "What Is Judicial Engagement?," available at https://ij.org/center-for-judicial-engagement/programs/what-is-judicial-engagement/, archived at https://perma.cc/BR2Y-83JZ.

8. South Dakota v. Wayfair, Inc., 138 S.Ct. 2080 (2018).

9. For a contrary view, Adam Feldman, "Empirical SCOTUS: The big business court," SCOTUSblog, Aug. 8, 2018, available at https://www.scotusblog.com/2018/08/empirical-scotus-the-big-business-court/, archived at https://perma.cc/Q3GM-F9RM, concludes that the "current Supreme Court is … perhaps as friendly [to big business] as any court dating back to the Lochner era."

Chapter 9. Deconstructing the Administrative State

1. Philip Rucker & Robert Costa, "Bannon vows a daily fight for 'deconstruction of the administrative state,'" Washington Post, Feb. 23, 2017.

2. Steven G. Calabresi & Gary Lawson, "The Depravity of the 1930s and the Modern Administrative State," Notre Dame Law Review 94 (Dec. 2018): 821–66, at pp. 839, 825, 861. William Baude, a rising star in the conservative legal academy, called

this article "a remarkable piece." William Baude @William Baude, Twitter (May 3, 2019, 1:51 PM) https://twitter.com/WilliamBaude/status/1124370914701918208.

3. Free Enterprise Fund v. Public Company Accounting Oversight Board, 561 U.S. 477 (2010); PHH Corp. v. Consumer Financial Protection Bureau, 881 F.3d 75, 164 (D.C. Cir. 2018) (Kavanaugh, J., dissenting).

4. Gordon Adams, The Iron Triangle: The Politics of Defense Contracting (Council on Economic Priorities, 1981).

5. Whitman v. American Trucking Ass'ns, Inc., 531 U.S. 457 (2001).

6. Industrial Union Department v. American Petroleum Institute, 448 U.S. 607 (1980).

7. David A. Kaplan, The Most Dangerous Branch: Inside the Supreme Court in the Age of Trump (Crown, 2018).

8. Cass A. Sunstein & Adrian Vermeule, "The Unbearable Rightness of Auer," University of Chicago Law Review 84 (Winter 2017): 297–321.

9. Justice Thomas, now joined by Justice Gorsuch, believes that "the judicial power, as originally understood, requires a court to exercise its independent judgment in interpreting and expounding upon the laws." Perez v. Mortgage Bankers Assn., 575 U.S. 92 (2015).

10. There's some thin evidence that judges appointed by Democrats are a little more faithful in applying Chevron than judges appointed by Republicans, in the sense that the Democratic-appointed judges uphold regulation and deregulation at about the same rate whereas Republican-appointed judges uphold deregulation more frequently than they do new regulations. Citations to the relevant studies are collected in John F. Manning & Matthew C. Stephenson, Legislation and Regulation (2nd ed., Foundation Press, 2013), p. 774.

11. Jody Freeman & David B. Spence, "Old Statutes, New Problems," University of Pennsylvania Law Review 163 (Dec. 2014): 1–93.

Chapter 10. Possibilities Thwarted and Revived

1. Coker v. Georgia, 433 U.S. 584 (1977) ("simple" rape); Atkins v. Virginia, 536 U.S. 304 (2002) (persons with intellectual disabilities); Roper v. Simmons, 543 U.S. 551 (2005) (juveniles); Kennedy v. Louisiana, 554 U.S. 407 (2008) (rape of a child).

2. Hurst v. Florida, 136 S.Ct. 616 (2016).

3. Bucklew v. Precythe, 139 S.Ct. 1112 (2019). For an "individual injustice" case decided in favor of the capital defendant in 2019, see Flowers v. Mississippi, 139 S.Ct. 2228 (2019).

4. Kelo v. City of New London, 545 U.S. 469 (2005); Ilya Somin, The Grasping Hand: "Kelo v. City of New London" and the Limits of Eminent Domain, University of Chicago Press, 2015).

5. Loretto v. Teleprompter Manhattan CATV Corp., Inc., 458 U.S. 419 (1982). For a peculiar case that the Court treated as involving a government seizure of raisins, see Horne v. Dep't of Agriculture, 135 S.Ct. 2419 (2015).

6. Dolan v. City of Tigard, 512 U.S. 374 (1994); Koontz v. St. Johns River Water Management Dist., 133 S.Ct. 2586 (2013).

7. Daniel A. Farber, "Murr v. Wisconsin and the Future of Takings Law," Supreme Court Review (2017): 115–67.

8. United States v. Lopez, 514 U.S. 549 (1995); United States v. Morrison, 529 U.S. 598 (2000); Alden v. Maine, 527 U.S. 706 (1999). But, for a dramatic example of how constitutional concerns about federalism (in connection with the treaty power) can affect statutory interpretation, see Bond v. United States, 572 U.S. 844 (2014).

9. Gonzales v. Raich, 545 U.S. 1 (2005).

10. Nathan Persily, Gillian E. Metzger & Trevor W. Morrison, eds., The Health Care Case: The Supreme Court's Decision and Its Implications (Oxford University Press, 2013), contains several valuable chapters dealing with conditional spending and federalism.

Chapter 11. The Weaponized First Amendment

1. American Beverage Ass'n v. City and County of San Francisco, 916 F.3d. 749 (9th Cir. 2019).

2. Jeremy Kessler, "The Early Years of First Amendment Lochnerism," Columbia Law Review 116 (Dec. 2016): 1915–2004, traces the history of First Amendment weaponization. Kessler emphasizes roughly a half dozen Supreme Court cases from the 1940s that held it unconstitutional for cities to require that Jehovah's Witnesses pay fees when they engaged in their door-to-door proselytizing that door-to-door salesmen of beauty products had to pay.

3. Sorrell v. IMS Health Inc., 564 U.S. 552 (2011) (Vermont prescription statute); American Meat Institute v. U.S. Dep't of Agriculture, 760 F.3d 18 (D.C. Cir 2014); Omri Ben-Shahar, "Vermont's GMO Labeling Law Violates the First Amendment," Forbes, June 1, 2016, available at https://www.forbes.com/sites/omribenshahar/2016/06/01/gmo-science-and-the-constitution-vermonts-labeling-law-violates-the-first-amendment/#1fec193051f1, archived at https://perma.cc/ASS3-5N7F; International Dairy Foods Ass'n v. Amestoy, 92 F.3d 67 (2nd Cir. 1996);International Dairy Foods

Ass'n v. Boggs, 622 F.3d 628 (6th Cir. 2010); National Ass'n of Manufacturers v. NLRB, 717 F.3d 947 (D.C. Cir. 2013).

4. David Cole, "Liberals, Don't Lose Faith in the First Amendment," New York Times, Aug. 1, 2018.

5. United States v. Stevens, 559 U.S. 460 (2010).

6. The Court has held that "simulated" child pornography—where the "child" depicted is an image generated by a computer—is constitutionally protected. Ashcroft v. Free Speech Coalition, 535 U.S. 234 (2002).

7. Matal v. Tam, 137 S.Ct. 1744 (2017).

8. Holder v. Humanitarian Law Project, 561 U.S. 1 (2010).

9. Zauderer v. Office of Disciplinary Counsel, 471 U.S. 626 (1985).

10. Jeremy K. Kessler, "The Search for an Egalitarian First Amendment," Columbia Law Review 118 (Nov. 2018): 1953–2010.

Chapter 12. Winning Elections, Enacting Statutes

1. Ronald A. Klain, "The first five things the Democrats should do with their House majority," Washington Post, Nov. 7, 2018; E. J. Dionne, "What House Democrats need to do," Washington Post, Nov. 11, 2018.

2. For overviews of possibilities for using state courts, see Matt Ford, "Can State Courts Save the Liberal Agenda?," The New Republic, Oct. 24, 2018, available at https://newrepublic.com/article/151640/can-state-courts-save-liberal-agenda, archived at https://perma.cc/EZ5S-V3HZ; Adam Feldman, "Empirical SCOTUS: State fault lines that might lead to big cases before the Supreme Court," Oct. 24, 2018, SCOTUSblog, available at https://www.scotusblog.com/2018/10/empirical-scotus -state-fault-lines-that-might-lead-to-big-cases-before-the-supreme-court/, archived at https://perma.cc/BZ23-HZTQ.

3. Jeffrey M. Kaban, "Alaska, The Last Frontier of Privacy: Using the State Constitution to Eliminate Pretextual Traffic Stops," Hastings Law Journal 55 (May 2004): 1309–28.

4. Michael C. Dorf, "Reinvigorating 'Defensive Crouch Liberal Constitutionalism'; Part I: Originalism and Searches," Dorf on Law, July 11, 2018, available at http://www.dorfonlaw.org/2018/07/reinvigorating-defensive-crouch-liberal.html, archived at https://perma.cc/9URF-EH9H. For similar arguments, see Daniel Hemel, "A Progressive Yankee in John Roberts' Court," Take Care, Oct. 17, 2018, available at https://takecareblog.com/blog/a-progressive-yankee-in-john-roberts-court, archived at https://perma.cc/8LTB-AMUF.

5. A lower court enjoined the plan's implementation, and the Supreme Court refused to vacate the injunction. The Trump administration proposed to repeal the plan, a process that takes a long time.

6. Good descriptions of the Democratic voting rights agenda are Lisa Manheim, "Shifting the Burden and Striking a Balance," Take Care, Nov. 16, 2018, available at https://takecareblog.com/blog/shifting-the-burden-and-striking-a-balance, archived at https://perma.cc/53HN-5KEH; Nicholas Stephanopoulos, "The Validity of Stopping Voter Suppression," Take Care, Nov. 14, 2018, available at https://takecareblog .com/blog/the-validity-of-stopping-voter-suppression, archived at https://perma.cc /SZ2V-PBKB; and Miles Rapaport & Cecily Hines, "The Good News from the Voting Wars," American Prospect, Oct. 3, 2018, available at https://prospect.org/article /good-news-voting-wars, archived at https://perma.cc/BS4H-CBRX. These articles either ignore or underestimate the possibility that the Court could devise creative grounds for holding unconstitutional statutes on the Democratic agenda.

7. King v. Burwell, 135 S.Ct. 248 (2015).

Chapter 13. Putting Courts on the Progressive Agenda

1. Jason Zengerle, "How the Trump Administration Is Remaking the Courts," New York Times Magazine, Aug. 22, 2018. For background, see Jennifer Bendery, "Trump Isn't Remaking the Supreme Court. Leonard Leo Is," Huffington Post, July 5, 2018, available at https://www.huffingtonpost.com/entry/leonard-leo-supreme-court -federalist-society_us_5b354230e4b0f3c2219f4082, archived at https://perma.cc/HP J6-9PC8.

2. Jon D. Michaels, "Advancing a Left-Liberal Jurisprudence," ACS Blog, Oct. 16, 2018, available at https://www.acslaw.org/acsblog/advancing-a-left-liberal-juris prudence/, archived at https://perma.cc/T9D9-NWCJ.

3. Kevin Drum, "No Liberal Equivalent of the Federalist Society? Please," Mother Jones, Jan. 24, 2019, available at https://www.motherjones.com/kevin-drum/2019/01 /no-liberal-equivalent-of-the-federalist-society-please/, archived at https://perma.cc /E7P7-C53Y.

4. Roger C. Cramton & Paul D. Carrington, Reforming the Supreme Court: Term Limits for Supreme Court Justices (Carolina Academic Press, 2005).

5. Steven G. Calabresi & James Lindgren, "Term Limits for the Supreme Court: Life Tenure Reconsidered," Harvard Journal of Law & Public Policy 29 (Summer 2006): 769–877; Jeffrey Rosen, "The Agonizer," The New Yorker, Nov. 11, 1996.

6. Richard Neuberger, "America Talks Court," Current History, June 1, 1937, p. 33. I thank Laura Kalman for this citation.

7. Amanda Driscoll & Michael J. Nelson, "These two arguments make Americans less opposed to court packing," Monkey Cage, March 27, 2019, available at https://www.washingtonpost.com/politics/2019/03/27/should-democrats-try-add-more-justices-supreme-court/?utm_term=.f1be73a26331, archived at https://perma.cc/MR6T-58RH. For progressive advocacy of Court-packing, see Ian Millhiser, "Let's Think About Court-Packing," Democracy, Winter 2019, available at https://democracyjournal.org/magazine/51/lets-think-about-court-packing-2/, archived at https://perma.cc/52BX-LS9V; David Leonhardt, "The Supreme Court Is Coming Apart," New York Times, Sept. 23, 2018 ("Democrats are right to be thinking about" Court-packing); Dahlia Lithwick, "A Political Scientist Explains Why Democrats Must Pack the Courts to Restore Democracy," Slate, Oct. 24, 2018, available at https://slate.com/news-and-politics/2018/10/why-the-democrats-need-to-pack-the-courts.html, archived at https://perma.cc/8ZDZ-76NZ. The last article describes the organization then known as 1.20.2120, of which I am chair of the advisory board.

8. Matt Ford, "The Weak Case for Packing the Supreme Court," The New Republic, March 12, 2019, available at https://newrepublic.com/article/153286/weak-case-packing-supreme-court, archived at https://perma.cc/8SV4-HH7R.

9. The literature on diffuse support is large. For a recent study, see James L. Gibson & Michael J. Nelson, "Reconsidering Positivity Theory: What Roles Do Politicization, Ideological Disagreement, and Legal Realism Play in Shaping U.S. Supreme Court Legitimacy?," Journal of Empirical Legal Studies 14 (Sept. 2017): 592–617. For summaries of the literature on diffuse support by a scholar of constitutional law, see Richard H. Fallon, Jr., Law and Legitimacy in the Supreme Court (Harvard University Press, 2018), pp. 156–57, and Tara Leigh Grove, "The Supreme Court's Legitimacy Dilemma," Harvard Law Review 132 (June 2019): 2240–76, at pp. 2252–53.

Chapter 14. Playing Constitutional Hardball

1. The usual reference for the introduction of the term is Mark Tushnet, "Constitutional Hardball," John Marshall Law Review 37 (Winter 2004): 523–53. The most important recent contribution is Joseph Fishkin & David E. Pozen, "Asymmetric Constitutional Hardball," Columbia Law Review 118 (April 2018): 915–82. See also Joseph Fishkin & David E. Pozen, "Evaluating Constitutional Hardball: Two Fallacies and a Research Agenda," Columbia Law Review Online 119 (May 20, 2019): 158–72 (responding to criticisms).

2. Later the subtitle became the more neutral "Democracy, the Trump Administration, and Reactions to It" and then, in a reverse, "Damage to Democracy and the Rule of Law."

3. For discussions of the filibuster's history, see Gregory Koger, Filibustering: A Political History of Obstruction in the House and Senate (University of Chicago Press, 2010); Josh Chafetz, "The Unconstitutionality of the Filibuster," Connecticut Law Review 43 (May 2011): 1003–40.

4. Daphna Renan, "Presidential Norms and Article II," Harvard Law Review 131 (June 2018): 2187–2282.

5. Aaron Blake, "Eric Holder: 'When they go low, we kick them. That's what this new Democratic Party is about,'" Washington Post, Oct. 10, 2018; Gregory Krieg, "Comey calls on Americans to 'use every breath we have' to oust Trump in 2020," CNN Politics, Dec. 10, 2010, available at https://www.cnn.com/2018/12/09/politics /james-comey-donald-trump-2020/index.html, archived at https://perma.cc/J8BS -EFZG.

6. Avishai Margalit, On Compromise and Rotten Compromises (Princeton University Press, 2009); Robert Mnookin, Bargaining with the Devil: When to Negotiate, When to Fight (Simon & Schuster, 2010).

7. Confidential memorandum in author's possession.

8. The classic source is Robert M. Axelrod, The Evolution of Cooperation (rev. ed. Basic Books, 2006; originally published 1984). The generalizability of Axelrod's result has been questioned. See for example Amnon Rapaport, Darryl Seale & Andrew M. Colman, "Is Tit-for-Tat the Answer: On the Conclusions Drawn from Axelrod's Tournaments," PLoS ONE 10(7): e0134128. https://doi.org/10.1371/journal.pone .0134128.

9. Kenneth A. Schepsle, "Congress Is a 'They,' Not an 'It,'" International Review of Law & Economics 12 (June 1992): 239–56.

10. David Pozen, "Hardball and/as Anti-Hardball," Balkinization, Oct. 11, 2018, available at https://balkin.blogspot.com/2018/10/hardball-andas-anti-hardball.html, archived at https://perma.cc/4ENY-CNGQ, describes several paths toward equilibrium, including playing hardball.

11. For useful discussions, see Perry Bacon, "The Six Wings of the Democratic Party," FiveThirtyEight, March 11, 2019, available at https://fivethirtyeight.com /features/the-six-wings-of-the-democratic-party/, archived at https://perma.cc/ZD D4-H9JR; David Atkins, "The Democratic Party Divide Is About Theories of Political Power," The American Prospect, March 1, 2019, available at https://prospect.org /article/democratic-party-divide-about-theories-political-power, archived at https:// perma.cc/8CNH-6D6V.

Part 4. Progressive Alternatives—The Long Run

1. "Democracy": Words and music by Leonard Cohen, copyright © 1992 Sony/ ATV Music Publishing LLC and Stranger Music Inc.; all rights administered by Sony/ATV Music Publishing LLC, 424 Church Street, Suite 1200, Nashville, TN 37219. International copyright secured; all rights reserved. Reprinted by Permission of Hal Leonard LLC.

Chapter 15. Popular Constitutionalism
Versus Judicial Supremacy

1. Larry Kramer, The People Themselves: Popular Constitutionalism and Judicial Review (Oxford University Press, 2004).

2. Joseph Fiskin & William E. Forbath, "The Anti-Oligarchy Constitution," Boston University Law Review 94 (May 2014): 669–96; David Rabban, Free Speech in Its Forgotten Years (Cambridge University Press, 1997); Laura Weinrib, The Taming of Free Speech: America's Civil Liberties Compromise (Harvard University Press, 2016).

3. News release, "Americans Are Poorly Informed About Basic Constitutional Provisions, Annenberg Public Policy Center, available at https://www.annenbergpub licpolicycenter.org/americans-are-poorly-informed-about-basic-constitutional -provisions/?utm_source=news-release&utm_medium=email&utm_campaign=2017 _civics_survey&utm_term=survey&utm_source=Media&utm_campaign=e5f213 892a-Civics_survey_2017_2017_09_12&utm_medium=email&utm_term=0_9e3d9 bcd8a-e5f213892a-425997897, archived at https://perma.cc/GJY9-3AN8.

4. For a useful discussion, see Jocelyn Simonson, "The Place of 'The People' in Criminal Procedure," Columbia Law Review 119 (Jan. 2019): 249–307.

5. The extent to which the Supreme Court responds to general popular approval or disapproval is contested, but the studies do not focus on the effects of more focused social movements. For a recent discussion, see Ben Johnson & Logan Strother, "Does the Supreme Court Respond to Public Opinion?," available at https://papers .ssrn.com/sol3/papers.cfm?abstract_id=3261668, archived at https://perma.cc/F9EZ -7N2J.

6. William N. Eskridge & John Ferejohn, A Republic of Statutes: The New American Constitution (Yale University Press, 2010).

7. Transcript of Oral Argument at 51, Nw. Austin Mun. Util. Dist. No. One v. Holder, 557 U.S. 193 (2009) (No. 08-322), 2009 WL 1146055.

8. Edwin Meese III, "The Law of the Constitution," Tulane Law Review 61 (April 1987): 979–90.

Chapter 16. Amending the Constitution

1. The books referred to are Rexford G. Tugwell, A Model Constitution for a United Republics of America (Center for the Study of Democratic Institutions, 1970); Richard Labunski, The Second Constitutional Convention: How the American People Can Take Back Their Government (Marley and Beck Press, 2000); Sanford E. Levinson, Our Undemocratic Constitution: Where the Constitution Goes Wrong (and How We the People Can Correct It) (Oxford University Press, 2006); Greg Abbott, "Restoring the Rule of Law with States Leading the Way," Jan. 8, 2016, available at link in https://gov.texas.gov/news/post/governor_abbott_unveils _texas_plan_offers_constitutional_amendments_to_rest, archived at https://perma .cc/SP93-7WJ8.

2. Labunski devotes almost ten pages to describing proposals to revise the Constitution quite substantially, running from 1877 through 1974.

3. See David A. Strauss, "The Irrelevance of Constitutional Amendments," Harvard Law Review 114 (March 2001): 1457–1505.

4. For a good presentation of these concerns, see David Super, "The Paradox of Liberal Fascination with an Article V Convention," Balkinization, Sept. 12, 2018, available at https://balkin.blogspot.com/2018/09/the-paradox-of-liberal-fascination -with.html, archived at https://perma.cc/WY9B-AKR3.

5. Even if we could have a single-topic convention, there's a question about how the applications are worded: Do two applications count toward the required two-thirds if they use different words to describe the single topic?

6. Eleanor LeCain, "How to Defend American Democracy," The American Prospect, Dec. 20, 2018, available at https://prospect.org/article/how-defend-american -democracy, archived at https://perma.cc/P3VQ-PZRU, refers to a "Koch brothers" convention.

7. Michael A. Neblo, Kevin M. Easterling & David M.J. Lazar, Politics With the People (Cambridge University Press, 2018).

8. Center for Deliberative Polling, "What is Deliberative Polling?," available at https://cdd.stanford.edu/what-is-deliberative-polling/, archived at https://perma .cc/4RF5-LNQ8.

9. For descriptions of the Icelandic process, see Jón Ólafsson, "Experiment in Iceland: Crowdsourcing a Constitution," available at https://www.academia.edu/1517443 /Experiment_in_Iceland_Crowdsourcing_a_Constitution, archived at https://perma .cc/9J4X-NAT3; Thorvaldur Gylfason, "Iceland's Ongoing Constitutional Fight," Verfassungsblog, Nov. 29, 2018, available at https://verfassungsblog.de/icelands -ongoing-constitutional-fight/, archived at https://perma.cc/PZP8-TUUK.

10. Eoin Carolan, "Ireland's Constitutional Convention: Behind the Hype About Citizen-Led Constitutional Change," *International Journal of Constitutional Law* 13 (July 2015): 733–48.

11. Richard D. Brown, Revolutionary Politics in Massachusetts: The Boston Committee of Correspondence and the Towns (Harvard University Press, 1970).

12. For an example of such a creative argument, see Eric W. Orts, "The Path to Give California 12 Senators, and Vermont Just One," The Atlantic, Jan. 2, 2019, available at https://www.theatlantic.com/ideas/archive/2019/01/heres-how-fix-senate/579172/, archived at https://perma.cc/4LA2-TD4T.

Conclusion

1. Adam Feldman, "Empirical SCOTUS: What to expect from Kavanaugh's first term," SCOTUSblog, Oct. 10, 2018, available at https://www.scotusblog.com/2018 /10/empirical-scotus-what-to-expect-from-kavanaughs-first-term/, archived at https:// perma.cc/42C7-3EZF.

2. For a representative discussion, see Mark Walsh, "Center Court," ABA Journal, Sept. 2018, pp. 20–21.

3. Once in a while a young scholar will dance onto the scene, presenting as new discoveries things that once were well known but have been forgotten. (I know, because I've been one of them.)

Index

Abbott, Greg, 66, 259

abortion, 102–3, 121–25, 197–98, 274; facilitation of, 106

accommodation of religion, 130–31

administrative agencies, independent, 149; presidential, 149

Administrative Procedure Act, 134–35, 148–49, 160

administrative state, deconstruction of defined, 147

affirmative action, 33–34, 70–74

Affordable Care Act (Obamacare), 206, 255; First Amendment and, 178; *Hobby Lobby* case and, 86–87; Supreme Court decision on, 171, 172, 199, 202–3, 279

Alaska, 193

Alito, Samuel, 14, 29–33, 115, 184–85

animal crush videos, 182–83

anti-commandeering doctrine, 195–96, 200

appeals courts, increasing number of judges on, 209–10

arbitration, 62

argument forms, 13–14, 16, 181–82, 186

Article V amendment process: described, 260; politics of, 262–63; problems associated with, 261–62

Articles of Confederation, 269–70

Avenatti, Michael, 59, 60, 61

balanced budget constitutional amendment, 259

Balkin, Jack, 270–71

Bannon, Steve, 147

Black Lives Matter movement, 74, 248

Blackstone, William, 39

Bladensburg cross case, 96, 128

Bork, Robert, 225, 235

bovine growth hormone (BGH), 177–78, 180, 181–82

Bowers v. Hardwick, 101

Brains Trust, 230

Brandeis, Louis, 191

Brennan, William J., 69

Brewer, Jan, 88

Breyer, Stephen, 69, 94–95, 121, 122, 186

Brown v. Board of Education, 27–28, 67

Bryant, Anita, 100

Buck capital punishment case, 66–67

Buckley, James, 51

Burger, Warren, 80, 101

Calabresi, Steven, 213
calling balls and strikes, in baseball, 3–5
campaign finance law, 46–51, 116–17
campaign spending, 48–49
campus speech controversies, 104–5
capital punishment, 164, 165–67; cases of individual injustice, 166; systematic challenges to, 165–66
Carrington, Paul, 212
Casey decision, 102
census (2020), 113–14
certiorari, writ of, 277
Chevron doctrine, 157–62; politics of, 161–62
Chief Justice's power to assign opinions, 280
child pornography, 183
Christian Right and Republican Party, 83, 95
church-related schools, government support for, 92–94
cigarettes, regulation of, 187–88
Citizens United decision, 28–29, 46, 49–50, 270
class actions, restrictions on, 61–62
Clean Air Act, 154–55, 157–59, 250
Cohen, Leonard, 241
Cole, David, 179–80
command-and-control regulation, 175
commissions for drawing constituency boundaries, 118–19
Committees of Correspondence, 269
common-law reasoning, 225–26. See *also* argument forms
conditional spending and federalism, 171–72
Congress's power to regulate commerce, 24

constituent power, 268
Constitution, public knowledge of, 246–47
constitutional amendments, outside of Article V, 264–70
constitutional constructions. See originalism
Constitutional Convention (France, 1792), 268–69
constitutional convention, runaway, 261
constitutional hardball: asymmetric, 236; defined, 224, 225; and game theory, 234–35
"constitutional jiu-jitsu," 194
constitutional norms: and compromise, 232–33; and regime shifts, 238–39
constitutional norms, 232, 233; death spiral of, 235–37; violations of, 237–38
constitutional orders/regimes/systems: defined, vii–viii; and judicial supremacy, 255–56; mechanisms for preserving, 44; role of Supreme Court in, 45, 111, 114, 116, 132, 255–56. See also New Deal/Great Society constitutional order; post-Trump constitutional order; Reagan constitutional order
Consumer Financial Protection Bureau, 150
coordination norms, 228
Cornyn, John, 66
corporations and the First Amendment, 187
corpus linguistics, 24–27, 195
corruption, role in campaign finance law of, 47–48, 116–17

Court packing, 210, 211, 214, 253; contemporary proposals for, 217–18; and legitimacy, 220–21; Roosevelt's, 215–16
Cramton, Roger, 212
crowd-sourcing constitutional amendment, 265–66

Deal, Nathan, 88
death penalty. *See* capital punishment
"deep state," 230
defunding the left, 59–64
delegation doctrine. *See* nondelegation doctrine
deliberative polling, 264
denominator problem, 169–70
departmentalism, 254
Department of Justice, presidential control of, 151–52
deregulation, 148–49
desegregation, voluntary, 34–35, 68–69
Dionne, E. J., 191
distinguishing cases and statutes, 12–13, 32–33
District of Columbia statehood, 201–2
districting commissions, 200–201
Dorf, Michael, 194
Douglas, William O., 14, 132
Douglass, Frederick, 33

e-commerce, 145
Eisenhower, Dwight, 95
Elections Clause, 199–200, 201
Electoral College, 204
eligible-vote rule for apportionment, 115
Employment Division v. Smith, 84, 91

Endangered Species Act, 250
Environmental Protection Agency, 149, 151
Establishment Clause, 92–98
Estrada, Miguel, 225
Evers, Tony, 223
exactions, 168–69

Federal Communications Commission, 149
federalism, 138, 141, 170–72; failed revolution of, 164; anti-commandeering doctrine in, 195–96
Federalist Society, 207, 220
felon disfranchisement, 117–18, 249
fetuses as persons, 124–25
Fifteenth Amendment and voting regulation, 200
filibuster, 196–97, 228–29
First Step Act (2018), 232
First Amendment: and campaign finance, 28–29, 46–51; and campus speech codes, 99–100; categorical rules as implementing, 179–80; and corporations, 187; and regulation of tobacco products, 187–88; and terrorism, 185; and trademarks, 183–85; and union dues, 29–32, 63–64, 123–24, 175, 194
Fishkin, James, 265
Fishkin, Joey, 236, 245
Forbath, William, 245
Fortas, Abe, vii
Fourteenth Amendment and voting regulation, 199–200
Frankfurter, Felix, 70, 257
Free Exercise Clause, 83–84; and free speech, 88–91

Garland, Merrick, 210, 225, 235, 255
gay marriage. *See* marriage equality
genetically modified organisms
  (GMOs), 177
gerrymandering: partisan, 53–55, 118,
  192–93; racial, 54
Ginsburg, Ruth Bader, 6–8, 14
good governance norms, 227–28
Gorsuch, Neil, 19, 155–56, 157, 255
Graham, Franklin, 79
Gramsci, Antonio, 274
gridlock, 153, 274
Griswold v. Connecticut, 132
Gundy v. United States, 155–56

hate speech codes on campus, 100
Heller decision, 80, 81–83, 125–26, 195.
  See also Second Amendment
Hobby Lobby decision, 86–87, 107
hunches, 10
Hunter, James Davison, 99

Iceland, constitutional change in,
  265–67
information regulation and the First
  Amendment, 175–76; examples of,
  177–78
Institute for Justice, 143
intellectual property law, 141–43; and
  Takings Clause, 70
interest groups, role in constitutional
  orders of, 79–80, 97–98
internet town meetings, 264
interregnum, ix, 189, 214, 237, 239
"iron triangle" of regulation, 153

Janus decision. *See* First Amendment:
  and union dues
Jellinek, Georg, 42

judicial appointments: by Democrats,
  207–8, 208–9; by Donald Trump,
  207
judicial elections, 192
"judicial engagement," 143–44
judicial philosophies, 10–11
judicial preferences, 10–12
judicial supremacy, 243–44, 246,
  252–53
judicial time, ix

Kagan, Elena, 8–9, 13–14, 175
Kavanaugh, Brett, 79, 121, 150, 155,
  211, 243, 255, 273
Kelo v. New London, 168
Kennedy, Anthony, 211, 213; in abortion cases, 103; in campaign
  finance cases, 28–29; and death
  penalty, 67; on gay rights, 90–91,
  100–101; on legislative prayer,
  95–96; and school desegregation,
  68–69
Klain, Ronald, 191
Koch brothers, 262
Kramer, Larry, 244–45

labor union fees case. *See* First
  Amendment: and union dues
Labunski, Richard, 258
Larsen, Don, 3
law all the way down, analyzed, 9–17
Lawrence v. Texas, 101, 102
legal materials, used in deciding cases,
  9–10
legitimacy of courts, 218–22
Leo, Leonard, 207
lethal injection case, 166
Levinson, Sanford, 258
Levitsky, Steven, 224, 231

licensing requirements for small businesses, 143
living constitutionalism, 19, 28
Lochner v. New York, 198
Locke, John, 39
Loesch, Dana, 79
Louisville, voluntary school desegregation, 68–69
Lucia v. SEC, 37

marriage equality, 38–39
Masterpiece Cakeshop v. Colorado Civil Rights Commission, 89–91, 107, 130–31
material assistance to terrorism statute, 185
McConnell, Mitch, 51, 224–25, 226
McGahn, Donald, 19
Medicare for All, 191, 198–99, 202, 206
Meese, Edwin III, 21, 254
minimum wage statute, 197
"moves." *See* argument forms
Mueller, Robert, 152
Mullenix v. Luna, 75–76

nation-of-origin regulations, 177, 182
National Labor Relations Board, 176, 178
National Popular Vote compact, 204–5
National Rifle Association, 45
net neutrality, 137, 140
Neuberger, Richard, 214
New Deal/Great Society constitutional order, vii, 1, 78, 143, 175, 217, 237, 239, 251, 254
NLRB v. Noel Canning Co., 36–37
nondelegation doctrine, 153–57

norms, constitutional, 216–18, 224, 227–28, 230–31
Norquist, Grover, 147

Obama, Michelle, 236
Obamacare decision, 171, 172, 199, 202–3, 279
Obergefell v. Hodges, 101–2, 199
O'Connor, Sandra Day, 73
one-person, one-vote rule, numerical basis for, 114–15
originalism: actual scope of, 37–38; constitutional constructions in, 26–28, 33–34, 36; faint-hearted, 30; liberal versions of, 42, 194–95; original expected applications version, 22–23; original-intent version, 21; original public meaning version, 23–27; political function of, 41–42; and precedents, 35–36, 195; and reasons for caring about original meaning, 40–41; as Shibboleth, 19–20
overruling prior decisions, 121, 122–24, 195

PACs (political action committees), 49, 63
paper money, 30
partisan entrenchment, 56–57; mechanisms for preserving, 44
Pelosi, Nancy, 206
Pena Rodriquez v. Colorado, 67
Pence, Mike, 88
Pinelli, Babe, 3
Pirate Party (Iceland), 265
political correctness and campus speech codes, 99–100, 172
political questions doctrine, 244

popular constitutionalism: clarity of, 252–53; as conservative, 248–49

post-Trump constitutional order, 107–8, 109–10, 148–49, 172–73

Powell, Lewis F., 101

Pozen, David, 236

prayers at city council meetings, 95–96; government-sponsored, 128

precedent, overturning, 121, 122–24, 195

preclearance, 56–59

preemption, 137–41, 203–4; express, 139; field, 140; implied, 140

Principal Officers Clause, 37

Prisoners' Dilemma, 234–35

private rights of action, 136–37

Progressive constitutional order, x

Progressive movement (early twentieth century), 253–54

property rights revolution, 164, 167–70

proportionality, 186–87

public acknowledgements of religion, politics associated with, 95

public monuments with religious content, 96–97

public school financing cases, 192–93

public sector unions, constitutional restrictions on, 63–64. *See also* First Amendment: and union dues

public support of religious institutions through historic preservation laws, 129

public use requirement, 167–68

public views of Supreme Court, 17

punitive damages, constitutional restrictions on, 60–61

qualified immunity doctrine, 76–77

quotas, in university admissions and hiring, 70

R.A.V. v. City of St. Paul, 100

Rabban, David, 245

Reagan constitutional order, viii, 1–2, 45, 65, 74, 80, 109, 119, 217, 237, 239, 251

Recess Appointments Clause, 36–37

Reed, Ralph, 79

regulatory takings, 169

Rehnquist, William H., 11, 14, 155

religious freedom protection acts, 88

Religious Freedom Restoration Act, 84–88; politics associated with, 85–86

Renan, Daphna, 229–30

Republican Party, composition of, 111

RFRA. *See* Religious Freedom Restoration Act

right to choose statute, 197–98

Roberts, John, 3, 16, 219, 273; in death penalty cases, 66–67; on e-commerce, 145; on First Amendment, 182–83, 185; on Obamacare, 199, 203, 279; on public aid to religious institutions, 93–94; on voluntary school desegregation, 68; on Voting Rights Act, 57, 58

Robinson, Joseph, 216

Roe v. Wade, 102, 111, 197, 252, 255, 279

Romney, Mitt, 232

Roosevelt, Franklin D., 214, 215, 230, 233

Ross, Wilbur, 113–14

runaway constitutional convention, 261

sanctuary cities, 195–96, 203

Sarbanes-Oxley Act, 6

Scalia, Antonin, 25–26, 27–28, 99, 107, 155

school prayer, 128

school vouchers and religiously-affiliated schools, 129–30

Seattle, voluntary school desegregation, 68–69

Second Amendment, 25, 30, 42, 111, 125–27, 195; and corpus linguistics, 25–26; interpretation of, 80–82; and popular constitutionalism, 245, 249, 254; standard of review for, 125–26

Securities and Exchange Commission, 149

Segall, Eric, 42

Senate, amending rules for the composition of, 271

Shelby County decision, 58, 65, 255

situation sense, 10

Slants (rock band), 183–84

social movements: and constitutional amendment, 263, 267; and popular constitutionalism, 247; role in constitutional orders of, 79–80, 97–98

soda regulations and the First Amendment, 174–75

Sotomayor, Sonia, 77, 93–94

Space Force, constitutionality of, 40–41

standing (Article III), 135–36

state courts, 192–93

Stevens, John Paul, 28–29, 52, 158–59

substantive due process and economic regulation, 144

Sunstein, Cass, 159

"super-statutes," 249–51

Supreme Court: changes in size of, 214–15; plenary docket of, 277–78; public support for, 220; strategic considerations in granting certiorari, 278–79; strategic decisions in assigning opinions, 280; summary ("shadow") docket of, 77

Takings Clause, 167–68

targeted regulation of abortion (TRAP) statutes, 121–22

Ten Commandments cases, 94–95

ten-percent plan, and affirmative action, 72–73

term limits for federal judges, 210–14

terrorism and the First Amendment, 185

Texas abortion decision. See *Whole Women's Health v. Hellerstedt*

textualism, 20–21

Thomas, Clarence, 33, 35, 39, 116

trademarks and the First Amendment, 183–85

transgender rights, 105

trial lawyers, role in Democratic Party, 59

Trump, Donald, 152, 219

Trumpist constitutional order, ix–x

Tugwell, Rexford, 258

Twenty-Third Amendment, 201–2

undue burden test in abortion cases, 102–3, 122, 279

union dues case. See First Amendment: and union dues

unitary executive theory, 37, 149–53, 157

University of Michigan affirmative
action programs, 71–72
University of Texas affirmative action
programs, 72–73
utopianism, realistic, 275

Vinson, Fred, vii
voter identification law, 51–53, 201
voter registration laws, 112; national
statute dealing with, 200–201
voter suppression, 199–200
Voting Rights Act (1965), 54, 55–59,
250

Walker, Scott, 223
"wall of separation," 92, 97
Wang, Sam, ix

wedding cake cases, 105–6
wedding photography cases, 89–90
Weinrib, Laura, 245
"whole file" review and affirmative
action, 71–72, 73
Whole Women's Health v. Hellerstedt,
103, 121
Wilson, James, 39
Wisconsin Republican Party, 223
Wright, Erik Olin, 267
writing opinions, 15

Yates v. United States, 5–9

Ziblatt, Daniel, 224, 231
zone of interests test, 135